T0333753

Real-Estate Derivatives

Real-Estate Derivatives

From Econometrics to Financial Engineering

Radu S. Tunaru

Great Clarendon Street, Oxford, OX2 6DP,
United Kingdom

Oxford University Press is a department of the University of Oxford.
It furthers the University's objective of excellence in research, scholarship,
and education by publishing worldwide. Oxford is a registered trade mark of
Oxford University Press in the UK and in certain other countries

First Edition published in 2017

Impression: 1

Published in the United States of America by Oxford University Press
198 Madison Avenue, New York, NY 10016, United States of America

British Library Cataloguing in Publication Data

Data available

Library of Congress Control Number: 2016956900

ISBN 978-0-19-874292-0

Printed and bound by
CPI Group (UK) Ltd, Croydon, CR0 4YY

This book is dedicated to my wife Diana, thanking her for her longstanding support and remarkable infinite kindness in the face of adversity.

■ PREFACE

Recently financial derivatives were portrayed as "weapons of mass destruction" by famous investors like Warren Buffett. This was not that long after he tried to buy Long Term Capital Management (LTCM) on the cheap, unsuccessfully. Should we really be worried about financial derivatives? First of all there is evidence that they were used as far back as 8000 B.C. by Sumer traders to lock in contracts in to the future and take advantage of seasonality. Thus, financial derivatives have been around for a long time and so far, there has not been a mass destruction. They could be used though to destabilize financial systems and in the last three decades almost all financial disasters involved financial derivatives. But this does not make Warren Buffett right. Antibiotics can also have a detrimental effect on millions of people if they are used wrongly. Still, I do not believe that we should eliminate antibiotics and likewise, I do not believe that we should stop using derivatives.

What famous people perhaps should argue for is not to use financial derivatives where they are not needed. Given that apart from forwards/futures and swaps the majority of financial derivatives have nonlinear payoffs, they can be used to leverage the positions and take high risk through financial markets. By the time the financial markets settle down large amounts of money can move into the hands of speculators.

Are derivatives needed by society? The most developed economies are dominated by real-estate which represents a very large part of total wealth. The crashing of property markets around the world has led to periods of recession and instability. It seems paradoxical that exactly where they are needed the most, in real-estate, derivatives are in infancy. Hopefully this book will motivate those in key positions to act immediately and help the expansion of real-estate derivatives. There is a general lack of knowledge of real-estate derivatives and this book is aiming at offering academics, investors, regulators, hedge-fund managers, risk managers, model validators, postgraduate and research students in Finance and Real-Estate, a valuable source of information that can serve them as a guide in their activities.

It is assumed that the reader has basic knowledge of financial markets, financial modelling, financial economics and statistics. The analysis presented in this book can be carried out with Excel and Matlab and many datasets used in this book are in the public domain.

While working on the RMBS desk in London at Merrill Lynch I came across a very interesting small portfolio in the aftermath of the subprime crisis. It was a set of property forwards on a real-estate index representative for the

UK market. Given the size of the residential mortgage backed securities I have thought that there *must* be a wide range of derivatives covering house prices offered by the banks. This proved to be wrong and there started my journey in this important area of finance.

At the time I have finished writing up this book the UK voted to leave in the Brexit referendum. There will be no doubt a lot of uncertainty over the years to come but I hope that the evolution of real-estate derivatives will not be hindered by the new political climate. There is a need for real-estate derivatives in order to stifle out speculation on property markets that are detrimental to us all. The big question is how to kick-start this market when the property markets stay for long time on a bull run reaching bubble states. The property owners would like to hedge the value of their properties and they would be naturally short on these property derivatives. The banks should be long property price risk since it is the only way they can be truly fully diversified. The recent stress exercises introduced by central banks and supervisory authorities will ask top banks to show the effects of a market downturn in real-estate on their portfolios. Property derivatives would help banks manage this enterprise risk management exercise. This seems to me to be the way forward.

Organization of the Book

This book can be used for a graduate class on real-estate finance and as an elective module on MBA and postgraduate research programmes in finance. Ultimately, the specialists working in investment area with exposure to real-estate price risk need to be aware of several facets of this type of risk, which are hopefully captured in the chapters of this book.

Chapter 2 presents the main real-estate indices used worldwide for investment purposes and on which derivatives contracts are very likely to be issued. For investors in financial markets, mortgages are the natural carrier of real-estate risk. Thus, an introduction to this asset class is given in Chapter 3. The distribution of risk resulting from holding mortgage loans has been done in recent years through the channels of securitization. The involvement of real-estate risk and description of some derivatives instruments directly related to the evolution of mortgages is covered in Chapter 4. A full description of real-estate derivatives is provided in Chapter 5 and some real-world applications are detailed in Chapter 6. The main models that have been proposed in the literature to help with this new important asset class are discussed at length in Chapter 7. A new frontier where real-estate derivatives are needed in relation to property price risk and negative equity insurance is highlighted in Chapter 8. The final chapter, Chapter 9, summarizes the main conclusions coming out of this monograph and also briefly discusses the outlook for real-estate derivatives.

ACKNOWLEDGEMENTS

This book took shape over a period of eight years, in the interesting times, for an academic, following the subprime crisis of 2007 and the series of events that followed. There are many people that helped me on this journey and to whom I will always be grateful. First of all, I would like to thank Robert Shiller for being a role model and for starting and persevering in advocating the promotion of real-estate derivatives as tools for stability in society. His contribution in this area over time has been truly outstanding and inspirational to myself. Secondly I would like to thank Frank Fabozzi for his constant help and advice on many issues related to this book.

I had the privilege to work with data on futures on IPD from their very beginning, after they were launched on EUREX. For this and for insightful discussions on the mechanics of the property futures, I am greatly in debt to Stuart Heath and Byron Baldwin and their team at EUREX in London for their support over the years. Special thanks are also owed to Tony Key at Cass Business School, for very interesting discussions on real-estate derivatives and for helping me contact other organizations who were doing actual business in real-estate derivatives. I would also like to acknowledge the help with data from Tradition Group in London, a market-maker in property derivatives, and the RBS real-estate desk, for help with unique datasets that are discussed in this book.

Some parts of this book emerged following joint research with some wonderful colleagues. To this end I am thankful to Silvia Stanescu and Made Reina Candradewi for their cooperation, particularly on the application on the arbitrage between total return swaps and futures markets on IPD. In addition, I would also like to thank participants at WHU Campus for Finance 2010, EFMA, Barcelona 2012, EFMA, Reading 2013, SUERF Property Prices and Real Estate Financing in a Turbulent World, Copenhagen 2013, for useful suggestions. I am indebted to Joao Cocco, Michael Dempster, Arturo Leccadito, Gianluca Marcato, Ekaterini Panopoulou, Hashem Pesaran for useful discussions and hints over the years, to Ana-Maria Dumitru, Jason Kynigakis, Tommaso Paletta, Sherry Zheng for help with data and to Filipa Tunaru for giving up her free time to proof-read the manuscript of this book.

Last but not least I have special thanks to the team at Oxford University Press, Aimee Wright, Gayathri Manoharan, and Adam Swallow in particular, for their dedication and help on this project.

CONTENTS

■ LIST OF FIGURES

■ LIST OF TABLES

"Buy land, they are not making it anymore."

Mark Twain

Quoted in *The Ladies' Home Journal*, Vol. 96 (1979), p. 10

1 An Overview of Real-Estate Prices

1.1 **Introduction**

In G7 countries, between 40% and 60% of total wealth is represented by real-estate. This is without a doubt one of the most important components in developed capitalist economies. Even after the introduction of new asset classes, the real-estate market still represents a substantial proportion of capital in the developed world. For example, the aggregate capital value of US stocks as of year-end 2008 was $10.3 trillion, while for the same period this was $20.5 trillion for residential housing and $6.0 trillion for commercial property. As opposed to bond markets or equity markets where an investor has a flurry of financial products to choose from for various risk-return profiles, financial innovation seems to be lagging for real-estate. Academics have identified a series of possible factors that are an impediment to the evolution of financial products related to real-estate such as a lack of fungibility and granularity, tax, legal, and trading costs issues for the spot markets, a long intermediation period and so on. Large banks hold vast portfolios of assets, yet they have a limited exposure to real-estate. Hence, it is difficult to accept that they are really diversified. Their lack of engagement in real-estate investments is the main reason for the lack of development in real-estate spot and derivatives markets. Furthermore, every time there is a financial crisis investors move almost invariably their capital from various high-yield assets to where the fundamental value is perceived to be, with real-estate a particular destination. Gorton (2009) cited the lack of understanding of housing price risk as one of the major contributing factors to the subprime mortgage crisis.

1.1.1 REAL-ESTATE MARKETS

The real-estate market can be dichotomized into residential or housing properties on one side and commercial properties on the other. The former category has similar characteristics to fixed income markets driven by general evolution of interest rates and individual credit evaluations. The residential property embeds intrinsically a consumption aspect since by de facto people need to live somewhere. The latter category can be viewed as a combination of bond and equity investments, the bond arising from the short-term lease. Supply and demand are very important for the price movements of both property markets. The relationship between storage and the commercial real-estate markets represented by the IPD index has been studied recently by Geman and Tunaru (2012).

US

At the turn of the new millennium Case et al. (2000) estimated the distribution of commercial real-estate in United States, with a total value of about $6 trillion. By type of property, office was worth $1.25 trillion, retail $1.35 trillion, industrial and manufacturing $0.8 trillion, apartments $2.3 trillion, hotels $0.22 trillion. From an owner perspective, commercial properties owned by corporate were valued at $1.68 trillion, commercial mortgages $1.43 trillion, $0.175 trillion in equity real-estate investment trusts and $0.110 in CMBS. Ruff (2007) pointed out that yields on commercial real-estate income in the US over the period 1965 to 2006 were always larger than 7% and averaged 9.6%.

UK

Baum (2001) has advocated the existence of cycles on property in the UK based on the evidence collated by IPD (RICS, 1999) for the period 1921 to 1998. Six cycles were identified given by the peaks in 1925–28, 1935, 1950, 1954, 1960–64, 1973, 1979–81, and 1989. Their research suggest that in the UK the cycles have a length between 4 to 12 years, with an average of 8 years.

Asian and Pacific countries

PWC (2016) describe the current trends in real-estate in Asian and Pacific countries.

The Japanese real-estate market is one of the largest in Asia. As with other developed economies, securitization connected the Japanese real-estate market with the financial investment market. However, in 2010 the securitized real-estate assets represented only 1.4% of the available real-estate assets. Japan suffers from a lack of inventory, having more buyers than available real-estate assets. Office values in Tokyo were up 20.6% year-on-year in the first half of 2015. Residential house prices look somehow stable, benefitting from a positive supply and demand balance. There is a a real possibility of refinancing risk with many existing mortgage loans having a high LTV ratio becoming overdue.

There are some specific risks that may impact in the near future the real-estate market in Japan. The concentration of real-estate investment in Tokyo is a major concern as well as the well-known exposure to earthquake and even tsunami. The ageing population may also cause problems in recirculation of real-estate inventory.

Singapore is another hot point for real-estate. The ten-year Urban Redevelopment Authority (URA) property price index generated an average capital return of almost 6% between 2005 and 2014. The hottest boom period was between 1989 and 1996, when real-estate prices in Singapore almost tripled in value.

Hong-Kong and Taiwan experienced periods of boom and bust in real-estate markets. They are very advanced in mortgage design and innovation. Given the problems posed by their ageing population needing long-term care is a significant problem. Thus, it is not surprising that new types of reverse mortgage type contracts are emerging from these areas.

Property market sentiment in China has turned negative in 2015, due to problems with the economy, a devaluation in the currency, and also the crash of the Shanghai stock exchange in the middle of 2015. Residential house prices decreased in the entire country with the exception of prime cities. Commercial property prices also dropped by 26% year on year in 2015. The cutting of interest rates, however, increased capital flows into real-estate in China. The difference between the real-estate market in China and that in other Asian countries like Japan, Australia, Hong Kong, Singapore, is that in China there is a need for more capital whereas in the other countries there is a need for more inventory.

1.2 Residential versus Commercial Property

As of 1999, Case et al. (2000) estimated that in United States there were approximately 103 million occupied houses, only two thirds being owned by their occupants. There were also an extra 13.4 million units that were occupied only seasonally or vacant. In United States, there have been periodic but localized housing price booms. In the 1980s the Massachusetts boom that occurred between the third quarter of 1983 until the third quarter of 1988 led to a total house value appreciation by $116.8 billion. Subsequently, Massachusetts lost $27.6 billion by the first quarter of 1991. Likewise, the California boom observed between the third quarter of 1985 to the third quarter of 1990 implied a total increase in house value of $544.8 billion, but then it also lost $121.5 billion by the first quarter of 1996. Furthermore, Texas also experienced a period of significant house value increase between the third quarter of 1986 and the third quarter of 1988 followed by a sharp fall. Other well-known property booms were the New England boom of 1983–88, the California boom of 1985–90, the Boston and Los Angeles booms in the late 1980s. In a series of papers Case and Shiller on one side (Case and Shiller,

1988, 1989, 1990) and also others such as Jim Clayton (Clayton, 1997) provide clear evidence that housing prices are sometimes driven by inertia and more-over, both housing buyers and sellers engage into house transactions based mainly on exuberant expectations. One of the main conclusions of the series of papers by Case and Shiller is that house price booms cannot be explained in terms of the value fundamentals, see Case and Shiller (1994) for a clear argument.

Case et al. (2000) reported that between 1988 to 1992 commercial real-estate values were falling dramatically on the north-eastern coast of United States and similar drops occurred all over Europe and in developed coun-tries in Asia. As an example they pointed out that the 1.4-million-square-foot Wang Towers in Lowell, Massachusetts, acquired for $107 million in 1988, was sold in 1992 for $525,000. The sharp drop in value of commercial real-estate assets caused problems to many banks, leading some of them to failure. The House Banking Committee's review on Bank of New England's collapse in 1991 cited as the main cause the disintegration of the bank's commercial real-estate portfolio.

1.2.1 CHARACTERISTICS OF RESIDENTIAL PROPERTY

In order to establish a correct relationship between projected house prices and cash reserves against housing loans, we envisage that a good understanding of the dynamics of Case-Shiller index will benefit a wide range of financial advisors to households and financial institutions. Case and Shiller (1989) find positive serial correlation as well as inertia in house prices and excess returns, concluding that in the United States the market for single-family homes is inefficient. These characteristics make the real-estate market unique and the financial economics arguments invoked for product design, pricing or hedging are bound to be different from other asset classes.

1.2.2 CHARACTERISTICS OF COMMERCIAL PROPERTY

There is a well documented cyclicality, see Case et al. (2000), associated with commercial real-estate markets caused mainly by the long lag period of time between getting planning approved and finishing the construction of the new building. This time period is on average between five to ten years and for an investor this can be a very long period of time to wait. Furthermore, all other markets may experience important shifts during this time, new policies may be introduced, and the real economy as a whole may be influenced by external shocks. Hence, the expectations of future rents may change significantly. Fur-thermore, the inventory of similar available buildings plays also an important role in determining price for properties.

1.3 **Empirical Characteristics of Real-Estate Prices Time Series**

1.3.1 DETERMINANTS OF COMMERCIAL PROPERTY PRICES

One of the earlier research studies on establishing the determinants of commercial property prices was Hoag (1980) who proposed a technique, called the fundamental valuation, to determine the value of a commercial property at any point in time. The valuation was based on fundamental features such as business inventories, construction costs, transportation access and population, on economic and demographic variables at national, regional and local level and some temporal variables such as transaction prices and cash flows. The model was implemented for industrial properties and it can be described (see Hoag 1980, p.576) as:

$$P_{it} = \alpha_0 + \alpha_f f + \alpha_n n + \alpha_r r + \alpha_l l + \alpha_q q + \varepsilon_{it} \tag{1.1}$$

where f denoted general fundamental characteristic of value, n was the national economic concomitants of value, r is the regional economic concomitants of value, l is the local characteristics of value and q shows the temporal characteristics of value.

In his study a sample of 463 industrial properties with transaction prices reported in various quarter times during the period between the first quarter of 1973 and the last quarter of 1978 was used. Hoag (1980) employed a pooled cross-section time-series regressions with generalized least squares estimation to show that the average compound returns for the industrial real-estate value were 3.38% per quarter with a quarterly standard deviation of 8.61%. Over the same period the return seems high while the risk remains comparable with stocks and corporate bonds. Dobson and Goddard (1992) developed a regression model to calculate the prices and rents of commercial property as a linear function of employment and real interest rates. Their dataset covered price and rent for three sectors; industrial premises, shops and offices, in four regions in Great Britain between 1972 and 1987. The model is described by the following equation:

$$\text{real-estate price or rent} = p^j_{(k,t)} + r^j_{(k,t)} + e^j_{(k,t)} + i_t + h_{(k,t)} + w + x + y$$

where: $p^j_{(k,t)}$ is the logarithm of the inflation-adjusted capital value index for sector j and area k in year t, $r^j_{(k,t)}$ is the logarithm of inflation-adjusted rent index for sector j and area k in year t, $e^j_{(k,t)}$ is the logarithm of employees in employment index in sector j and area k in year t, i_t is the logarithm of (1+real interest rate), where the real interest rate is the difference between the average yield on long-dated (20 year) British government securities and the rate of increase in the retail price index in year t, $h_{(k,t)}$ is the logarithm of inflation-adjusted house price index for area k in year t, w is the dummy variable for area w; x is the dummy variable for area x, y is the dummy variable for area y. Based on OLS estimation with and without restrictions Dobson and Goddard (1992) reveal that employment has an important influence on price, for industrial property in particular. Furthermore, both price and rents are also sensitive to interest rates. In a different study, Ling and Naranjo (1996) found evidence that the excess returns on commercial property is determined by the growth rate in real per capita consumption, the real T-bill rate, the term structure of interest rates, and unexpected inflation. Their study used data between the 1978 and 1994. The model they proposed, called the Multifactor Asset Pricing Model (MAP) is:

$$\tilde{r}_{it} = \lambda_0 t + \sum_{k=1}^{K} \beta_{ikt}\lambda_{kt} + \sum_{k=1}^{K} \beta_{ikt}[\tilde{F}_{kt} - E_{(t-1)}(F_{kt})] + \tilde{\varepsilon}_{it} \qquad (1.2)$$

where the tilde ( ) denotes a time t random variable and $\tilde{r}_{it}$ is the excess return for the i-th asset, λ_{0t} is the zero-beta excess rate of return, $E_{(t-1)}(z_t)$ is the expected value of z_t, F_{kt} is the kth of the K risk factors at time t, β_{ikt} is the possibly time-varying sensitivity of the ith asset to the kth risk factor, λ_{kt} is the risk premium (price of risk) corresponding to the k-th risk factor, $\tilde{\varepsilon}_{it}$ is a disturbance idiosyncratic to the ith asset. They reveal that the existence of a consistently significant risk premium on consumption suggests that previous literature highlighting significant abnormal returns (either positive or negative) but that have ignored consumption could be biased due to an omitted variables problem.

De Wit and Van Dijk (2003) searched for the determinants of office real-estate returns made of rents, capital appraisal, and total returns. The data under their analysis covered real-estate type variables such as the capital value, net rent, vacancy and office stock expressed in square meters but also macroeconomic indicators, such as GDP for Asia and Europe and GMP for the United States, unemployment on a national level for Asia and Europe and MSA employment for the United States, for 46 major office districts in Asia (13), Europe (24) and the United States (9) on quarterly basis between 1986 and 1999. The model they proposed as a vehicle for their analysis is a dynamic panel-data model that can prove to be very useful in accounting for a time lag to changing economic conditions. The model is specified as:

$$R_{it} = \beta_0 R_{i,t-1} + \beta_1 x_{1it} + \ldots + \beta_K x_{Kit} + \mu_i + \nu_{it} \qquad (1.3)$$

where R_{it} is the return of office district i in period t, x_{Kit} is a non-stochastic macroeconomic, supply or demand variable, β is the vector of parameters,

μ_i is the parameter accounting for the office district specific intercept, v_{it} is the error term. Their conclusion was that the property vacancy rate or availability and change in unemployment rate are essential for a long-term return analysis, from a worldwide perspective. A very important idea was put forward by Clayton et al. (2009) who disentangle the fundamentals drivers from the investor sentiment when valuing in commercial real-estate. Their analysis focuses on the going-in capitalization rates for nine property types: apartment, hotel, industrial research and development, industrial warehouse, central business district (CBD) office, suburban office, neighbourhood retail, power shopping centres, and regional malls for the period starting in the first quarter of 1996 until the second quarter of 2007. This is one of the first studies that clearly assigns an important role to investors sentiment vis-à-vis property prices. Based on some survey data the authors are able to consider both direct and indirect measures of investor sentiment for property pricing purposes. The model does not pinpoint the investor sentiment as a driver of the observed cap rates. Thus, Clayton et al. (2009) augment the specification of the second equation with several measures of investor sentiment and successfully show that investor sentiment has a significant impact on pricing.

1.4 Summary Points and Further Reading

Real-estate markets constitute a very important part of economies worldwide. The property prices, house prices in particular, have become a major concern in all developed countries. This asset class exhibits unique characteristics that must be taken into consideration when new financial models are proposed to capture the dynamics of price time-series.

Compared to other asset classes such as equity, foreign exchange, or fixed income, financial modelling for real-estate prices is clearly underdeveloped. The focus of modelling for real-estate prices seems to be on forecasting future prices. Most of the models in this area are regression type models that try to identify linkages to various covariate information.

Most of the effort regarding financial modelling of real-estate time series takes place in the US and the UK with notable exceptions for some countries in Europe and Far East Asia. Given the role played by mortgages and house prices in the last subprime crisis, regulators have identified this asset class as being very important and they have included the outlook on house prices in their stress exercises on most important banks.

This book is focused on real-estate derivatives modelling. Complementary readings on financial modelling of real-estate that are recommended are Brooks and Tsolacos (2010) and Staiger (2015). Other useful readings are

Baum (2001) on real-estate cycles and Baum and Hartzell (2012) on looking at real-estate from an investment perspective. Case et al. (2000) discusses the link between real-estate and macroeconomy. Black (1986) investigates what contributes to the success or failure of futures markets and Stulz (2004) discusses whether we should fear derivatives.

2   A Review of Real-Estate Indices

2.1 Introduction

The underlying for a financial derivative can be a single asset, a basket of assets, a market index, and even variables that are only observable but not traded in the market. In the equity market, for example, there are derivatives on individual stocks, industry sectors, and broad-based market indices. The same is true for fixed-income derivatives. In the case of property or real-estate derivatives, the underlying is usually not an individual property but a broad-based real-estate index. Hoag (1980) presented a conceptual framework for the calculation of real-estate value and return similar to what has been done in the equity market. Since then[1] numerous methodologies have been proposed by researchers for constructing indices that are representative of the performance of real-estate markets, residential and commercial.

In this chapter, we describe the main real-estate indices that have been generally used, with various derivative contracts or be analysed from a risk management point of view towards derivatives or embedded options in other financial products. We highlight the historical evolution of these indices in both price levels and in percentage returns, emphasizing the nature of the serial correlation that is inherent with indices constructed for this asset class. This is important because before discussing how to price real-estate derivatives we need to understand the stylized facts of the indices that are representative for this asset class and which are selected as the underlying asset in property derivative contracts. The main question addressed in this chapter is whether property price indices behave like equities, bonds, commodities, or foreign exchange. As we emphasize in this chapter, real-estate is not actually like any of the other standard assets widely used as the underlying for derivatives.

We will show that while there are some common characteristics for all real-estate market indices, there are also some distinctions between more frequent and less frequent indices.[2]

---

[1] Real-estate indices were constructed long before 1980 but the connection with derivatives contracts started in the 1980s.

[2] Real-estate indices are constructed traditionally with information updated at low frequency such as annually. Over time, indices have been constructed with a quarterly and even monthly update. Recently, indices revised on a more frequent basis such as daily have been introduced. Kinlaw et al. (2014) point out that the estimation of parameters such as volatilities and correlations can be very different depending on whether high or low frequency data are used.

Therefore, it would be *wrong to directly apply* pricing models that proved to be successful for equities, bonds, commodities or foreign exchange, to real-estate. Any model proposed for pricing real-estate derivatives should try to account for the stylized features about real-estate that we identify in this chapter. The main problem, as we will see, is serial correlation which is the correlation of a random variable with itself over successive time intervals. We will see that serial correlation for real-estate price indices is in general positive for short time horizons and negative for medium to longer time horizons. In some cases, the serial correlation may turn positive again followed again by negative for even longer horizons. Serial correlation will cause a higher degree of predictability for real-estate price indices and, in turn, this will make it more challenging to find an appropriate models for pricing real-estate derivatives.

2.2 A Classification of Real-Estate Indices

The easiest classification of real-estate indices is in residential property indices and commercial property indices. There are clear differences between those two types of index that will be emerging by the end of this monograph.

Perhaps more important is another type of classification generated by the method of index calculation. Fisher et al. (1994) classify real-estate indices into two categories: transactions-based indices and appraisal-based (or valuation-based) indices. We discuss each in the following section.

2.2.1 TRANSACTION-BASED INDICES

Transaction-based indices take the actual transaction prices over the period into account. Indices that fall into this category can be good choices for the underlying for property derivatives if there is sufficient granular information and state-of-the-art statistical procedures to control for differences arising from trading in different periods and to minimize noise in the index returns. Two methodologies have been developed to deal with the statistical problems associated with transaction-based indices: the hedonic value methodology and the repeat-sales regression methodology. Transaction based indices have been proposed in the literature by Hoag (1980); Miles et al. (1990); Webb et al. (1992); and Fisher et al. (2004).

The hedonic value methodology, first introduced by Adelman and Griliches (1961) and then extended by Rosen (1974), involves regressing property prices on a function of various characteristics of the properties, such as size, age, location, and quality. The repeat-sales methodology, proposed by Bailey et al.

(1963) takes into account that individual properties are sold more than once. As opposed to appraisal-based indices discussed below that may deduct capital expenditures from the appreciation return of the index, the repeat-sales indices do not subtract the effect of capital improvement expenditures. The foundations of the methodology for constructing a repeat-sales house index are often attributed to Bailey et al. (1963). Shiller (2008a) has pointed out that the origins of the methodology were provided in the works of Wyngarden (1927) and Wenzlick (1952). A repeat-sales regression has been used for quotation of the Office of Federal Housing Enterprise Oversight House Price Index and the Standard & Poors (S&P)/Case-Shiller Home Price Index. Case and Shiller (1989) note that one major advantage of the repeat-sales indices is that they are not subject to the noise caused by a change in the mix of sales. The hedonic indices, by contrast, inherit all the pitfalls associated with regression methods, including multicollinearity, model misspecification, and parameter estimation error.

2.2.2 APPRAISAL-BASED INDICES

Appraisal-based indices, also referred to as valuation-based indices, are constructed from valuation models using continuously updated property characteristics. In a traditional appraisal-based index, all of the properties of the index population are appraised regularly, and the index returns are calculated from a simple aggregation of those appraised values in each period.

The appraisal-based indices have some basic flaws. They are difficult to maintain accurately for large or dense populated areas and are more subjective in their construction due to the same experts evaluating the properties year after year. For this reason the repeat-sales index seems to be the best choice for managing residential risk. This view appears to be supported by a recent Supervisory Capital Assessment Program initiated to determine whether the largest US banking organizations have sufficient capital buffers to withstand the impact of an economic environment that is more challenging than is currently anticipated. For this stress exercise, the Case-Shiller index, a repeat-sales index, has been designated as the representative index for housing prices in the United States.

Appraisal indices generally have a lower volatility than hedonic indices. In addition appraisal indices tend to lag behind the actual observed changes in the property markets because the valuation process is not carried out often enough. Furthermore, the appraisals do not reflect the real transaction prices as the information on the actual traded prices is opaque. Hence, a sudden change in market conditions is not immediately reflected in the appraisal process. This leads to an underestimation of appraisal indices in a bull market and in an overestimation for the same indices in a bear market.

2.3 **Main Real-Estate Indices Worldwide**

In this section we shall discuss the main econometric properties of real-estate indices, with a focus on United States and United Kingdom since they host the largest property derivatives markets. We are restricting our coverage to only the real-estate indices of these two countries for two reasons. Firstly, they are the most frequently used real-estate indices for investment purposes. Secondly, they are indices for which derivatives contracts have been designed, thereby allowing a different type of more leveraged trading to be executed.

2.3.1 THE INVESTMENT PROPERTY DATA INDEX

The Investment Property Databank (IPD) is a London-based entity that provides information about commercial real-estate in the United Kingdom and worldwide. This commercial real-estate index is constructed on directly owned investments in completed and available for rent property assets held in investment portfolios. Assets that were not fully owned or available for utilization during the period of measurement are excluded. The costs of trading, management fees, taxes, the impact of debt and cash are also excluded.

The IPD index family is now part of the MSCI group. The IPD family of indices are appraisal-based indices. The IPD UK Annual Property Index covered approximately 21,175 directly held UK property investments with a market value close to £152.7 billion as of December 2013. This index can be tracked back to December 1980, and, for a much smaller sample of assets, to December 1970. Reflecting the cumulative value of roughly 70% of the property assets held by UK institutions, trusts, partnerships and listed property companies, and almost 50% of the total professionally managed UK property investment market, the composition of the index is spread unevenly across various sectors of the real-estate market. Approximately 46.8% of the properties (4,156 properties worth £71 billion) are retail properties, 26.5% office properties (2,663 properties worth £40 billion), 15.4% industrial properties (2,850 properties worth £23.5 billion), 3.8% residential compound properties (9,127 properties worth £5.75 billion), and 7.5% (2379 properties worth £11.5 billion).

Indices from the IPD family are value-weighted measures, this means that each asset contributes to the index according to its monetary weight. The investment performance used to assess the performance of the index which is the total return, calculated with the formula:

$$TR_t = \frac{CV_t - CV_{t-1} - CE_t + CR_t + NI_t}{CV_{t-1} + CE_{t-1}} \times 100 \qquad (2.1)$$

where TR_t is the total return in month t, CV_t is the capital value at the end of month t, CE_t is the total capital expenditure in month t, CR_t is the total capital receipts in month t and NI_t is the day-dated rent receivable in month t, net of property management costs, ground rent and other irrecoverable expenditure.

The total return index value starts with a base value of 100 and is calculated by multiplying the previous index value using the formula

$$I_{t+1} = I_t \left(\frac{1 + TR_{t+1}}{100} \right) \tag{2.2}$$

where TR_{t+1} is the total return in month $t + 1$.

There is also an IPD UK Monthly Property Index started in 1986 that has a reduced representation given by a portfolio of 3,479 properties worth around £43.3 billion at year-end 2014, covering about 40%-50% of the market. The IPD UK Monthly index is employed for marking to market positions on derivatives taken on IPD UK Annual Property Index. The latest IPD UK index is a quarterly index, IPD UK Quarterly Property Index tracking the performance of a portfolio of 9,712 properties worth £134.5 billion as of September 2014. This index covers about 45%–55% of the market and the historical data goes back to 2000.

There is an entire family of IPD indices, all of which are exclusively determined by the open market appraised valuations of actual buildings by property professionals. All properties that are directly owned by the organizations providing appraisals to IPD are included; however, properties held indirectly through investment vehicles are excluded, as well as any bonds, cash or derivative holdings.

In Figure 2.1 we show the tests for serial correlation for the returns on the IPD UK Monthly index. As with other real-estate indices analysed below, there is an alternation of serial correlation, positive short term followed by negative autocorrelation which appears after year three.

Figure 2.1 displays an upward trend up to the end of 2006 combined with a significant market crash in 2008 in the level series and positive serial correlation short term followed by negative serial correlation longer term. Serial correlation, also referred to as autocorrelation, is a very important feature of time-series data. In its presence, standard statistical models may produce unreliable estimators and standard statistical tests may become biased. In other words, if there is serial correlation but it is ignored, the data analysis conclusions may be wrong. Typical examples are those of spurious correlations and spurious regression whereby an analyst finds statistically significant results when in fact the opposite is true.

Since real-estate property lacks granularity and the average time period to complete a real-estate transaction is three months, it is understandable that real-estate prices are sticky and one may expect a high degree of serial

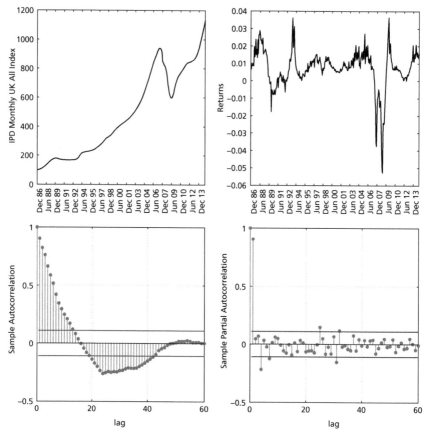

Figure 2.1. The IPD UK All Property Total Return Monthly Price Index between December 1986 and December 2014.

Notes: The IPD UK All Property Total Return Monthly Price Index level and percentage returns for monthly series between December 1986 and December 2014. The lower graphs show the ACF and PACF plots. The upper graphs show the index levels and percentage returns for the monthly series. The lower graphs show the sample autocorrelation and partial autocorrelation functions plots over the same time period.

correlation. The sample autocorrelation function (ACF) and partial autocorrelation function (PACF) are statistical measures that can be used to indicate the existence of autocorrelation at individual lags. It is important to test for autocorrelation at various time lags to see how long it takes for this effect to disappear. The ACF and PACF plots help in realizing after how many lags the information on those real-estate indices is not relevant for the current index value and also see if the relationship with past values is one of positive or negative correlation. Fortunately, there are statistical tests that can be used to test for the presence of serial correlation. The most commonly used statistical test is the Ljung-Box test.[3] The application of this test to the historical returns in Figure 2.1 using 6, 12, 30, 48, and 96 monthly lags clearly indicates that there is autocorrelation present even after eight years. The Q statistic for each lag and the corresponding critical value for determining if the computed Q value is statistical significant shown in parentheses is as follows: 6 months, 1064.5 (12.6), 12 months, 1245.7 (21.0), 30 months, 1470.6 (43.8), 48 months, 1643.3 (65.2), and 96 months, 1674.0 (119.9). Since the computed Q values are less than the corresponding critical value, we conclude that the observed serial correlation exhibited in Figure 2.1 is statistically significant. It is noteworthy that between January 1993 and September 2007, *all IPD monthly returns were positive*, representing one of the longest bull periods observed in an asset class, as pointed out by Tunaru (2013).

The IPDETRAI Monthly index represents the monthly estimates of the annual return of the IPD All Property Return. The values for this index for the period January 2005 to January 2014 are shown in Figure 2.2. Notice that the level of the index declined after the crisis of 2007–2008 to almost the initial level of 2005. The autocorrelation plots are very similar to the autocorrelation plots of the IPD Monthly UK All Return Index in Figure 2.1. Applying the Ljung-Box Q test to the monthly returns for this index indicates the existence of serial correlation at 6, 12, 30, 48, and 96 monthly lags. The Q statistic for each lag and the corresponding critical value for determining if the computed Q value is statistically significant shown in parentheses is as follows: 6 months, 299.00 (12.6), 12 months, 327.27 (21.0), 30 months, 504.11 (43.8), 48 months, 565.13 (65.2), and 96 months, 693.87 (119.9). Since the computed Q values are less than the corresponding critical value, we conclude that the observed serial correlation exhibited in Figure 2.2 is statistically significant.

From the autocorrelation graph in Figure 2.2 one can see that for the IPDE-TRAI monthly index the serial correlation is strongly positive for short-term periods of up to about one year, then negative for medium-term periods of length two years, and switching again to positive correlation for longer-term periods such as after five years. This type of behaviour of the real-estate index will pose some theoretical problems when we seek to develop pricing models for derivatives contingent on this index. For example, assuming a geometric Brownian motion for the continuous-time dynamics of such an index will be in flagrant contradiction with the stylized features revealed in this chapter.

---

[3] The Ljung-Box Q-test is helpful to quantitatively test the existence of autocorrelation at multiple lags. The null hypothesis for this test is that the first d autocorrelations are jointly zero; that is, $H_0 : \rho_1 = \rho_2 = \ldots = \rho_d = 0$.

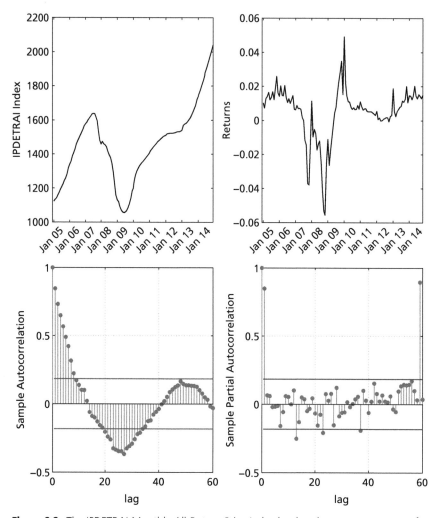

Figure 2.2. The IPDETRAI Monthly All Return Price Index level and percentage returns for monthly series between January 2005 and December 2014.

Notes: The lower graphs show the ACF and PACF plots. The upper graphs show the index levels and percentage returns for monthly series between January 2005 and December 2014. The lower graphs show the sample autocorrelation and partial autocorrelation functions plots over the same time period.

2.3.2 NCREIF PROPERTY INDEX

The National Council of Real Estate Investment Fiduciaries (NCREIF) is a not-for-profit trade association in the US that, according to its website, seeks to serve the institutional real-estate investment community as a non-partisan collector, processor, validator, and disseminator of real-estate performance information.[4] The indices produced by NCREIF are appraisal indices. The family of NCREIF indices includes, in addition to the most widely known classic national index, five property types (Apartment, Industrial, Office, Retail, and Hotel) and four main regions (East, South, Midwest, and West). There are also subindices for the eight subregions (Northeast, Mideast, Southeast, East North Central, South West, West North Central, Mountain, and Pacific). For each of these indices, three different types of return are calculated: (1) total return; (2) income return; and (3) capital appreciation return.

The data used in constructing the indices are obtained as follows. The members of NCREIF who have qualifying data on properties under management submit their valuations each quarter to the NCREIF Property Index (NPI). Then NCREIF aggregates the individual property data it receives and constructs indices such as the NPI. There is historical data that starts with the fourth quarter of 1977 and covers all types of property, including Industrial, Office, and Retail. In the third quarter of 1984 the NPI was expanded by the NCREIF to include Apartments and in 1995 leveraged properties were added to the NPI on a deleveraged basis with historical data being added back to 1982. The database from which the NPI was generated was expanded in 2000 to include alternative property types such as self-storage, seniors' housing, and others. In the first quarter of 2007, the database underpinning the NPI contained almost 5,500 properties with an estimated aggregate market value of $267 billion.

The National Property Index (NPI) is an appraisal index from the NCREIF family and the composite index includes income generated by the properties included in the index. The capital returns are derived from changes in appraised values. However, NCREIF returns tend to lag "true" market returns because not all properties are re-evaluated each quarter. The index is determined from the performance of institutional class properties owned by investment managers and pension funds. It is a quarterly index giving unlevered returns (total, income and appreciation) at the national and regional level by property type beginning in 1978. The methodology employed to construct this index is relatively simple. The index is set to 100 in the fourth quarter of 1977 and then quarterly returns of individual properties before the deduction of portfolio-level management fees but inclusive of property level management fees, are applied to derive the new property values. Each property's return is weighted by its market value (value-weighted).

The appraisal process that is used to construct the NPI is based on the market value that should be conceptualized as the most likely selling price for that particular property. As of the second quarter of 2013, the NCREIF database included almost 30,000 properties historically. There is an

---

[4] http://www.ncreif.org/about.aspx.

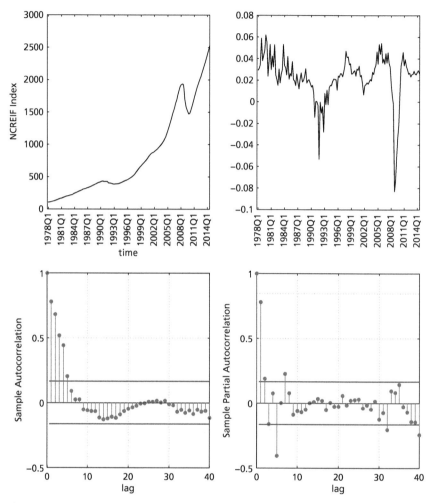

Figure 2.3. The NCREIF National House Price Index level and percentage returns for quarterly series between Q1 1978 and Q3 2014.

Notes: The upper graphs show the index levels and percentage returns for the quarterly series between Q1 1978 and Q3 2014. The lower graphs show the sample autocorrelation and partial autocorrelation functions plots over the same time period.

independent appraisal at least once a year, with the NCREIF members focusing on the discounted cash flow analysis.

It is known from the real-estate literature that NCREIF, as any other appraisal index, is subject to random appraisal error and appraisal smoothing error.[5] Both errors determine stale values, seasonality, smoothing, and lagging. Figure 2.3 shows a large market drop in commercial property values at the

---

[5] See, for example, Webb (1994), Fisher et al. (1999), and Cannon and Cole (2011).

beginning of the 1990s and the massive decline at the end of 2008/beginning of 2009. There is also large positive autocorrelation up to eight quarterly lags or two years and a subsequent weaker negative autocorrelation. Hence, any model proposed for pricing derivatives, such as futures or swaps, on this real-estate index must be capable of producing serial correlations of this nature. Otherwise, the flawed dynamics resulting from the model put forward for this index may lead to erroneous derivatives prices and risk measures. Application of the Ljung-Box Q-test for autocorrelation indicates that there is autocorrelation at 4, 8, 12 and 36 quarterly lags. The Q statistic for each lag and the corresponding critical value for determining if the computed Q value is statistical significant shown in parentheses is as follows: 4 months, 232.5 (9.48), 8 months, 240.3 (15.5), 12 months, 242.76 (21.02), and 36 months, 262.46 (50.99). Since the computed Q values are less than the corresponding critical value, we conclude that the observed serial correlation exhibited in Figure 2.3 is statistically significant.

The reliability of appraisal indices has been questioned by researchers since the late 1990s. Fisher et al. (1999) analysed 2,739 properties sold between 1978 and 1998 which were also covered in the NCREIF database. They were able to compare the values produced by the appraisal process with the actual trade values. The average absolute percentage error they found was between 9% and 12.5%, and the average percentage error was 2.64% over the entire period, being positive during up markets and negative during down markets. Cannon and Cole (2011) uncovered new evidence on the performance measurement and reporting of commercial real-estate returns and measure the accuracy of commercial real-estate appraisals reported before the sale of properties included in the NCREIF database between 1984 and 2010, a period covering two up-and-down cycles of the market. They found that, on average, appraisals are more than 12% above or below subsequent sales prices that take place two quarters after the appraisal. Even in a portfolio context where netting[6] will occur, appraisals have an error that is on average 4% to 5% of the actual transacted value, even after adjusting for capital appreciation during those two quarters. Furthermore, they point out that their analysis indicates that appraisals appear to lag behind the true sales prices, falling significantly below in hot markets and remaining significantly above in cold markets. They argue that the appraisal error is largely systematic and not due solely to property-specific heterogeneity.

While the NCREIF index covers unsecuritized real-estate, the cousin index NAREIT covers securitized real-estate. The latter index includes non-core

---

[6] By netting we mean that in a portfolio of real-estate assets some may increase in value while some other assets may decrease in value over the same period of time. The appraiser will give some estimates for the value of the properties and, because ultimately it is the overall estimate of the portfolio value that matters, positive errors will be cancelled out by negative errors and therefore in theory the overall error may be smaller.

properties and it has a much larger volatility than the former index which may be explained by the fact that it allows leverage. The MIT Center for Real Estate, in cooperation with the NCREIF, began publishing in 2006, the first regularly produced hedonic index of commercial property based on the prices of the properties sold from the NCREIF database.

2.3.3 MOODY'S/RCA COMMERCIAL PROPERTY PRICE INDEX

The Moody's/RCA Commercial Property Price Indices (CPPI) are transaction-based indices that measure property prices at a national level. Indices cover apartment, retail, office, and industrial properties. The RCA family of indices is produced by Real Capital Analytics (RCA), a data vendor tracking commercial real-estate transaction activities and prices in partnership with the MIT Center for Real Estate (MIT/CRE) and the firm Real Estate Analytics LLC (REAL). The series of price indices and capital returns have been published monthly on a national level since 2000. In addition, there are quarterly indices for the main property types and annual indices for select metropolitan statistical areas (MSAs).[7] The indices are transaction-based, constructed using a repeat-sales methodology similar to the one employed to produce the Case-Shiller/S&P housing prices indices. The majority of properties included in these indices are properties sold for more than $2.5million. Geltner (2007) describes how property derivatives contingent on the Moodys/RCA Index could be used to hedge CMBS risk.

Figure 2.4 shows that the CPPI exhibits a similar evolution for the level series and for the return series as does the IPD and NCREIF indices. However, the autocorrelation plot shows that the positive short-term serial correlation is followed by some weaker negative correlation on medium-term periods and an even stronger negative correlation for longer-term periods. There is no surprise then that the Ljung-Box Q-tests strongly reject the hypothesis of no autocorrelation at various lags such as 6, 12, 30, 48, and 96 monthly lags.

2.3.4 S&P CASE-SHILLER INDEX

The S&P/Case-Shiller family of Home Price Indices are the product of a partnership that includes S&P Dow Jones Indices LLC, Core Logic, and Macro-Markets LLC. They were developed using the research of Karl Case and Robert Shiller. This family of home price indices is the most representative for United States, covering 20 major MSAs and widely used as a benchmark for house prices there. The indices are based on the repeat sales pricing method, which

---

[7] MSAs are geographical entities that the US Office of Management and Budget specifies and is used for the collection, tabulation, and publication of Federal statistical agencies.

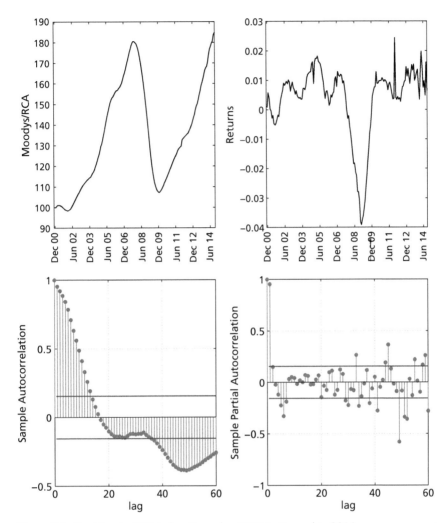

Figure 2.4. The Moodys/RCA Index: December 2000 to November 2014.

Notes: The upper graphs show the index levels and percentage returns for monthly series. The lower graphs show the sample autocorrelation and partial autocorrelation functions plots over the same time period.

has been recognized as a reliable methodology to account for housing price movements by the Office of Federal Housing Enterprise Oversight (OFHEO). A full description of the methodology behind this family of real-estate housing indices is described in S&P Dow Jones Indices (2014).[8]

The S&P/Case-Shiller Home Price Indices are calculated monthly and the indices for different MSAs are aggregated to form a 10 areas composite

---

[8] An historical account of the introduction of this index is given in Shiller (2008a).

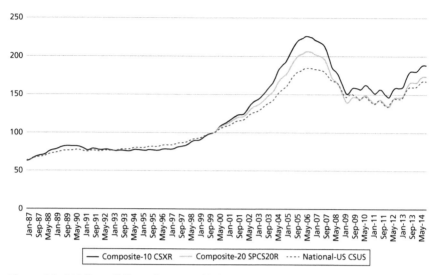

Figure 2.5. S&P/Case-Shiller Indices monthly between January 1987 and October 2014.

Notes: Historical evolution of S&P/Case-Shiller Indices: Composite 10, Composite 20, and National-US, monthly between January 1987 and October 2014.

index (Composite-10 CSXR) and a 20 areas composite index (Composite-20 SPCS20R). The S&P/Case-Shiller US National Home Price Index (the US national index National-US CSUS) represents the price of single-family homes in the United States. The historical data goes back to January 1987 for CSXR and National-US CSUS and to January 2000 for the SPCS20R. The three series are illustrated in Figure 2.5. The peak of all three indices occurred during the months of August and September in 2006. Some market observers have taken the moment of downturn in the S&P/Case-Shiller indices as an essential signal to a possible property market downturn.

The S&P/Case-Shiller family of indices measure changes in housing market prices without taking into account changes in the type of houses or in their physical characteristics and leaving out newly constructed houses, condominiums, coops/apartments or multi-family dwellings. The indices are calculated monthly based on rolling three-month periods, using a sample of sale pairs, representing the change in price between two consecutive sales of the same single-family home. The quality and size of the house is ensured to be the same. Sale pairs for the current month and the previous two months are employed in order to compensate for the delay in reporting house sales data. The sale pairs are weighted, by the repeat sales index model, to account for increasing variation in price changes due to transactions occurring over greater time periods.

Case and Shiller (1989) find positive serial correlation as well as inertia in house prices and excess returns, concluding that in the United States the market for single-family homes is inefficient. These characteristics make the real-estate market unique and the financial economics arguments invoked for product design, pricing, and hedging are bound to be different from other asset classes. The standard way to reduce or eliminate serial correlation effects is to work with the data on a returns scale. Even if serial correlation is not completely eliminated, the time series of returns is hopefully stationary whereas the price level series of real-estate is more trend-following.

As can be seen from Figure 2.6 the Case-Shiller Composite 10 index is highly autocorrelated, exhibiting a degree of predictability with a forecast R-squared at a one-year horizon of about 50%. This forecasting characteristic is attributed

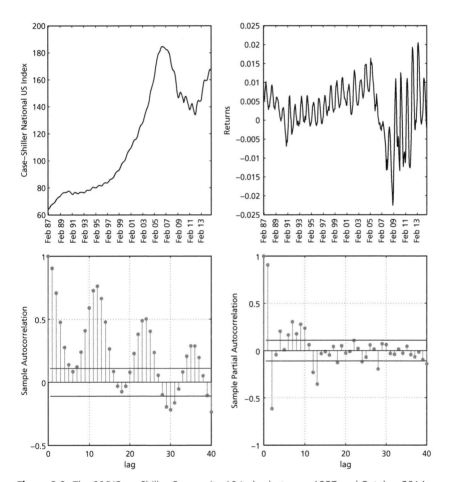

Figure 2.6. The S&P/Case-Shiller Composite 10 Index between 1987 and October 2014.

Notes: The upper graphs show the index levels and percentage returns for monthly series between 1987 and October 2014. The lower graphs show the sample autocorrelation and partial autocorrelation functions plots over the same time period.

to the profound illiquidity of the market. Furthermore, there seems to be a clear seasonality effect present in the returns series as well as in the autocorrelations, which are positive up to 2.5 years but turn negative afterwards. The visual inspection is confirmed by the Ljung-Box Q test that we conduct at 6, 12, 30, and 48 lags that correspond to the six months, one year, 2.5 years, and four years, which strongly reject the hypothesis of no autocorrelation.

A similar conclusion can be drawn for the S&P/Case-Shiller National US index over the same period. The only observable difference, see Figure 2.7, is that the decline in the National US index that seems to occur around the third quarter of 2007 is not so large as for the Composite 10 index. The S&P/Case-Shiller Composite 20 index has a shorter history starting in January 2000. Nevertheless, this index has similar characteristics to the other two indices from the same family as can be seen in Figure 2.7. There is high positive auto-correlation on the short term and negative autocorrelation on the longer term.

The S&P/Case-Shiller US national home price index is calculated using the formula:

$$H_t = \frac{\sum_i \frac{H_{it}}{H_{id}} V_{id}}{Divisor_d} \qquad (2.3)$$

where H_t is the value of the US national index in period t, H_{it} is the value of the home price index for the census division i in period t, H_{id} is the value of the home price index for the reference period d and V_{id} is the aggregate value of single-family housing stock in division i in the reference period d. The $Divisor_d$ is taken to make sure that the level of the composite index does not change due to changes in the reference period weights. The reference periods are: January 1990, January 2000 and January 2010. The national index is set equal to 100 at its base period in January 2000.

As with the S&P/Case-Shiller Composite-10 index, the Ljung-Box Q-test for the S&P/Case-Shiller Composite-20 index indicate that the hypothesis of no autocorrelation is strongly rejected at monthly 6, 12, 30, and 48 lags. There-fore, any model for the price dynamics of an index from the S&P/Case-Shiller family should be able to produce these empirical characteristics. For example, a geometric Brownian motion for the index levels would not be a suitable model because it does not hold the capacity to generate these kind of autocorrelations.

2.3.5 RESIDENTIAL PROPERTY INDEX

Developed by Radar Logic Incorporated, the Residential Property Index (RPX) is a relatively new residential index covering owner-occupied housing in 25 US MSAs. The RPX, updated daily, is measured in terms of price per square foot. This is probably the only real-estate index that is published on a daily basis.

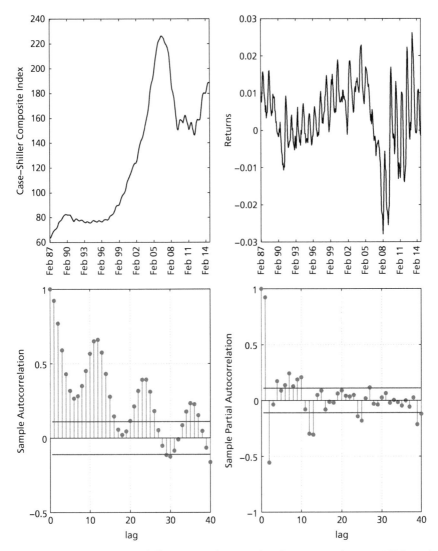

Figure 2.7. The S&P/Case-Shiller National US Index between February 1987 and October 2014.

Notes: The upper graphs show the index levels and returns for monthly series between 1987 and October 2014. The lower graphs show the sample autocorrelation and partial autocorrelation functions plots over the same time period.

This index can be used to account for values paid in arms-length residential real-estate transactions on a price per square foot basis. There is a family of RPX indices such as the MSA 25 Composite index covering the top 25 MSAs, as well as indices for each MSA.

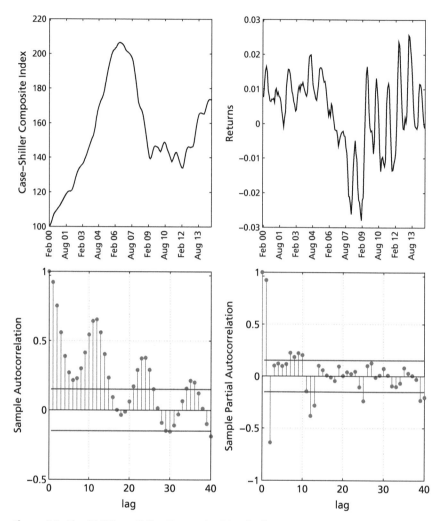

Figure 2.8. The S&P/Case-Shiller Composite 20 Index between 1987 and October 2014.

Notes: The upper graphs show the index levels and percentage returns for monthly series between 1987 and October 2014. The lower graphs show the sample autocorrelation and partial autocorrelation functions plots over the same time period.

The RPX family of indices includes three daily price values based on 1-day, 7-day, and 28-day time periods. Although the 7- and 28-day prices are not moving averages, they are calculated with the same methodology as the 1-day price, but using an aggregate of all transactions for the current published transaction date plus the prior 6 or 27 calendar days.

Because the RPX family of real-estate indices is the only family with a daily update, the historical evolution for these indices shown in Figure 2.9 exhibits

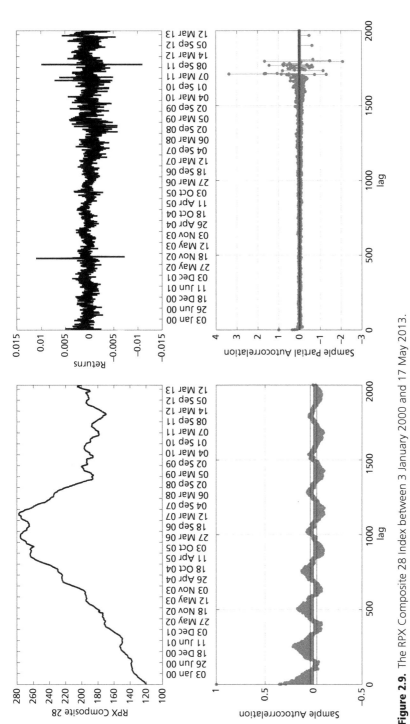

Figure 2.9. The RPX Composite 28 Index between 3 January 2000 and 17 May 2013.

Notes: The upper graphs show the index levels and returns for monthly series between 3 January 2000 and 17 May 2013. The lower graphs show the ACF and PACF plots.

a more dynamic change for the levels of these indices, particularly in the aftermath of the subprime mortgage crisis that began in the late summer of 2007. There is a clear spike in the returns series in 2002, both upwards and downwards. Furthermore, the RPX Composite 28 series after 2007 is clearly more volatile. The sample autocorrelation plot is quite surprising, showing a clear seasonal pattern. The Ljung-Box test for no serial correlation strongly rejects the hypothesis of zero autocorrelation. The Q statistic for each lag, and the corresponding critical value for determining if the computed Q value is statistically significant shown in parentheses are as follows: 20 days, 4,741 (31.4), 60 days, 8,007 (79.1), 90 days, 8,645 (113.1), 1,300 days, 32,831 (138.5), and 2,600 days, 44,520 (271.97). Since the computed Q values are less than the corresponding critical value, we conclude that the observed serial correlation exhibited in Figure 2.9 is statistically significant.

2.3.6 HALIFAX HOUSE PRICE INDEX

The Halifax House Price Index (HHPI) is constructed from the monthly values recovered from the mortgage database of the Halifax which is part of Lloyds Banking Group. Typically the HHPI covers an average of 15,000 house purchases per month. The index is constructed using the hedonic approach whereby a "standardized" house price is derived and seasonal adjustments are applied. The seasonal factors are updated monthly. In a similar fashion, a quarterly index series is also produced. The methodology for establishing this index is based on the research carried out by Fleming and Nellis (1981). The main idea in constructing this hedonic index was not to use averages but to take into account the property characteristics, taking advantage of the large pool of mortgage data managed by Halifax. In a nutshell the price of a house is estimated using a regression model that includes both qualitative and quantitative variables that include location (region), type of property (house detached, semi-detached or terraced bungalow, flat), age of property, tenure (freehold, leasehold, feudal), number of rooms (habitable rooms, bedrooms, living-rooms, bathrooms), number of separate toilets, central heating (none, full, partial), number of garages and garage spaces, garden, land area if greater than one acre, road charge liability.

The regression model used for calculation is specified as

$$\ln(P_i) = \beta_0 + \beta_1 X_{1i} + \beta_2 X_{2i} + \ldots + \beta_{ji} X_{ji} + \varepsilon_i \qquad (2.4)$$

The average house price within a particular period is influenced by the number of observations on each characteristic in the same period. Therefore, the house price could rise simply due to an increase to the number of houses sold relative to total house number. One way to solve this problem is to keep the mix of

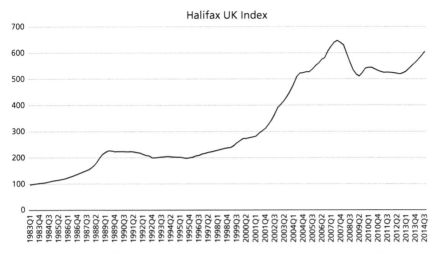

Figure 2.10. The Halifax House Price Index, quarterly between Q1 1983 and Q3 2014.

Notes: The historical price of Halifax All Property index, quarterly between Q1 1983 and Q3 2014, all houses, all buyers, seasonally adjusted.

house characteristics constant across time, by choosing a representative set of weights based on the number of observations of each characteristic for a chosen time period. The set of weights are fixed to the base period of 1983. The numerical value of this is derived by comparing the current mix-adjusted price to the base period weighted average price.

The evolution of the quarterly Halifax All Property SA is shown in Figure 2.10. The monthly version of the same index is illustrated in Figure 2.11. As can be seen by comparing the two figures, there is very little difference between the two indices, confirming the known empirical characteristics of the housing markets regarding price stickiness, inertia, strong short-term positive autocorrelation, and so on. One possible explanation is that it takes on average three calendar months to complete a property sale. Therefore, the speed of transactions in the housing market is very slow and structural changes to property prices may be observed only after periods longer than three months. Another possible explanation is based on the methodology used to construct the index. The hedonic approach is essentially a regression type approach. The variables used to construct the quarterly and the monthly indices, respectively, are the same and they are likely to have the same or very close values for all months within a quarter. This may lead to roughly the same path evolution of HHPI.

As with the IPD indices, the graphs illustrated in Figure 2.11 indicate that there is positive autocorrelation of returns up to about three years and then negative autocorrelation after five years. Although the Halifax UK SA monthly index levels show a similar evolution to all other real-estate indices,

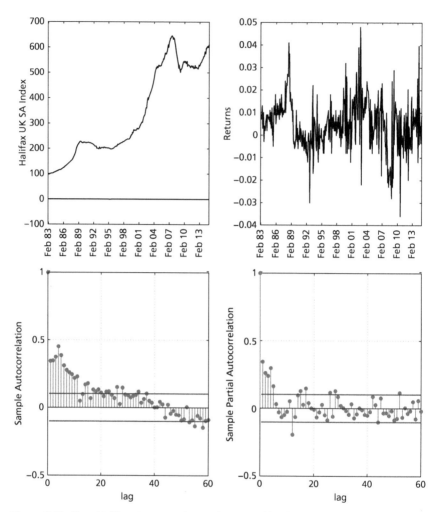

Figure 2.11. The Halifax House Price Index monthly between January 1983 and December 2014.

Notes: The historical price of Halifax All Property index, quarterly between Q1 1983 and Q3 2014, all houses, all buyers, seasonally adjusted. The upper graphs show the index levels and returns for monthly series between January 1983 and December 2014, all houses, all buyers, seasonally adjusted. The lower graphs show the ACF and PACF plots.

the percentage returns series seems to be a lot more volatile than the other property indices, but otherwise quite stationary. The Ljung-Box Q-test strongly rejects the absence of no autocorrelation at 6, 12, 30, and 96 monthly lags. Hence, this UK housing price index has similar stylized features as the US commercial and housing price indices. There are also 12 regional indices as well as a subindex dedicated to first time buyers, all calculated with the same hedonic methodology.

2.3.7 NATIONWIDE HOUSE PRICE INDEX

As of December 2014, the Nationwide Building Society (Nationwide hereafter) was the third largest mortgage lender in the United Kingdom, with a market share of almost 15%. The family of house price indices produced by Nationwide is comprised of 140 different indices. In the United Kingdom, the Nationwide House Price Index (NHPI) and the Halifax House Price Index (HHPI) are the most frequently used house price indices.

The methodology employed for calculating the NHPI index has evolved over time from a simple average of purchase price between 1952 and Q4 of 1959, to a weighted average depending on floor area for the period Q1 1960 to Q4 of 1973, progressing to a weighted averages using floor area, region and property type for the period between Q1 1974 to Q4 1982. Finally, the hedonic methodology of Fleming and Nellis (1981) was implemented in 1989 for all data after Q1 1983.

Interestingly, the market decline following the subprime mortgage crisis in 2007 did not come after a sudden market increase but after a sustained bull period of almost 20 years of growth. From an econometric perspective, the path of the UK house prices observed here leads to an oscillation in percentage returns around a long-run mean level of zero. Note that the volatility of this index increased after 1970, largely due to the increase in frequency and the size of jumps as can be seen in the upper-right panel of Figure 2.12 where more spikes occurred after 1970. Therefore, for modelling purposes, any continuous-time modelling for this index may consider incorporating jumps. There is a

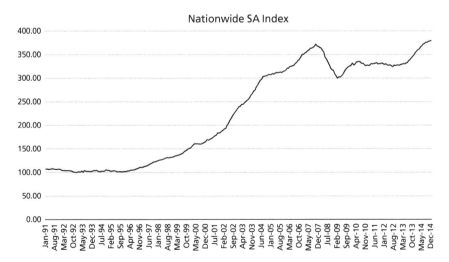

Figure 2.12. The Monthly Nationwide House Price Index: January 1991 to December 2014.

Notes: The historical evolution of the monthly Nationwide House Price Index seasonally adjusted between January 1991 and December 2014.

monthly version of the Nationwide seasonally adjusted index, starting with January 1991. This index series is illustrated in Figure 2.12. Compared to its quarterly counterpart, this index seems to show a smoother evolution. However, the period covered is not the same and the starting value of 100 is not setup at the same point in time.

The historical data plot for the quarterly NHPI depicted in Figure 2.13 shows a similar pattern to the Halifax index. Hence, the current methodology used

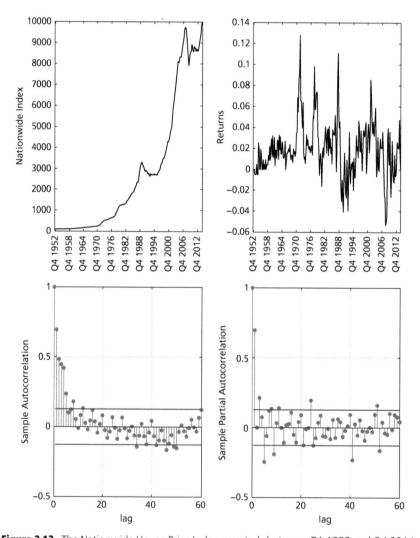

Figure 2.13. The Nationwide House Price Index, quarterly between Q1 1953 and Q4 2014.

Notes: The upper graphs show the index levels and returns for quarterly series between Q1 1953 and Q4 2014. The lower graphs show the ACF and PACF plots.

by Nationwide is also hedonic and very similar to the one used by Halifax. The variables used in the regressions are: location, type of neighbourhood, floor size, property design (detached house, semi-detached house, terraced house, bungalow, flat, etc.), number of bathrooms (1 or more than 1), type of garage (single garage, double garage, or none), number of bedrooms (1, 2, 3, 4, or more than 4), and new build (yes, no).

The graphs in Figure 2.13 appear to indicate that there is a clear indication of strong positive autocorrelation until lag 8, which corresponds to two years. On the longer term there appears to be a weaker but negative autocorrelation. This conclusion is confirmed using the Ljung-Box Q-test at 5% critical level. Furthermore, the graph depicting returns indicates two sharp upward spikes in the 1970s and one in the 1980s, followed by large market corrections. There is also a downward spike associated with the subprime crisis of 2007.

2.4 **Other Indices**

We conclude this chapter with a brief discussion of other indices:

- FTSE NAREIT Composite Total Return Index
- FTSE NAREIT Residential Property Sector Total Return Index
- S&P/GRA Commercial Real Estate Indices
- Rexx Index
- MSCI IPD UK Quarterly All Property Index

The FTSE NAREIT Composite Total Return Index (FNCOTR) includes both price and income returns of all publicly traded real-estate investment trusts, REITS (equity, mortgage, and hybrid). The index began on 31 December 1971 with a base of 100 and provided monthly data from January 1972 to December 1998. Since 4 January 1999 the index has been reported on a daily basis. In Figure 2.14 we present the daily version of the index that started when FNCOTR was 1115.11. The evolution of this index shows a slightly different type of plot compared to the plots for the real-estate indices presented earlier. Although the Ljung-Box Q-test strongly rejects the hypothesis of no autocorrelation at 20, 60, 90, 1,300 daily lags, it fails to reject at 2,600 daily lags. The Q statistic for each lag and the corresponding critical value for determining if the computed Q value is statistical significant shown in parentheses is as follows: 20 days, 225.6 (31.4), 60 days, 442.8 (79.1), 90 days, 639.4 (113.1), 1300 days, 1988.4 (138.5), and 2600 days, 2370.2 (271.97). The p-values for the 20, 60, 90, and 1300 days are all 0.00 but the p-value for 2600 days is 0.995. Hence, the serial correlation disappears at long horizon for this particular real-estate index. Therefore, this index seems to have a different behaviour, possibly caused by the equity REITS included in the index.

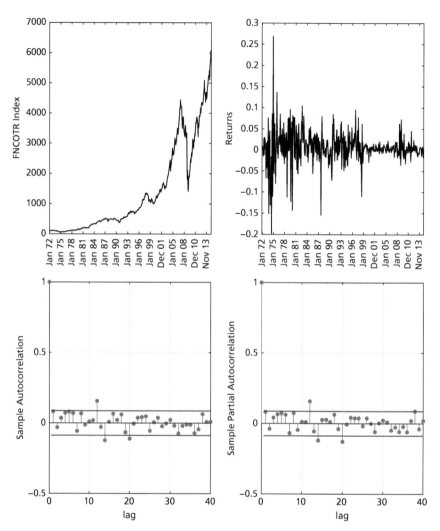

Figure 2.14. The FTSE NAREIT Composite Total Return Index, daily between 4 January 1999 and 2 February 2015.

Notes: The upper graphs show the index levels and returns for daily series between 4 January 1999 and 2 February 2015. The lower graphs show the ACF and PACF plots.

A related index is the FTSE NAREIT Residential Property Sector Total Return Index for which a daily series between 6 March 2006 and 2 February 2015 is available. This index has a similar historical evolution to the FTSE NAREIT Composite TR Index as can be seen in Figure 2.15. There is evidence of serial correlation, short term and medium term but, for this particular index the autocorrelation disappears in the long term (10 years). The Q statistic for each lag and the corresponding critical value for determining

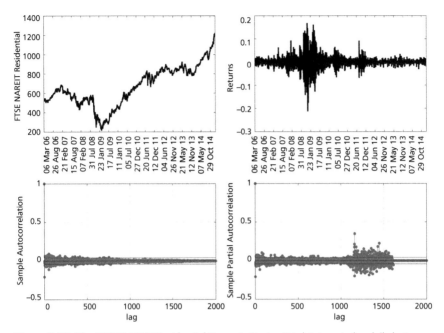

Figure 2.15. The FTSE NAREIT Residential Property Sector Total Return Index daily between 5 March 2006 and 2 February 2015.

Notes: The upper graphs show the index levels and percentage returns for daily series between 5 March 2006 and 2 February 2015. The lower graphs show the ACF and PACF plots.

if the computed Q value is statistical significant shown in parentheses is as follows: 20 days, 166.5 (31.4), 60 days, 337.7 (79.1), 90 days, 463.14 (113.1), 1300 days, 1427.4 (138.5), and 2600 days, 1516.1 (271.97). The p-values for the 20, 60, 90, and 1300 days are all 0.00 but the p-value for 2600 days is 1. Hence, once again the serial correlation disappears at long horizon for this particular real-estate index.

The S&P/GRA Commercial Real Estate Indices (SPCREX), produced by S&P and Global Real Analytics (GRA)/Charles Schwab, is a transaction-based index derived as a three-month moving average of average sale price per square foot. It is reported quarterly and it does not include income. A proprietary algorithm is applied to property-level transaction price per square foot data. The SPCREX indices are traded on CME.

The Rexx Index was developed by Cushman & Wakefield and Newmark, Knight, Frank for office properties only in 1994. This index is calculated quarterly and it provides returns (total, rent and capital) at the national level as well as for 15 major MSAs. The valuation for the index is based on a proprietary model using variables such as rents, vacancy rates and leasing activity, jointly with macroeconomic variables such as interest rates and inflation.

The DIX (Deutscher Imobilien Index) is Germany's only real-estate performance index based on an extensive databank covering 55 different portfolios of institutional portfolios, representing 44% of the relevant institutional property market. The performance for DIX is measured as a total return that is extracted from the net cash-flow yields and value-change yields for real-estate properties.

In the UK MSCI has taken over the IPD family of indices. The IPD UK Quarterly All Property Index is being offered by MSCI with a view to having information on commercial property markets in the UK being provided more frequently at quarterly steps. This index measures the performance of unlevered direct commercial property in UK, covering 9,618 properties with a value of £145 bn as of 2015 (PDIG, 2015). The index has 30 years of historical index performance and it is commonly used for many UK property funds. The index is also used after 2015 as the underlying index for property futures on EUREX. The MSCI IPD UK Quarterly family of indices are available at composite level (UK All Property), sector level (UK Office, UK Retail, UK Industrial) and subsector levels (UK Retail Warehouses, UK Shopping Centres, London City Offices).

Other real-estate indices include Chambres Des Notaires/INSEE which is a residential index covering Paris, calculated on a transaction basis, with a semi-annual frequency and a price return and Hong Kong University RE (HKU), which is a residential index covering Hong Kong, on a transaction basis, monthly on a price return.

2.5 **Summary Points and Further Reading**

There is a wide range of real-estate indices covering commercial as well as residential property. The majority of indices that have been in use in the real-estate investment finance are either in United States or United Kingdom. Real-estate derivatives are currently traded on some of these indices, such as NCREIF, S&P/Case-Shiller, RPX, IPD and Halifax, but since the market of property derivatives is only in its infancy we can envisage a growth of these products being introduced in relation to the other indices revised in this section and possibly other indices not mentioned here.

It is important to know the type of real-estate index based on its method of construction. The methodologies underpinning the real-estate indices described here, hedonic, repeat sales, appraisal or transaction based should be taken into consideration when modelling real-estate indices. We envisage that the frequency of publication may play a role in accelerating the development of real-estate derivatives markets. The historical annual frequency may be a deterrent to the evolution of real-estate derivatives, since the information flow on real-estate indices at an annual frequency seems to be too slow for financial markets and it may even induce herding and other behavioural undesirable effects.

The stylized facts about the real-estate indices are important not only for a better understanding of the real-estate investment market per se but also for better model construction for pricing real-estate derivatives. Serial correlation is a major feature of real-estate indices as demonstrated comprehensibly in this chapter and in general this is positive short-term, and negative medium-term. Longer term serial correlation may switch back to being positive, albeit weakly positive, or disappear as in the case of daily calculated indices. Taking into account the stylized features of real-estate indices is necessary to avoid model risk.

Kuo (1996) studied the serial correlation and seasonality of residential property prices in four US metropolitan areas from 1971 to 1986 and found that the US indices have strong autocorrelation, therefore rejecting the random-walk hypothesis. Hill et al. (1999) combined hedonic and repeat sales data and test for the presence of a random walk on the data from the four metropolitan areas from Case and Shiller (1989) and on 347 repeat sales from Baton Rouge. The hypothesis of random walk is rejected in both Case and Shiller and Baton Rouge data. Gu (2002) studies the autocorrelation in house price movements using the quarterly Conventional Mortgage Home Price Index for all US states between 1975 and 1999. He suggests that autocorrelation differs across geographic areas and over time periods, in periods when there is negative autocorrelation in the house price indices, the autocorrelation having a positive relationship with volatility and negative with the rate of return; while in the periods when the autocorrelation between longer periods is positive, it is negatively related to the volatility and positively with the rate of return. Schindler (2013) analysed the predictability of the S&P/Case-Shiller Index, for the national level and across 20 metropolitan areas, using the real and log price indices over the period from 1987 to 2009, employing parametric and non-parametric independence tests. They found empirical evidence of strong persistence in price changes for both real and nominal indices allowing both autocorrelation and moving average based strategies to be profitable, depending on the size of the transaction costs.

3 Financial Modelling for Mortgages

3.1 Introduction

Financial markets are dominated by fixed income markets which, in turn, evolve mainly around the large family of swaps. Interest rate swaps were invented in the 1980s as a solution to the interest rate risk posed by the very large mortgage portfolios in the US. Mortgages were contracts that allowed social emancipation and spot real-estate is arguably the largest asset class, in essence representing the major part of the market. In the US mortgages were arranged mainly as up to five year balloon-payment mortgages before the 1930s, although long-term fixed-rate self-amortizing mortgages were also available but not taken by borrowers.[1] After the first US national housing crisis between 1925–1933 when house prices dropped by almost 30%, people started taking the self-amortizing mortgages.

The US, UK, and Japan are probably the largest mortgage markets in the world. Kamra et al. (2012) reported that the total outstanding mortgage loans for the US, UK and Japan were about 6.625, 1.214, and 1.475 trillion GBP, respectively, representing as a proportion of GDP 74.3%, 89.5%, and 37.6%, respectively. The home ownership is roughly 65%, 70% and 60% for these three countries.

In spite of the importance of real-estate market to the overall economy and despite the sophisticated quantitative finance evolution experience by all the other asset classes, housing finance is still in its infancy and there are still many barriers to housing finance innovation as highlighted by Shiller (2014). One can argue, that closing down the mortgage markets will have a domino effect leading to a closure of the swap markets and ultimately the fixed income market, at least partially.

Investors in mortgages are exposed to two types of options. First there is a call option on long-term debt generated by the early prepayment that is allowed in the mortgage contract. Mortgage houses have introduced early repayment charges to deter the exercising of this option when interest rate levels change over time in favor of the mortgagors. The second option is a put option on real-estate prices and is given by the possibility that the mortgagor will default on her mortgage contract. This put option may be guaranteed

---

[1] For a historical discussion of the American mortgage please see Green and Wachter (2005).

by law in states where mortgage contracts are nonrecourse. In other states, the option may not be guaranteed by law but court decisions in favor of lenders recouping their losses from non real-estate assets of mortgagors are very rare.

Negative equity, occurring when the current value of the house is below the value of the mortgage loan, seems to be the root of all evils in house price crashes. Whenever housing price risk appears, the negative equity risk is the major factor deeply embedded in any product that is exposed to house price risk, including actuarial related contracts such as reverse mortgages. In the UK there has been a budget proposal suggesting that the first half of the negative equity losses to be covered by the private insurance sector and the government to be a kind of lender of last resort for the second half (Quantum Alpha Limited, 2013). However, the government has adopted a different scheme called *Help to Buy Mortgage Guarantee*. Under this scheme the maximum LTV was raised to 95%, but it does not provide automatic workouts and there is no cover provided by the private sector. Moreover, the lender will be refunded if there is any default up to the seventh year, the taxpayer gets losses up to 15% of the loan and the government is also charging a premium for facilitating this scheme. It is not clear how this premium is calculated.

Over time several solutions have been proposed to mitigate house price risk between the owners and lenders. This is very important from a social point of view for people trying to get on the property ladder such as first-time buyers, but also for the people towards the end part of their working life who put most of their money into bricks and mortar and are faced with lack of cash to serve their needs. The Dodd-Frank act recommended a study of shared appreciation mortgages (SAMs), which were marketed by Bank of Scotland and Bear Sterns in the 1990s. This type of mortgage received bad press in UK because of homeowners that used them for speculation and then lost. However, Iacoviello and Ortalo-Magné (2003) studied the benefits of introducing property derivatives which allowed households to hedge their house price risk exposure and they showed that the existence of property derivatives can improve welfare, particularly for the house owners with lower income.

Shiller (2008c) introduced continuous workout mortgages (CWMs), designed with a pre-specified workout mechanism that rebalances the outstanding balance constantly in accord to a real-estate index of house prices that is representative for the local area. It was proved (Shiller et al., 2013) that this product can be priced efficiently and that their introduction will lead to a significant welfare gain. Syz et al. (2008) proposed an index-linked mortgage where the payments are directly related to the corresponding housing performance. These type of mortgages, developed for Switzerland, could link the principal to a housing index and keep interest payment fixed or fix the principal and link the interest rate payments.

The purpose of this chapter is to familiarize the reader with the concept of mortgages and to describe the behavioural factors behind decisions to prepay and default on mortgages that ultimately influence the evolution of real-estate markets. The other scope of this chapter is to highlight the complexity of the financial modelling related to real-estate area, and to mortgages in general.

3.2 **Mortgages**

The exposure to mortgages is the main driver for the need of real-estate derivatives. The channels through which real-estate price risk is finding its way out in the financial markets are mainly defined by mortgages. Hence, a minimal understanding of the main characteristics of mortgages is helpful for appreciating the requirements for modelling arising with real-estate derivatives. In this chapter, we describe the commercial and residential mortgages including their main drivers. Furthermore, the focus in the second part of this chapter is on prepayment models since they are used intensively in the area of real-estate investment banking and are needed in relation with balance guaranteed swaps discussed later on in Chapter 4.

3.2.1 COMMERCIAL MORTGAGES

Commercial mortgages are loans that are secured by commercial properties such as apartment buildings, shopping malls, warehouse facilities, offices, hotels and so on. The borrowers typically pay only interest and are due a balloon payment on principal at the end of the mortgage that has a maturity usually between seven to ten years. The notional in these loans is quite large, in US this ranges between $2 million and $100 million.

Commercial mortgages do not have prepayment risk since it is unusual for a commercial mortgage to prepay. The only form of prepayment risk occurring for this asset class is marginalized to lockouts (after one year typically) or penalties triggered by covenants in the contract. The main risk here is default risk.

The risk coming out of the commercial mortgage loan is defined by the collateral rather than the borrower. From this point of view commercial mortgage loans are closer to corporate loans. The majority of commercial mortgages were fixed rate loans traditionally although flexible rate loans are increasingly common.

Commercial mortgage prices and residential mortgage prices show similar time-series patterns with autocorrelation and mean reversion over long time periods. There seems to be more volatility present in commercial property prices than in the corresponding housing prices. Gyourko (2009) calculated the correlations between various commercial real-estate indices in the US and one residential real-estate index for almost 30 years before 2008 and he found evidence of substantial correlation between the two sectors of real-estate markets. This was 38% between NAREIT and the Federal Housing Finance Agency (FHFA), 39% between NCREIF and FHFA and 65% between the Transactions-Based Index (TBI), which is computed by the MIT Center for Real Estate based on sales out of the NCREIF index, and FHFA.

There is also upward bias or positive market sentiment in these markets, which pushed the prices higher up prior to the subprime crisis.

3.2.2   RESIDENTIAL MORTGAGES

By definition a *mortgage* is a loan that is secured by underlying assets (collateral) that can be repossessed in the event of default. The collateral is the property (+ improvements if any) *and* the land. These loans are serviced by specialized units that will collect the fees and pass them to the investors. The key characteristics of a mortgage are

- Lien status: implying the loan's seniority in case of default
- Original loan term: previously 30 years, also linked to fixed mortgages; shift towards shorter terms in recent years
- Credit quality: *prime loans* and *subprime loans*; in between you have *alt-A* loans, which are considered to be prime (hence the A rating).
- Interest rate type: fixed rate and floating rates
- Amortization type: amortizing or interest only
- Credit guarantees: conventional loans and government backed loans
- Loan balances: the agencies have set limits for loan balance that can be part of a pool they back up
- Prepayment and prepayment penalties

In the UK the subprime mortgages are called *nonconforming*. We assume that in what follows subprime and nonconforming are used interchangeably although there are subtle legal differences between the two. In the UK the main type of interest rates charged to mortgages are a) *standard variable rates* (SVR), which is lender specific and typically linked in a non-explicit way to the Bank of England Base Rate (BBR) b) *fixed rates*, these rates are fixed only for a period of time and then they revert to the banks SVR, c) *tracker* this is a rate linked explicitly to BBR or SVR or some other public rate, d) a *cap and/or collar rate* where interest is allowed to vary within boundaries, and e) *discount rate* this is a low interest rate applicable for a very short period of time to allow first-time buyers enter the market, it then reverts to a higher rate or SVR after the discount period.

Mortgages can also be classified by the purpose of the loan into purchase mortgages, discussed in this chapter, and reverse mortgage or equity release mortgages, which are the subject of Chapter 8. They can be also classified as buy-to-let (when the owners buy the properties to rent them out) and primary (when the buyers use the property as their residence). Self-certified mortgages refer to the fact that the documentation regarding income is not verifiable by a third party as an employer. An offset mortgage is a product where the loan is linked with a savings account and the interest is paid only on the net notional between the loan and the savings account.

Many of the securitized deals contained future exposure to SVR rates and were therefore exposed to interest rate risk. Rating agencies insisted that as part of the securitization the deal also contained hedges of interest rate risk when assets where moved to the SPV. However, since the future SVR rates where idiosyncratic to the banks they could not be part of the derivatives contracts aimed at hedging interest rate risk. This is still a problem for the regulator to solve!

Prime vs. Nonconforming Mortgages

A *prime* mortgage is characterized by the following attributes:

- clean credit history
- an HPI equal to three times the earnings
- full documentation of earnings
- owner occupancy (owner lives in)

The *nonconforming* mortgage is defined by

- any breach of the criteria for prime moves the mortgage into nonconforming territory
- self-certified: borrowers are self-employed, new workers, economic migrants
- credit repair: problems in the past but which are now resolved
- credit impaired: CCJs, repossessions
- BTL: borrowers are individuals or property companies
- right-to-buy: former council tenants

A revision of mortgage calculus

A quick revision of mortgage calculus is useful in order to appreciate the interlinkages between various cash-flows generated in relation to a mortgage. We shall denote for each month t: $c(t)$ the MBS cash flow for month t; $MP(t)$ the scheduled mortgage payment; $TPP(t)$ the total principal payment; $IP(t)$ the interest payment; $SP(t)$ the scheduled principal payment; $PP(t)$ the principal payment; $B(t)$ the balance at end of month t; WAC the weighted average coupon on the pool of mortgages, weighted by the balance of each mortgage; WAM the weighted average maturity, weighted by the balance of each mortgage; $SMM(t)$ the single monthly mortality for month t observed at the end of the month; $CPR(t)$ is the conditional prepayment rate for month t, observed at the end of month t.

Then the following formulae are used routinely in mortgage markets.

$$c(t) = MP(t) + PP(t)$$
$$= TPP(t) + IP(t)$$
$$MP(t) = SP(t) + IP(t)$$
$$TPP(t) = SP(t) + PP(t)$$
$$MP(t) = B(t-1)\left(\frac{WAC/12}{1 - (1 + WAC/12)^{-WAM+t}}\right)$$
$$IP(t) = B(t-1)\frac{WAC}{12}$$
$$PP(t) = SMM(t)[B(t-1) - SP(t)]$$
$$B(t) = B(t-1) - TPP(t)$$
$$SMM(t) = 1 - (1 - CPR(t))^{1/12}$$

The *single mortality rate* (SMM) has nothing to do with the mortality of the borrowers. Sometimes, a different convention is used, employing the total monthly principal prepayments on a pool as a percentage of the balance at the beginning of the month in question

$$SMM = 100 \times \frac{\text{scheduled balance} - \text{actual balance}}{\text{scheduled balance}} \tag{3.1}$$

The *conditional prepayment rate* (CPR) is then given by

$$CPR = 100 \times \left[1 - \left(1 - \frac{SMM}{100}\right)^{12}\right] \tag{3.2}$$

The CPR are annualized SMM rates. They are widely used for communicating risk related to MBS.

A CPR of 20% is translated into the monthly mortality rate SMM

$$SMM = 1 - (1 - 20\%)^{1/12} = 1.8423\%$$

The PSA model (Public Securities Association– now the Securities Industry and Financial Markets Association) is the simplest standard model taking into

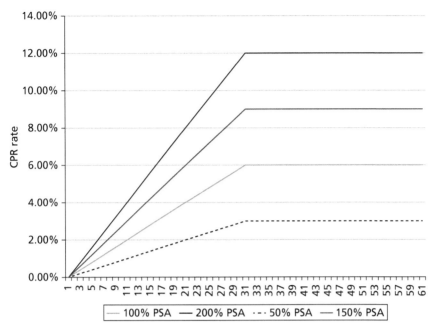

Figure 3.1. The PSA CPR curves.

account that in the very first months the prepayments will ramp up. The 100% PSA specifies that prepayments start with 0.2% in the first month and increase by 0.2% per month until they reach 6.0% CPR in month 30; after that they stay flat at 6% for the life of the portfolio. A 200% PSA has double the speed, 0.4% in ramp-up period to the terminal 12% speed from month 30.

The formula for PSA curve generation is

$$PSA = 100 \times \frac{CPR}{min(age, 30) \times 0.2} \tag{3.3}$$

The PSA model is sensitive to the age of the loan, or the weighted average loan age (WALA). Hence a 4.0% CPR in month 20 is equivalent to 100% PSA, while a 4.0% CPR in month 6 is equivalent to 333% PSA. When the prepayment ramps shorten, as has happened historically, the PSA model may distort the actual prepayment rate behaviour. When interest rates go down prepayments increase and the price of MBS goes down, underperforming bonds without prepayment exposure, while when interest rates go up, prepayments go down so average life and duration of MBS bonds increase. This phenomenon is called *extension risk*. Mortgage borrowers are called *mortgagors* by analogy with corporate borrowers who are called *obligors*. The Figure 3.1 shows various PSA curves.

3.3 **Main Drivers of Mortgage Rates**

3.3.1 PREPAYMENT RISK

Prepayment risk is seen as a major risk in good times when the economy is doing well and the interest rates may not be too high. The investor does not want his money not being paid at all but he also does not like being paid too soon either because of reinvestment risk. The rate at which borrowers in a pool prepay their mortgages is defined as prepayment speed.

What causes prepayment?

Home sales Homes that are on a mortgage loan, when sold will lead to the prepayment of the mortgage.

Refinancings Another major cause of prepayments refers to mortgagors taking advantage of lower rates by refinancing out of an existing loan into a new one. This factor is the most volatile component of prepayment speeds, and causes the bulk of prepayments when speeds are very high.

Defaults A prepayment caused by a foreclosure and follow up liquidation of a mortgage. This is a minor component in good times, averaging less than 0.5% per year in US in normal times for moderately seasoned loans, and is close to zero for very seasoned loans; however it may become a major component during periods of market downturns and recessions.

Curtailments Some borrowers may occasionally pay more than the scheduled monthly payment in an effort to increase their equity in their property. These extra payments, called partial prepayments or curtailments, contribute in the aggregate to the prepayments of principal and, for fixed rate loans it will shorten the loan maturity.

Full payoffs Historical evidence suggests that many borrowers pay off their mortgage in full when the loan is very seasoned and the remaining loan balance is small. Full payoffs may also occur because of insurance related payments to natural disasters such as hurricanes and earthquakes.

Refinancing Incentive Related to the difference between the current mortgage rate and the prevailing loan rate. Although some believe that the larger the difference the greater the incentive to prepay, the ratio between the two rates seem to be more determinant.

Burnout effect This is the tendency for prepayment to decay over time even when refinancing is possible.

- If the mortgage rates decrease below a given threshold then rise up and then go down below this threshold again, the burnout effect means that there would be fewer prepayments second time round because the borrowers with highest likelihood to prepay have done it first time.

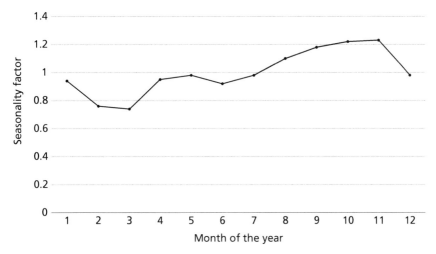

Figure 3.2. Seasonality as used by Richard and Roll in the Goldman Sachs model.

Notes: The graph is constructed from the numerical values detailed in Richard and Roll (1989).

- The pool factor defined as the total mortgage balance outstanding divided by the original mortgage balance is an important ratio for assessing the level of prepayment; a lower ratio means that prepayments have already occurred.

Seasoning This means that new loans will prepay slower than older ones. Over time, prepayment rates are low immediately after issuance and increase after some seasoning . Fixed rate mortgages season quicker than adjustable-rate mortgages slowing down prepayments. At the end of the fixed rate period the remortgage rate is close to the market rate and this prevents prepayments.

Seasonality House trading is higher in the spring and peaks in late summer, so there are higher prepayments in those months. There are fewer sales in autumn and winter with lower prepayment rates then.

3.3.2 DEFAULT RISK

Default is easy to define for corporates but it is not so straightforward for home-owners. In general we have default when the lender has already repossessed the property. This can only be done following:

- a court order
- the borrower informing the lender that he is no longer paying and is prepared to hand over the property

It takes time to repossess and for risk management calculation purposes the timing of actual default is difficult to be determine. The main factors influencing default are

Ability to pay This factor is generated by common reasons such as divorce, disability or increase in family members, which are more idiosyncratic. The other common reason is unemployment and this is a systematic risk related to the economic cycle.

Willingness to pay If a borrower gets into negative equity then he/she has a strong incentive to default on the mortgage and let the lender take over the house. This is a put option that is in the money once the loan-to-value (LTV) exceeds 100%. Thus LTV is a major indicator of default.

3.3.3 ARREARS

A borrower may be in arrears by any number of months. Arrears are measured by the number of overdue monthly payments. From the risk management perspective, there is a cutoff point after which the loan is considered in default. In practice, the loan can be in arrears for a few months, then clear, then in arrears again, and so on.

For modelling purposes it is best to define a transition matrix for the arrears, with two states (prepayment and default) as absorbent states. The transition matrix technique is similar to the rating transition matrix estimation used in credit. Arrears are signalling that the loan is on its path to default. Very little has been done for efficient modelling of arrears and defaults.

The Office of Thrift Supervision (OTS) classified loans as being in arrears (delinquent) as follows

- payment due date up to 30 days late: current
- 30–60 days late: 30 days delinquent
- 60–90 days late: 60 days delinquent
- more than 90 days late: 90+ days delinquent

3.3.4 LOSS SEVERITY

Upon failure to make the monthly payments the property that is the collateral to the loan will be repossessed. The outstanding debt has three components

1. the remaining mortgage balance
2. the overdue interest payments
3. any fees incurred in connection with arrears servicing, property repossession and property sale.

If the sale proceeds are greater than the outstanding debt the excess is returned to the former home owner. However, if the opposite is true then the lender has a loss The loss severity can be measured as expected loss divided by the remaining mortgage balance.

3.3.5 DRIVERS OF LOSSES FOR NONCONFORMING MORTGAGES

There are several drivers of losses for nonconforming[2] mortgages. Firstly, supply and demand is very important. An indicator of housing market demand is the number of loans approved by lenders, as reported by the Council of Mortgage Lenders (CML). Secondly, property markets are known to exhibit a mean-reversion effect, so the longer a residential market has been on a bull run the higher the probability of a downturn. The geographic location also plays a role since in many developed economies there is a clear north/south or west/east divide. The vintage of the borrowers, their location and their LTV at origination also plays an important role. High inflation or deflation can both lead to losses, reflecting major problems in the real economy. Interestingly, mass-media (always referring to nominal prices!!) and market sentiment (if my neighbour is safe then I am safe) can also skew the views of borrowers and trigger default decisions.

Lenders apply to court for a possession order, which will legally enable them to repossess and sell the property used as security, once a mortgage is three months in arrears. Usually there is a period that can reach even 12–18 months from the mortgage falling into default to the property being sold.

Individual voluntary arrangements (IVAs) are similar to bankruptcy: the borrower is protected from unsecured creditors and interest stops accruing if she/he pays an agreed amount for a limited period (usually five years). IVAs are not the same as bankruptcy because the primary residence can be retained. Thus, IVAs do not crystallize losses as opposed to bankruptcies, they only impair the credit quality of the borrower.

3.3.6 RISK MANAGEMENT CONSIDERATIONS FOR MORTGAGES

Since the risk drivers for the main options embedded in mortgage portfolios are interest rate risk and house price risk, one may think that buying some options or entering into futures contracts on these two markets would be enough to offset the risks of early prepayment option and default option. However, mortgage portfolios have different maturity and rates characteristics and they are very large. In order to manage interest rate risk related to prepayment the investors in mortgages would have to buy thousand of options with different strikes and maturities. Buying a basket option is not feasible either because of the large number of mortgages (in thousands). A similar rationale occurs for

---

[2] Nonconforming is the term used in the UK for subprime mortgages in US.

house price risk. Combine that with the fact that for one amortizing mortgage there is a pre-specified vector of strike prices at monthly dates and it becomes clear that it is not feasible to use bespoke options. Furthermore, the options are not exercised as in capital markets because the holders of those options may exercise them following a mixture of rational decisions and forced events.[3]

As discussed in detail by Case and Shiller (1996) a better solution to risk management of prepayment risk and default risk is to use futures contracts. The first interest rate futures market was established in 1975, the Government National Mortgage Association (GNMA), in order to cover prepayment risk and interest rate risk. The GNMA futures market perished because the delivery option in the contract led to poor hedging of prepayment risks.

Any GNMA bond is collateralized by a pool of mortgages. There is no default risk because it is guaranteed against default by the full faith and credit of the US government, but actually what this means practically is that if there is a default the GNMA will prepay the mortgage. Hence, for GNMA bonds, the government guarantee transforms default risk into prepayment risk.

The subprime crisis has highlighted that default risk can lead to catastrophic losses, well beyond the losses caused by prepayment. As house prices fall the losses to mortgage lenders increase non-linearly. There is ample evidence[4] that the main predictor of default is the LTV ratio. As emphasized by Case and Shiller (1996), regional house prices can exhibit large swings, making it difficult to hedge mortgage default risk in the absence of national and regional derivatives markets on house price indices.

Prepayment and default risks are competing risks and perhaps the state of the art modelling in this area should consider modelling these two risks jointly. Even better, by analogy with rating transition matrices, a total view on risks would be obtained by modelling mortgages in several states: a normal paying state, several arrears states (up to six or twelve months), a prepayment state and a default state. The last two states are absorbent state in the sense that when a mortgagor enters this state they will never leave it. This approach would be data intensive but it will provide early warnings for both prepayment and default.

3.4 An Overview of Prepayment Models

Prepayment models are at the heart of valuation and risk management in RMBS markets and securitization. We have seen a description of the static cash-flow models (PSA). However, under this model the pricing is unrealistic

---

[3] Even prepayments can be forced by events. If a house is ruined by fire or an earthquake the borrower will get money from his insurance to redo his house and the money obtained from insurance may be used to pay in full the mortgage first.

[4] See Foster and Order (1984), Kau et al. (1994), and Quercia and Stegman (1992) for early evidence.

and it gives misleading price-yield and duration-yield curves. Here we review briefly some of the models developed by academics in partnership with banks and other financial institutions.

3.4.1 THE ARCTANGENT MODEL

This is called the *arctangent* model, see an example in Asay et al. (1987)

$$CPR_t = \alpha_1 - \alpha_2 \arctan[\alpha_3(\alpha_4 + SPD_t)] \qquad (3.4)$$

where *CPR* is the conditional prepayment rate, *SPD* is the difference between the prevailing market loan rate and the loan coupon rate and arctan is the arctangent function.

Example 3.1. *A calibrated model done in the past is*

$$CPR_t = 0.3 - 0.16 \arctan[123.11(0.02 + SPD_t)] \qquad (3.5)$$

With these parameter values the CPR rates as a function of the new available mortgage rate on the market, generated by this model, are illustrated in Figure 3.3.
   When the loan rate is high, such as 8% and 5%, the CPR can be very high if the new offered rate is close to zero and it decreases rapidly with the increase of new mortgage rates.

Example 3.2. *The following calibrated model is from the Office of Thrift Supervision.*

$$CPR(t) = 0.2406 - 0.1389 \arctan\left[5.9518\left(1.089 - \frac{WAC}{r_{10}(t)}\right)\right]$$

where WAC is the weighted average coupon on the pool of mortgages and $r_{10}(t)$ is the 10 year swap rate that proxies the market mortgage rate.
   The CPR calculations depicted in Figure 3.4 show overall a similar picture with the CPR produced by the arctangent model. When the loan rate is high, such as 8% and 5%, once again the CPR can be very high aproaching 45% if the new offered rate is close to zero and it decreases rapidly with the increase of new mortgage rates.

However, comparing the two graphs in the above two examples for the case when the loan rate is 2% we can see that the modified arctangent model used by the Office of Thrift Supervision can produce CPR values close to 45% whereas the original arctangent model for the same loan rate 2% can only generate a CPR of maximum 16% when the new rate is almost zero. Hence, using the ratio of the contracted loan rate to the new mortgage rate as opposed to their difference may generate very different values of CPR.

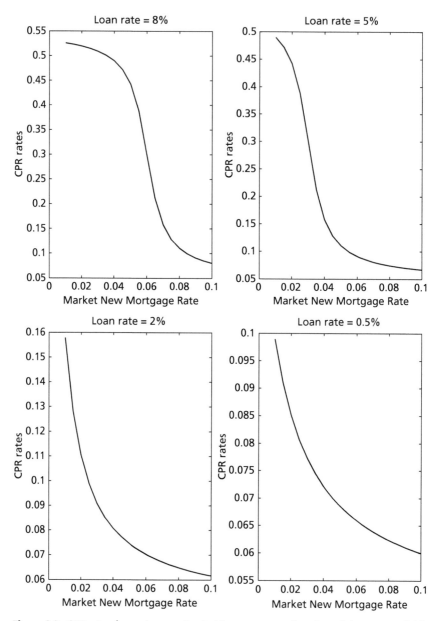

Figure 3.3. CPR rates for various contracted loan rates as a function of the new available mortgage rate on the market using the Asay et al. (1987) model.

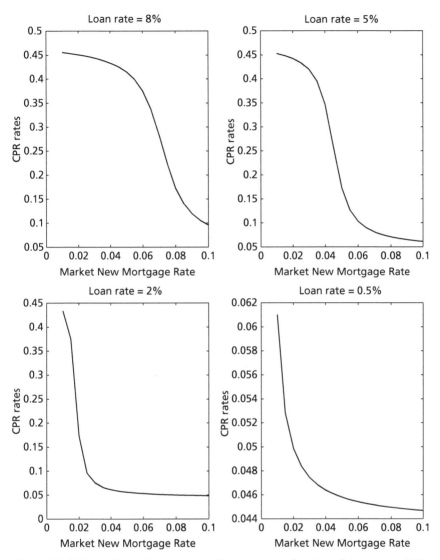

Figure 3.4. CPR rates for various contracted loan rates as a function of the new available mortgage rate on the market using the modified arctangent model used by the Office of Thrift Supervision.

3.4.2 THE CHINLOY MODEL

Chinloy (1989, 1991) proposed the prepayment model

$$CPR_t = \alpha_1 - \alpha_2 \times r + \alpha_3 \times R + \alpha_4 \times \tau \tag{3.6}$$

where r is the average market rate on newly originated fixed rate mortgages, R is the contracted rate and τ is the seasoning or age of the loan.

Example 3.3. *A calibration on GNMA mortgage backed securities from Jan 1986 to May 1989 produced*

$$CPR_t = 0.0813 - 1.7951 \times r + 0.9063 \times R + 0.0012 \times \tau \qquad (3.7)$$

Chinloy remarked that seasoning does not affect the probability of prepayment.

One major deficiency of this model is the fact that the two important rates contributing to the prepayment activity, the loan rate R and the refinancing rate r are linked to the CPR linearly. This is illustrated by the graphs in Figure 3.5 and it is in contradiction with market experience.

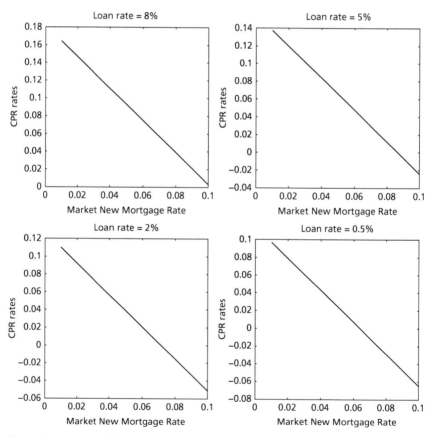

Figure 3.5. CPR rates for various contracted loan rates as a function of the new available mortgage rate on the market using the Chinloy model.

3.4.3 THE SCHWARTZ AND TOROUS MODEL

This is a proportional hazard model proposed by Schwartz and Torous (1989) and given by

$$SMM(t) \equiv \pi(t; V, \beta) = \pi_0(t; \lambda, p) \exp \left[\sum_{i=1}^{4} \beta_i V_i(t) \right]$$

$$= \frac{\lambda p (\lambda t)^{p-1}}{1 + (\lambda t)^p} \exp \left[\sum_{i=1}^{4} \beta_i V_i(t) \right] \qquad (3.8)$$

where

1. $V_1(t) = c - l(t - s), s \geq 0$, with c is the contracted mortgage rate, l is the long-term treasury rate for month t with an s-month lag. In general $s = 3$ is used.

2. $V_2(t) = [c - l(t - s)]^3, s \geq 0$ represents an acceleration factor when the refinancing rates are sufficiently lower than the mortgage contract rate.

3. $V_3(t) = \ln \frac{B(t)}{B^*(t)}$ accounts for the burn-out effect where $B(t)$ is the dollar amount of the pool outstanding at time t and $B^*(t)$ is the pool's principal that would prevail at t in the absence of prepayments but would consider the amortization of the underlying mortgages.

4. $V_4(t)$ is +1 if t is May to August and 0 if t is September to April.

Here $\pi_0(t; \lambda, p)$ is the baseline function which explains the CRP when the factor vector $V = 0$. The baseline value of π_0 shows us that the mortgage will suffer a baseline risk at any time of the mortgage. The factor $\exp(\beta V)$ represents the mortgage specified risk.

The explanatory variables in the Schwartz and Torous (1989) model may include the costs of refinancing, borrowers characteristics, property characteristics. By using a proportional hazard model the explanatory variables impact equi-proportional at all mortgage ages.

Focusing only on the covariate variables listed above as in the original paper, one should expect $\beta_1 > 0$ because a larger value of V_1 implies a greater incentive to prepay; $\beta_2 > 0$ since if the proxy of a new mortgage rate l indicates that lower available rates increase further the incentive to refinance; $\beta_3 > 0$ because the covariate V_3 is likely to be negative and higher in absolute value when more mortgages in the pool have been prepaid already, so there will be less mortgage borrowers looking to prepay. Clearly, $\beta_4 > 0$ because it is well known that prepayment activities are higher in the spring and summer due to the effects of the school calendar year.

Example 3.4. *Calibrating on Ginnie Mae 30-year single-pool family prepayment rates for the period Jan 1978 to Nov 1987 the following values* were reported[5] in Schwartz and Torous (1989) when the covariates included the seasonality covariate,

$$\lambda = 0.0149 \ (0.001), \ p = 2.312 \ (0.139), \ \beta_1 = 0.380 \ (0.064), \quad (3.9)$$

$$\beta_2 = 0.003 \ (0.001), \ \beta_3 = 3.577 \ (0.345), \ \beta_4 = 0.266 \ (0.329)$$

Another estimation carried out by leaving out the seasonality covariate gave the estimation results

$$\lambda = 0.0157 \ (0.002), \ p = 2.350 \ (0.121), \ \beta_1 = 0.397 \ (0.043) \quad (3.10)$$

$$\beta_2 = 0.004 \ (0.001), \ \beta_3 = 3.743 \ (0.447)$$

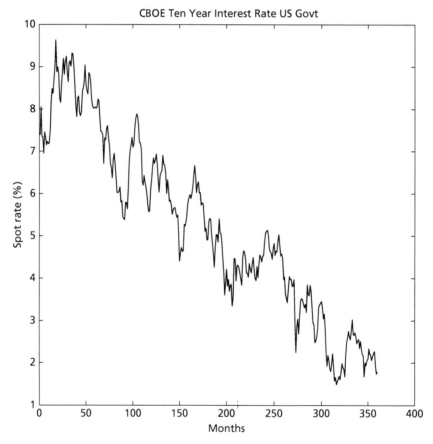

Figure 3.6. Historical 10 Year US Government Interest Rates, monthly between April 1986 and May 2016.

Source of Data: CBOE

[5] The estimates are maximum-likelihood estimates with jacknifed standard deviation estimates in parentheses.

In order to see how the Schwartz-Torous model would be applied, we take as a proxy for the new mortgage market rate the 10 Year US Government Spot Rate. This is illustrated in Figure 3.6. Then we calculate the baseline hazard rate, scheduled balance, prepayment rates amortizing balance for a hypothetical 200,000 USD 30-year fixed rate mortgage. Issued in April 1986. There are 360 months for which we calculate the SMM rate and their corresponding CPR rates. We must remark that the general trend between 1986 and 2016 was a clear downward trend.

For a mortgage with a contractual fixed mortgage rate of $c = 15\%$ the prepayment calculations are depicted in Figure 3.7. For reference calculations of baseline hazard rate, scheduled balance, prepayment rates and amortizing

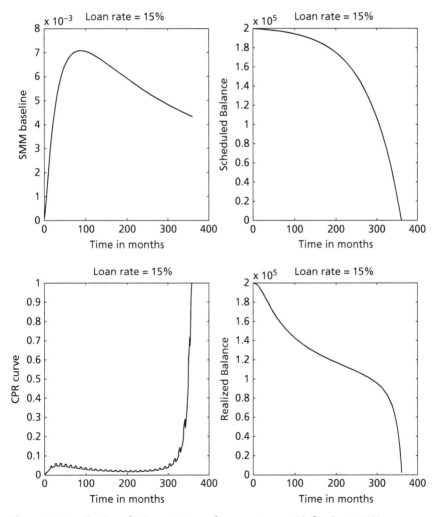

Figure 3.7. Application of Schwartz-Torous for a mortgage with fixed rate 15%.

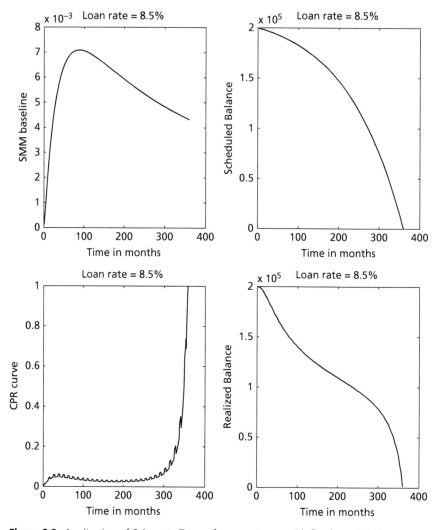

Figure 3.8. Application of Schwartz-Torous for a mortgage with fixed rate 8.5%.

balance are done for a hypothetical 200,000 USD 30-year fixed rate mortgage, issued in April 1986. For comparison we repeat the prepayment calculations for different contractual mortgage rates $c \in \{8.5\%, 5\%, 1\%\}$. The results are presented in Figures 3.8-3.10, respectively.

It can be observed that while the baseline hazard rate curve is the same in all four scenarios – as it should be by design,– the prepayment curve is also very much the same in all four scenarios. The amortization of the scheduled balance changes from a concave shape at high contractual mortgage rates to an almost linear amortization for the 1% mortgage rate. The realized balance

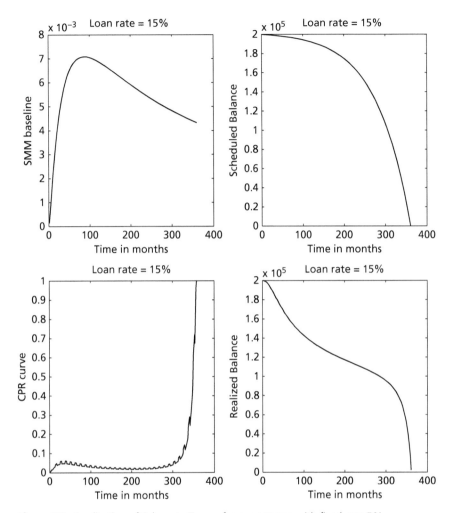

Figure 3.9. Application of Schwartz-Torous for a mortgage with fixed rate 5%.

has a similar shape in all four scenarios, amortizing faster in the first part of the mortgage life, in contrast with market evidence showing that borrowers do not refinance early on but rather in line with the refinancing incentive, given that the new rates were going lower over time. The prepayment balance slows down in the middle—this was the period of late 1990s and beginning of 2000s when rates increased for a while, and then finally the prepayment rates increase exponentially towards the end leading to a fast amortization of the balance.

One major advantage of the Schwartz-Torous model is that it can be used for a loan-by-loan analysis and for specialized mortgage portfolios such as buy-to-let or first time buyers that exhibit different behaviour to the other borrowers.

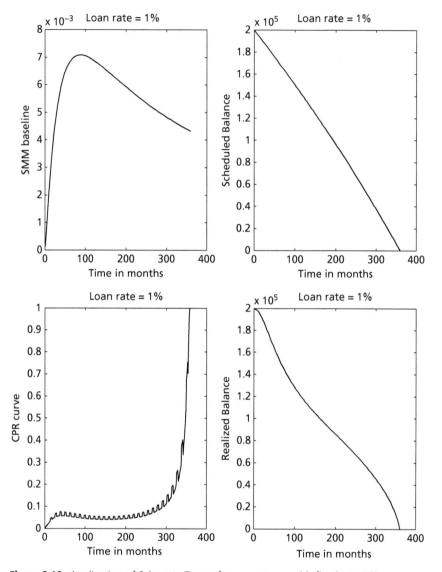

Figure 3.10. Application of Schwartz-Torous for a mortgage with fixed rate 1%.

3.4.4 THE GOLDMAN SACHS MODEL (RICHARD AND ROLL, 1989)

Richard and Roll (1989) developed a prepayment model used by Goldman Sachs. The Richard-Roll model was given by

$$CPR_t = RI_t \times SF_t \times M_t \times BF_t \tag{3.11}$$

where *CPR* is the conditional annual prepayment rate, RI_t is the refinancing incentive, SF_t is the seasoning factor and M_t is the month factor BF_t is the pool burnout factor.

Here

$$RI_t = \alpha_1 + \alpha_2 \arctan[\alpha_3 + \alpha_4(WAC - R_t)] \qquad (3.12)$$

where $\alpha_1 = (maxCPR + minCPR)/2$, $\alpha_2 = 100\frac{max\ CPR - \alpha_1}{\pi/2}$, $\alpha_4 = maxslope/$ α_1 and $\alpha_3 = \alpha_4$ midpoint difference. WAC is the weighted average coupon rate or the contracted loan rate while R_t is the available new market mortgage rate. It is assumed generally that max CPR = 50%, min CPR 0%, the midpoint 25% CPR is at diff = 200 bps and at midpoint max slope is 6% CPR for a 10 bps shift.

The seasoning multiplier is $SF_t = min(\frac{t}{30}, 1)$ while the monthly multiplier is given by the vector (taken from Richard and Roll 1989)

$$M(t) = (0.94, 0.76, 0.74, 0.95, 0.98, 0.92, 0.98, 1.10, 1.18, 1.22, 1.23, 0.98)$$

The burnout factor is specified as

$$BF_t = \beta_1 + \beta_2 \frac{B(t)}{B(0)}$$

where $B(t)$ is the balance at time t. Some calibrations gave $\beta_0 = 0.3$ and $\beta_1 = 0.7$.

For the evolution of interest rates we use the ten year government spot rate historical data described and used above in Section 3.4.3. We calculate the CPR curves working with a hypothetical 200,000 USD 30-year fixed rate mortgage issued at the beginning of the year in 1986. There are 360 months for which we calculate the CPR rates for various contractual fixed mortgage rate of $c \in$ {15%, 8.5%, 5%, 1%}. The CPR curves generated by the Goldman-Sachs model are illustrated in Figure 3.11.

This model has some design deficiencies. First of all, the refinancing factor may become negative depending on the values of the calibrated parameters and the evolution of interest rates used as a proxy for the new mortgage rates. Secondly, a decrease of the CPR due to burnout effect may be cancelled out by the existence of a lower interest rate. As with previous models, perhaps the ratio of the two competing rates, the contracted mortgage rate and the market available rate, is more relevant than the difference in rates.

3.4.5 THE MODIFIED GOLDMAN SACHS MODEL

In this extended model the refinancing incentive factor is modelled as

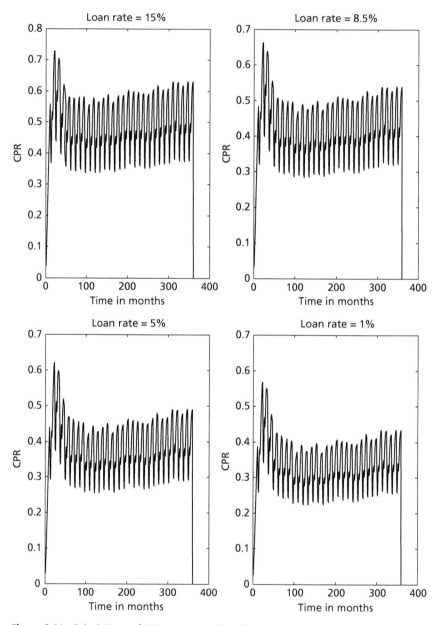

Figure 3.11. Calculations of CPR curves produced by the Goldman Sachs model.

$$RI_t = \alpha_1 - \alpha_2 \arctan \left\{ \alpha_3 \left[\alpha_4 - \frac{C_t + S_t}{P_t + F_t} \right] \right\} \tag{3.13}$$

where C is the MBS average coupon rate, S is the loan-servicing rate taken out of the pool, P is the refinancing rate and F is the additional refinancing cost associated with refinancing the mortgage. Hence, this model pays more attention to the various payments that need to be made in the case of a voluntary prepayment.

The seasoning factor begins at 0 at month 0 and linearly approaches 1 over a specified seasoning period; a loan is fully seasoned after 30 months. The idea behind this model is that new mortgages are not likely to be prepaid for a number of months because homeowners will not relocate immediately. New buyers are unlikely to refinance immediately because of transactions costs and inconvenience.

Observing that the prepayments are higher in the later summer months. The month factor is a sine wave given by

$$M_t = 1 + 0.2 \sin \left[\frac{\pi}{2} (m + t - 3)/3 - 1 \right] \tag{3.14}$$

where m is the month $\{1, 2, \ldots, 12\}$ in which the MBS is priced.

Pool burnout means that not all mortgagors in the pool prepay identically. In reality there are faster payers and slower payers. The more often the option has been in the money the more rapidly pool burnout will happen. The burnout factor proposed in this model was

$$BF_t = \exp(-\alpha B_t) \tag{3.15}$$

where B_t is a function of the ratio of the mortgage coupon rate to the refinancing rate.

3.4.6 A NUMERICAL EXAMPLE OF USING THE RICHARD AND ROLL MODEL

In this section we shall highlight how to implement the Richard and Roll model for prepayment rates. The model is given by (3.11) with the Refinance Incentive modelled as in (3.13), but taking $S_t \equiv 0$ and $F_t \equiv 0$. The version we apply here is the one described by the Office of Thrift Supervision that calibrated the refinancing parameters to

$$\alpha_1 = 0.24, \quad \alpha_2 = 0.14, \quad \alpha_3 = 5.95, \quad \alpha_4 = 1.09$$

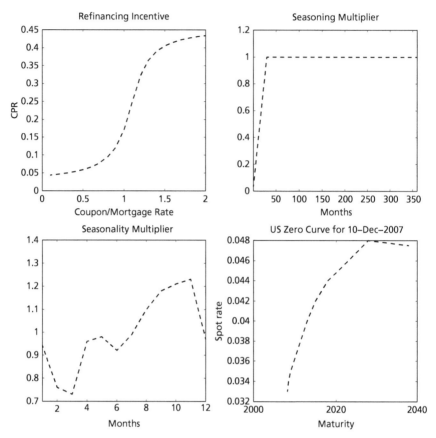

Figure 3.12. Input Curves for CPR Calculations by the Modified Richard and Roll Goldman Sachs Model.

We consider pricing an RMBS deal on 10 December 2007 with 15 years maturity. The coupon rate is 4.5%. The graphs in Figure 3.12 show the main components of this model, the refinancing incentive, the seasoning, seasonality and the zero spot curve on the day of calculation.

It is crucial for this model implementation to be able to generate future paths of interest rates. Some of the rates will be used as a proxy for the future mortgage market rate and also, for valuation purposes one would need the discount factors represented by the zero spot rates curve. Here two popular interest rate models are implemented, the LIBOR Market Model (LMM) and the two-factor Hull-White short rate model. These models are described succinctly in Appendix 3.8.

The model is specified once the volatility and correlation functions are given. Using the popular volatility specification described in 3.24, the volatility and correlations are calibrated to the caps/floors/swaptions market data on the

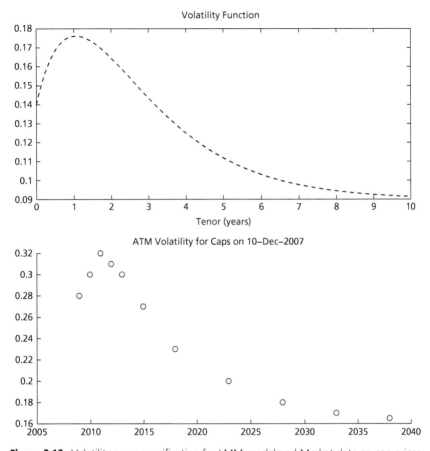

Figure 3.13. Volatility curve specification for LMM model and Market data on cap prices.

day. The volatility function and the cap market at-the-money volatilities are depicted in Figure 3.13. The fit of the LMM model is depicted in Figure 3.14. indicating a very good fit.

After fitting the LMM model, we can simulate various paths of interest rates in the future. Two such simulations are described in Figures 3.15–3.16.

Similarly, after calibrating the Hull-White two factor model, one can simulate interest rate scenario paths interest rate scenario paths for interest rates with different tenors. We also provide here two such paths, under this different interest rate model. Two such simulations are described in Figures 3.17–3.18.

The simulated interest rates can be very different under the same model and across different models. A Monte Carlo simulation analysis would be able to account for these uncertainties.

Once we have a tool to simulate future interest rates of different tenors, we can continue and start constructing future possible mortgage rates. The Office

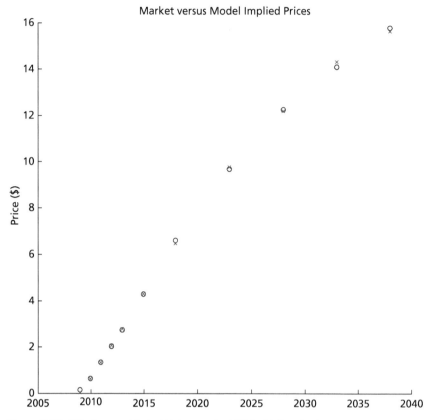

Figure 3.14. Fitted versus Market Values under LMM of interest rates.

of Thrift Supervision has calculated the mortgage rate as a linear combination of the two year spot rate and the ten year spot rate. For the sake of exemplification, suppose that the new mortgage rate is given by the specification

$$\omega_t = 0.024 + 0.2R(2) + 0.6R(10)$$

where ω_t is the new mortgage rate, $R(2)$ is the two year spot rate and $R(10)$ is the ten year spot rate.

Using the simulators for spot interest rates will give future values for the market mortgage rate which can then be fed into the Richard and Roll arctan model to produce the CPR values. In Figure 3.19 we illustrate the CPR curves resulting from the LMM model and from the two-factor Gaussian Hull-White model. For comparison we also add the PSA curves. For most of the mortgage life the CPR rates given by the two interest rate models are very similar. However, towards the end of the mortgage, the LMM implied CPR values are a lot higher

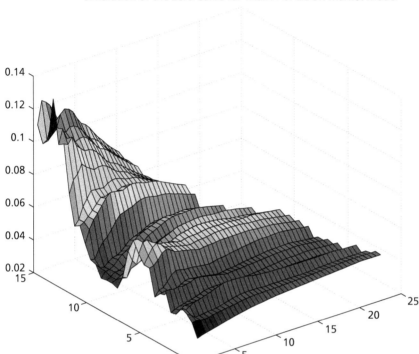

Simulation of the Zero Curve for Trial:11 of LIBOR Market Model

Figure 3.15. One Simulated Interest Rate Surface under LMM.

than the Hull-White model. Moreover, as can be seen in Figure 3.20 from a different Monte Carlo simulation under the same model parameters, it is also possible that the CPR values under the Hull-White model are significantly higher than the CPR values of the LMM.

The RMBS deal is then priced as 1.0178 under 100 PSA prepayment assumption, as 0.9874 under the CPR curves given by the LMM and as 0.9869 under the CPR curves given by the Hull-White model.

3.4.7 CITIGROUP MODEL

The Citigroup model for prepayments and defaults of nonconforming the UK mortgages (Kamra et al., 2012) starts from the standard assumption that the prepayments are generated by the *turnover*, defined as the selling of a house, the *refinancing rate*, which is the new mortgage rate available on the market, and occurring *defaults*. Turnover and refinancing mortgage lead to voluntary prepayments, whereas defaults are caused by forced events. The model calculates

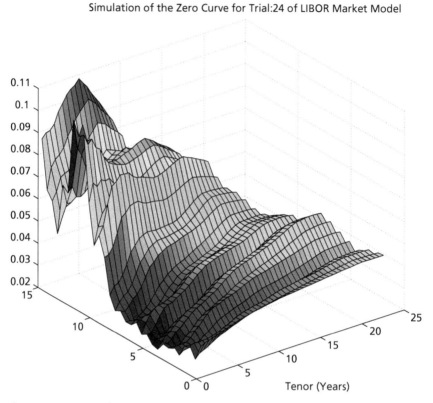

Figure 3.16. A Second Simulated Interest Rate Surface under LMM.

the prepayment monthly rates due to each source, adds them up and then annualizes the results into CPR rates.

Under this model, the turnover rate $\psi(t)$ at month t is calculated from the formula

$$\psi(t) = HS(t) \times \xi(t) \times f(Age, HPAM) \tag{3.16}$$

where $HS(t)$ is the projected base house turnover rate, $\xi(t)$ is the seasonality factor, *Age* represents the time since the loan has been taken and *HPAM* is a term accounting for the 12-month change in house prices.

The refinancing rate $\varrho(t)$ is constructed from the refinancing rates of different mortgage products, with fixed, discount and variable rates. Thus

$$\varrho(t) = \left[\varrho_{fixed}(t) + \varrho_{discount}(t) + \varrho_{variable}(t) \right] \times f(LendingSqueeze)$$
$$\times \Lambda(t) / \Gamma(t) \tag{3.17}$$

Simulation of the Zero Curve for Trial:25 of G2++ Model

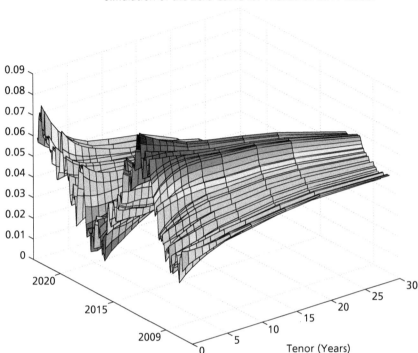

Figure 3.17. One Simulated Interest Rate Surface under two-factor Hull-White Model.

where $\Lambda(t)$ is for seasoning, $\Gamma(t)$ is for prepay penalty and LendingSqueeze is a term calculated as a function of the spread between LIBOR and the average mortgage rate at time t. Each of the three refinancing rates is modelled separately as follows

$$\varrho_{fixed}(t) = \delta_{fixed}(t) \times f(bmRate(0) - bmRate(t))$$

where $\delta_{fixed}(t)$ is the proportion of fixed rate mortgage loans in the total portfolio outstanding collateral and $bmRate(t)$ is the benchmark rate of the loans at time t;

$$\varrho_{discount} = \sum_{\tau=-3}^{\tau=3} \delta_{discount}(t+\tau) \times c_{\tau}$$

where $\delta_{discount}(t)$ is the proportion of discount rate loans in the outstanding collateral that is due to reset at time t and c_{τ} are some normalization constants enforcing that the amount of refinancing resulting from discount-rate mortgages is less that the total discount rate mortgages due to reset; and finally

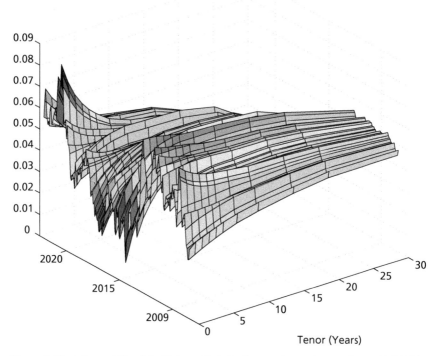

Simulation of the Zero Curve for Trial:50 of G2++ Model

Figure 3.18. A Second Simulated Interest Rate Surface under under two-factor Hull-White Model.

$$\varrho_{variable}(t) = \delta_{variable}(t) \times f(\Delta bmRate \times [Mrate_{variable} - Mrate_{discount}])$$

where $\delta_{variable}$ is the proportion of variable-rate loans in the outstanding collateral and $Mrate$ is the mortgage rate for the type of mortgage.

The Citigroup model calculates the default rate from a multiplicative model generated by various factors such as LTV, low documentation level, CCJs,[6] unemployment and a rate payment shock. The formula for the default rate $\eta(t)$ is

$$\eta(t) = \eta^*(t) \times f_1(LTV) \times f_2(LowDoc) \times f_3(CCJ) \times f_4(Unemployment)$$
$$\times f_5(RateShock) \qquad (3.18)$$

where $\eta^*(t)$ is a base case default rate.

---

[6] These are court rules to repay outstanding debts. The number of CCJs is indicative for the credit worthiness of the borrower, with more CCJs showing higher risk.

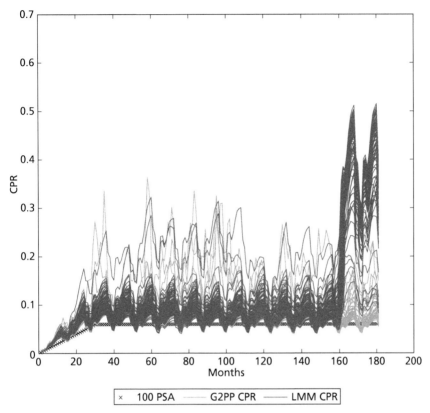

Figure 3.19. CPR curves under the 100 PSA, the LMM, and the two-factor Hull-White Model (G2PP).

The Citigroup model is a top-down model that is calibrated directly on the securitized collateral portfolio. It could be applied as a loan-by-loan model if all data is available for all loans, but Kamra et al. (2012) consider that this is highly unlikely.

In their paper models are not fully specified, in the sense that all functions f are not disclosed. Thus, this model as described above is only generic, the investors can take any functions, linear or not, that they consider are suitable given the factors involved.

3.4.8 LEHMAN BROTHERS LOGISTIC REGRESSION MODEL

Before their spectacular collapse in 2008, Lehman Brothers was one of the most pro-active players on the securitization of RMBS. One of the models they used for prepayment was an econometric model making use of the historical data

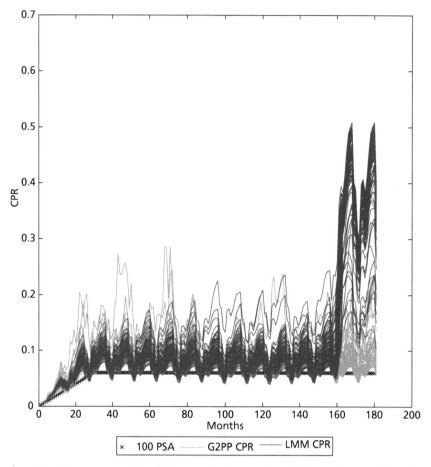

Figure 3.20. CPR curves under the 100 PSA, the LMM, and the two-factor Hull-White Model (G2PP).

at loan level. The Lehman Brothers logistic regression model uses financial markets information, credit borrowers information, borrower characteristics information and loan characteristics information. The model can be calibrated for either prepayments or defaults.

The predictor variables in the logistic regression model of prepayments for subprime or nonconforming mortgages were:

Second Lien mortgages Second lien mortgages are in general very expensive to the borrower so the borrower will prepay at the first opportunity.

Annual Regional House Price Appreciation Upon house prices appreciation the effective LTV falls and the equity borrowers have locked in their properties increase. Owners can crystalize this equity by taking out new mortgages at higher LTVs and prepaying the old loans. Thus, house price appreciation leads to higher prepayment speeds.

Switch Date For the initially fixed-rate loans or floating-rate loans with an initial discount period, the fixed-rate and the discount mortgages switch to being regular floating-rate loans. At the switch date fixed-rate borrowers may want to refinance into a new fixed mortgage, while discount borrowers will consider a new discount mortgage, so prepayment speeds increase.

Buy-to-let Mortgages These will prepay more slowly because they do not have to move out of property if the owner circumstances change.

Refinancing Incentive Lower fixed interest rates make the borrower to prepay and take out a new one at a lower fixed rate. The larger the difference the stronger the impact. Conversely, if rates rise, there is no refinancing risk.

Monthly Mortgage Balance The smaller the remaining mortgage balance, the lesser the savings from refinancing. Thus only borrowers with a larger outstanding balance should be willing to prepay.

Financial Markets Variables : LIBOR rates, BBR rates, HPI, CPI, inflation index, market mortgage rate (or proxy).

Loan Characteristics : LTV, DSCR (the number of times monthly household income covers the monthly mortgage payment), BTL, maturity of loan, house quality, ERC, time to end of ERC.

Borrower Characteristics CCJ info, credit card info, self-certified, number of payments missed in the last 24 months.

The idea is to link the probability of prepayment (SMM or CPR) to a set of covariates such as those enumerated above. The link functions usually applied are *logit, probit, tobit*. The fit can be done very easily with standard statistical packages such as SPSS, EVIEWS, S-Plus, Matlab, even Excel. The main difficulty is with data cleaning and preparation. One major drawback of these model is that they are single period models!

Model specification looks something like

$$logit(p_{it}) = \alpha_0 + \alpha_1 X_1 + \alpha_2 X_2 + \ldots + \alpha_d X_d + \varepsilon_{it} \qquad (3.19)$$

where $logit(p) = \log \frac{p}{1-p}$ and X denotes the covariate information such as LIBOR rates, LTV, maturity, BTL, and so on.

Once the model has been fitted it can be used for forecasting purposes. There are two ways to forecast. First computations can be carried out at the observation level, i.e. a new set of covariate information for a single new observation. This is the case for a loan-by-loan model that works in a bottom-up fashion. On the other hand the model can be also applied in a top-down approach at the pool level where the average covariate information is kept fixed and the model is extrapolated for a given future period.

This approach is very easy to implement once data is in place. The theoretical statistical framework underpinning the logistic model does not apply 100% here since the same loans are used in subsequent periods until prepayment or default. For example the sample size is not fixed over time. It is quite common to have loans issued at various points in time so the same covariate information will marginally impact on the probability of prepayment (default) differently. Default and prepayments should be modelled jointly as one loan may leave the sample because of defaults when we are modelling prepayments and vice verse.

3.5 Default Models

Lehman Brothers' logistic regression model was used for mortgage defaults as well and even for arrears, obviously with slightly different drivers.

3.5.1 CASE-SHILLER MODEL

Here we describe one of the main models proposed for mortgage defaults, proposed by Case and Shiller (1996). The Case-Shiller default model is linear on the log-scale motivated by the fact that default rates are small when the LTV is small and increase rapidly when the LTV is larger than one, corresponding to a drop in current house prices.

The model assumes that the mortgagor i buys a house at time t_i with a log-price P_{it} that is spanned by three components

$$P_{it} = C_t + H_{it} + N_{it} \tag{3.20}$$

where C_t is the log of the region wide level of house prices, H_{it} is a Gaussian random walk with zero mean, variance σ_H^2 and uncorrelated to C_t, and N_{it} is an idiosyncratic error term that is house specific, with zero mean, variance σ_N^2 and uncorrelated with C_t and H_{it} at all leads and lags.

If M_{it} is the log of the current mortgage balance then the log of the current LTV is $L_{it} = M_{it} - P_{it}$. The Case-Shiller default model links the probability of default p_{it} at time t for mortgagor i to L_{it} and a vector of covariates X_{it} that reflect macroeconomic factors such as rate of unemployment, GDP, and so on. The link function $p_{it} = f(L_{it}, X_{it})$ is non-linear.

The probability that the mortgagor i will default in time period t is then given by

$$p_{it} = f(M_{it} - (C_t - C_{t_i} + H_{it} - H_{it_i} - P_{it_i}), X_{it}) \tag{3.21}$$

For a given vintage of mortgages, that is all houses were bought at the same time t_i for the same price P_{it} under the same contract conditions and same macroeconomic factors, the fraction of the portfolio that will default at time t is given under this model by

$$\delta = \int_{-\infty}^{\infty} f(M_{it} - (C_t - C_{t_i} + s\sqrt{t - t_i} - P_{it_i}, X_{it})n_H(s)ds \qquad (3.22)$$

where n_H denotes the normal density function with zero mean and variance σ_H^2. Under the assumption that the expected loss upon default is given by $V(M_{it} - P_{it}, X_{it})$, the expected average loss caused by defaults for the entire portfolio can be calculated as

$$\Xi = \int_{-\infty}^{\infty} V(M_{it} - (C_t - C_{t_i} + s\sqrt{t - t_i}) - P_{it}, X_{it})f(M_{it} - (C_t - C_{t_i}$$
$$+ s\sqrt{t - t_i} - P_{it_i}, X_{it})n_H(s)ds \qquad (3.23)$$

This type of analysis can be carried out on a vintage by vintage basis and for different geographic areas.

3.6 Supervisory Stress Tests: The OFHEO Experience

The Supervisory Capital Assessment Program (SCAP) was introduced on February 9, 2009, in US and it was focused on a stress test of the 19 largest US banking companies; those with over $100 billion in total assets, testing whether each company carried sufficient capital to get through a possible new recession. The test found 10 banking organizations with insufficient capital. After that, the Federal Reserve has imposed stress tests as an important ongoing component of its supervision program for the systemically relevant banking companies. In 2010, the Dodd-Frank Act made stress testing compulsory for all banking companies with more than $50 billion in total assets, in addition to "systemically important non-bank financial institutions".

Fannie Mae and Freddie Mac are the main government-sponsored enterprises (GSEs) in the US mortgage market, covering $5.8 trillion of the $10.0 trillion home mortgage debt outstanding as of 2013. Frame et al. (2013) highlighted that the risk-based capital stress test model for Fannie Mae and Freddie Mac failed comprehensively. In this section we review the findings in Frame et al. (2013), who demonstrate that the OFHEO models for default and prepayment forecasting were extremely poor and that OFHEO "never re-estimated the model and hence left parameters static for almost a decade".

Furthermore, they also demonstrate that the stressed scenario for house prices under the OFHEO model was significantly less stressful than the actual recent US experience.

The Office of Federal Housing Enterprise Oversight (OFHEO) was charged to supervise Fannie Mae and Freddie Mac for a long period before the sub-prime crisis, between 1992 and 2008. The two GSEs will have to use a risk-based capital calculation based on a stress test determined by OFHEO. It took OFHEO almost ten years to finalize the model and risk-based capital rule. Surprisingly, the stress test proposed by OFHEO was considered to be state of the art, Stiglitz et al. (2002) arguing that if Fannie Mae and Freddie Mac were using the OFHEO risk-based capital stress test their risk of insolvency would be effectively zero. As it happened, Fannie Mae and Freddie Mac maintained capital in excess of the risk-based capital rule throughout the 24 quarters up to June 30, 2008. Nevertheless, this was not sufficient to stop severe problems appearing for both GSEs, Fannie Mae and Freddie Mac being helped with $187 billion of taxpayer's money.

Frame et al. (2013) revealed that the OFHEO model was unreliable for pre-dicting 30-year fixed rate mortgage defaults and prepayments, in the downturn period following the subprime crisis. OFHEO omitted risk factors, such as credit scores and loan documentation. Hence, even supervisory authorities cannot be trusted to manage reliable stress tests being exposed to model risk emerging from model misspecification, parameter estimation error, lack of reliable data and even coding problems.

3.7 **Summary Points and Further Reading**

Mortgage loans are contracts carrying real-estate risk. They represent a large part of the assets in the banking systems worldwide and banks find it difficult to hedge this asset class against real-estate risk.

Prepayments and default models are essential to any risk management enter-prise looking to contain this type of risk. There are many models proposed in the academic and practitioner literature, there is not a single model that is widely acceptable.

In normal times investors are worried mainly about prepayment risk while in turbulent and crises time default models gain in importance. Prepayment and default are generated by different economic factors but they should be modelled and monitored as a pair in relation to real-estate risk.

A very interesting design of a mortgage contract, an adjustable rate mortgage with variable tenor (VRT), is discussed in Chow et al. (2000). In this contract when the interest rates change the loan is adjusted in maturity and principal payment such that the monthly installment remains the same. This product is used in Hong Kong, where 35% of residential mortgages are of this type.

Moreover, Cocco (2013) argues convincingly that alternative mortgage products may be a valuable tool for households who expect increased income in the near future and that are looking to smooth consumption.

Ghysels et al. (2007) developed a log-linearized discounted rents model for commercial real-estate valuation that is better than hedonic type models. Using an advanced econometric methodology they validate that cap rates forecast commercial real-estate returns and they show that commercial real-estate prices can be modelled as financial assets.

3.8 **Appendix**

3.8.1 THE LIBOR MARKET MODEL

This model is constructed on discrete forward rates, each forward rate F^i being lognormal distributed from the model specification

$$dF_t^i = -\mu_i(t)F_t^i dt + \sigma_i(t)dW_t^i$$

where dW is an N dimensional geometric Brownian motion with $E[dW_t^i dW_t^j] = \rho_{ij}dt$.

This is a no-arbitrage model with the drifts calculated under the spot LIBOR measure by

$$\mu_i(t) = -\sigma_i(t) \sum_{j=q(t)}^{i} \frac{\tau_j \rho_{ij}\sigma_j(t)F_t^j}{1 + \tau_j F_t^j}$$

where τ_i is the time fraction associated with the ith forward rate and $q(t)$ is such that $T_{q(t)-1} < t < T_{q(t)}$.

In essence the LIBOR Market Model (LMM) is about volatility and correlation specification, the drift being automatically calculated. The most popular specification for volatility and correlation are

$$\sigma_i(t) = \phi_i[a(T_i - t) + b]e^{c(T_i-t)} + d \qquad (3.24)$$

$$\rho_{i,j} = e^{-\beta|i-j|} \qquad (3.25)$$

3.8.2 THE TWO-FACTOR ADDITIVE GAUSSIAN MODEL

This model for short rates is a two-factor model specified by

$$r_t = x_t + y_t + \varphi(t) \qquad (3.26)$$

$$dx_t = -ax_t dt + \sigma dW_t^1 \tag{3.27}$$

$$dy_t = -by_t dt + \eta dW_t^2 \tag{3.28}$$

where the two Wiener processes are correlated such that $E[dW_t^1 dW_t^2] = \rho dt$ and the calibrating function given by Hull-White model is

$$\varphi(T) = f^M(0, T) + \frac{\sigma^2}{2a^2}(1 - e^{-aT})^2 + \frac{\eta^2}{2b^2}(1 - e^{-bT})^2$$
$$+ \rho\frac{\sigma\eta}{ab}(1 - e^{-aT})(1 - e^{-bT})$$

where $f^M(0, T)$ is the market forward rate observed on 10 December 2007.

4 Mortgage Securitization; Pricing and Risk Management

4.1 **Introduction**

Long before the subprime crisis, there were major losses in MBS space, such as Merrill Lynch losing $377 million in 1987, Askin Capital Management $600 million in 1994, Cargill Minnetonka fund $100 million in 1994, Bank of Montreal Harris Trust & Savings Bank $51.3 million in 1994, due to bad investments in collateralized mortgage derivatives, Odessa College $11 million in 1994, Paine Webber Bond Mutual Fund $33 million in 1994 , Piper Jaffray Cos. $700 million in 1994, Capital Corporate Federal Credit Union $126 million in 1995, Connecticut Pension fund $25million in 1995, Postipankki $110 million in 1995, National Australia Bank $1.75 billion in 2001, and Freddie Mac $4.48 billion in 2004.

The majority of mortgages worldwide allow for early prepayment. This condition generates convexity for the fixed-income of a bank or financial house holding mortgages. A bank typically borrows at a fixed rate and issues a mortgage loan that is carried on the asset side of the balance sheet. The prepayment option embedded in the mortgage is equivalent to a short position in a swaption because the prepayment option is usually exercised when interest rates fall below a certain limit. The mortgage borrower is long in this option and they may exercise this option on a monthly basis, making the option a Bermudan exercising style. Hence, the holder of the mortgage loan (warehouse, SPV, agency, etc.) indirectly has sold an option on a swap contract and therefore it is short convexity, while the mortgage borrower is long convexity. This convexity can be hedged with swaptions but these swaptions must be hedged dynamically.

This chapter captures an overview of how real-estate risk is transferred to investors through securitization channels. A large part is dedicated to a less known financial instrument called the balance guaranteed swap, that is a type of multi-period derivative contingent on cash-flows generated by a pool of mortgage loans. We emphasize the problems arising from modelling cash-flows and we reveal the difficult task of dynamically managing the risk of balance guaranteed swaps.

4.2 **Mortgage Backed Securities**

4.2.1 BRIEF OVERVIEW

There are various classifications of mortgage backed securities. The most common one is based on the type of cash-flow payments.

Pass-through MBS This security will pass-through principal and interest payments from mortgages, after subtracting the servicing and guarantee fee, to the investors.

CMO In this structure, the original pass-through MBS is tranched into several classes, generally named A, B, C, D, etc. Tranche A will get the principal payment first, and class B will get principal paid back only when tranche A has been paid off. Tranche C will get a principal payment after tranche B has been paid off, and so on and so forth. The interest payment for each tranche is proportional to its remaining balance.

Stripped MBS This structure divides the payment of pass-through MBS into two classes: Interest Only (IO), and Principal Only (PO). *Each piece is more risky than the original pass-through*. For example, with high prepayments the IO investor may not recoup his par investment.

The nonagency RMBS typically has the CMO structure.

Another classification is after the type of issuer:

- Agency MBS: loans with guarantees backed by the US. Treasury, that have the full faith and credit of the US government. They are called *government loans* and are securitized by Ginnie Mae (GNMA). There are also *conventional loans*, issued through government-sponsored enterprises (GSEs), namely Freddie Mac and Fannie Mae.
- Private label MBS.

The mortgage balance may determine the type of securitization the loan will go into. In the US, agency guaranteed pools have a cap on the balance of the loans; this increased from $410,000 in 2006 to $625,000 in 2008 and even temporarily to $730,000 in 2010. Loans with larger balances are called *jumbo* loans (or nonconforming in the US) and they are securitized through private labels. *Prime* loans are those loans for which there is extensive documentation and the borrower has strong credit quality. *Subprime* loans are for borrowers with weaker credit quality. *Alt-A* or alternative-A loans are nonstandard loans with incomplete documentation and occupancy requirements; they are between prime and subprime.

4.2.2 PRIVATE LABEL

Not all mortgages are issued from agencies. Many mortgages in recent years have been issued by private banks or financial houses. There are major differences between standard mortgages issued by agencies and mortgages launched by *private label*. There is no guarantee fee. Credit risk is managed through subordination, the senior tranches are supported by junior tranches that absorb the first losses. All unscheduled principal prepayments are directed to senior tranches while the subordinated tranches are locked out from prepayments, although regular payments are still made. The deal's coupon is a function of market conditions including the investors' required rate of return and the prepayment outlook. Given a target pool coupon, the loans are split into discount and premium and after taking out the fees the net note rate can be calculated. Discount loans are particular bonds with a net rate lower than target coupon. This is also the case for the premium loans.

The plot in Figure 4.1 shows the exponential increase in mortgage issuance prior to the subprime crisis in the US. Please note that the notional stays high even after the subprime crisis. This means that the real-estate risk is till embedded in those mortgages and this risk needs to be managed by banks and investors. The evolution of outstanding mortgage notional mirrors the evolution of the Case-Shiller index, suggesting that the exponential increase

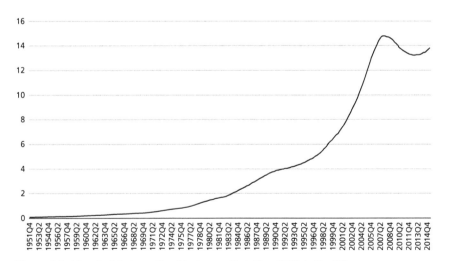

Figure 4.1. Historical Outstanding Mortgages (in trillion USD) in the US.

Source of Data: Board of Governors of the Federal Reserve System.

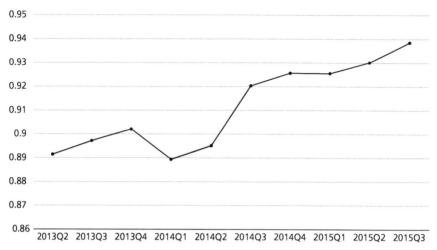

Figure 4.2. Historical Outstanding Mortgages (in trillion GBP) in UK.

Source of Data: Council of Mortgage Lenders.

in house prices works in tandem with the exponential increase of loans being made available.

The outstanding mortgage notional in the UK, depicted in Figure 4.2, is much smaller than its US counterpart but still approaches the 1 trillion benchmark, showing that this market is very important in the UK as well.

4.3 Commercial Mortgage Backed Securities

4.3.1 BRIEF OVERVIEW

The residential mortgage backed securities asset class is called RMBS. The commercial mortgage backed security is called CMBS. Most CMBS deals are *conduit* or fusion transactions, with collateral diversified geographically and by type. The property types considered in CMBS are: office, retail, industrial, hotel, multifamily compounds. The analysis of CMBS deals requires a bottom-up approach of properties in the portfolio and an understanding of the associated credit and extension risk. The loans in a CMBS are typically much larger than in RMBS, the largest 10–15 loans in a CMBS can represent 30%–50% of collateral.

Conduit transactions are securitizations of fixed-rate commercial mortgage loans where no loan is bigger than 5% of the transaction and the largest 10 loans represent less than 30%. Fusion transactions are securitizations of fixed-rate commercial mortgage loans where the largest 10 loans represent more than 30%. There are floating-rate transactions covering loans on transitional properties (renovations etc.), with short maturities but with several extensions.

The idiosyncratic risk of component properties is important for CMBS. Most owners of CMBS will borrow 50% to 80% of the value of the property and CMBS originators will provide loans up to 75%–80% of LTV. CMBS loans typically restrict prepayment locking out all loans during the first two to four years. After the lock-out period, the borrowers can eschew the underlying mortgage property by substituting the loan with the US government securities. Some CMBS originators may allow borrowers to prepay but impose prepayment penalties.

CMBS spread levels depend on supply and demand in this sector but also on the other fixed income sectors. Seasoned deals may trade differently depending on the credit quality left in the pools. Spreads tend to widen when there is a lot of issuance coming up. Changes in spreads of RMBS or corporate bonds may drive changes in CMBS spreads.

4.3.2 MODELLING ISSUES FOR CMBS

The main risks for CMBS are driven by interest rate risk and credit risk. Many investors assume the 0/0 framework, i.e. 0 prepayments and 0 defaults. Drivers of CMBS performance are taken as deterministic functions of debt service cover ratio (DSCR) and the LTV. The most important risk is the extension risk at maturity, if the payment of principal cannot be made the loan is either extended ($LTV < 100\%$) or put in default ($LTV > 100\%$). Another important specific risk here is the pay-off risk, whether property will pay if LTV is sufficiently low ($LTV < 80\%$) or not.

As opposed to RMBS where portfolios are more granular there is no granularity with CMBS, idiosyncratic risk is key. External factors influencing CMBS value are macro risks: interest rates, inflation; sectorial risks: job growth, outsourcing, skype, consumer spending, disposable income, demand and effective rent, vacancy, and diversification of commercial loans in the deal.

4.4 **Securitization**

The Federal National Mortgage Association (Fannie Mae) was founded in 1930s, to buy and sell government insured loans. Before the 1950s the government had provided explicit guarantee of loans, helping the secondary market where whole loans were actively traded. In 1968 Fannie Mae split into two, Fannie Mae, as a shareholder-owned government-sponsored enterprise (GSE) and Ginnie Mae (GNMA), were created to continue providing a secondary market for government-insured loans.

In 1970s, Ginnie Mae issued the first mortgage pass-through security, with full repayment guaranteed in case of default while Fannie Mae changed its activity to conventional mortgages. At the same time the government introduced the Federal Home Loan Mortgage Corporation (Freddie Mac) to help a shortage of credit for single-family houses. Fannie Mae and Freddie Mac guarantee the timely payment of principal and interest but their guarantees are corporate guarantees and are not backed by the full faith and credit of the US government, whereas Ginnie Mae does have the full backing of government.

Securitization allowed an issuer to issue notes with a higher rating than itself, jumping from non-investment to investment grade.

4.4.1 FEDERAL AGENCY SECURITIES – US

These securities represent debt of entities chartered by Congress to provide funding for large national projects like housing or agriculture. The largest issuers are government sponsored enterprises (GSEs), Fannie Mae, Freddie Mac, Tennessee Valley Authority and Federal Home Loan Banks, and Federal Farm Credit Banks.

It is important to realize that debt by GSEs is NOT guaranteed by the US government, smaller agencies may have full or partial "full faith and credit" guarantees but that is not an automatic cover in case of default. About 97% of outstanding federal agency market debt is issued by GSEs and in 2007, the year of the subprime crisis, the outstanding non-mortgage backed debt of the GSEs and all federal agencies made up 94% of the US debt market.

4.4.2 FACTORS INFLUENCING THE MBS PORTFOLIOS

The major factors affecting the valuation and risk management of mortgage backed securities portfolios are

Amortization schedule The majority of mortgages are amortizing loans and pay down a minimum amount of principal according to a schedule. The amortization schedule does not account for prepayments which are an option given to the borrower.

Prepayments The borrower has the option to pay down principal on top of the scheduled amortization schedule. Prepayments tend to increase when interest rates are low and refinancing is cheap.

Arrears The borrower may miss some payments but technically he/she has not defaulted yet.

Defaults The borrower stops paying his mortgage or is declared insolvent and the repossession process begins.

Loss severity Upon default, the property that is the collateral to the mortgage loan will be repossessed and sold on the market. Friction costs and market conditions may lead to only a partial recovery of the entire outstanding debt, in which case a mortgage default results in a loss.

4.5 Valuation of Mortgage Cash-Flows

The key ingredients for implementing a simulation model for pricing MBS securities are

1. an *interest rate model*
2. a *prepayment model*
3. *if* there is a liquid market, an OAS model may be used for tuning the market risk factors

The interest rate model must produce the short-term rate and the long-term rate, the latter sometimes being an input into the prepayment models.

A Monte Carlo simulation will simulate interest rate paths and prepayment paths, then combine them to cover a wide set of market scenarios and ultimately calculate the price of the MBS along each dual path by simple discount cash-flow calculus. The price of the MBS is then the average of all those prices.

4.5.1 PRICING MBS FRAMEWORK

The general discounting cash-flow techniques are based on the formula

$$MBS_0 = E\left[\sum df(t)c(t)\right] \tag{4.1}$$

where $df(t)$s the discounting factor for tenor t and $c(t)$ is the cash-flow realized at time t.

The discount factor is determined from the short-term interest rate process

$$df(t) = df[0,1]df[1,2]\ldots df[t-1,t] \tag{4.2}$$

$$= \prod_{k=0}^{t-1} exp(-s_k\Delta t) = exp[-\sum_{k=0}^{t-1} s_k\Delta t] \tag{4.3}$$

where $df[k-1,k]$ is the discount factor calculated at time k−1 for time k, $r(k)$ is the short-term rate used to generate df[k,k+1], observed at the end of period k, and Δt is the time step used in simulation.

The cashflows are given by standard calculations with mortgage payments.

4.5.2 BOND-EQUIVALENT MBS YIELD AND THE OAS ADJUSTMENT RATE

The cash-flows on MBS are typically monthly. Some investors compare the yield on MBS with the yield on a treasury coupon. If r_i = the monthly interest rate that will equate the present value of the projected cash-flows for the MBS security to the market price of that security plus accrued interest. Then the MBS bond-equivalent yield is $2[(1+r_i)^6 - 1]$.

There are two problems with this measure. Firstly, there is reinvestment risk: cash-flows must be reinvested at the rate r_i on the market. Secondly there is interest rate maturity risk because the bond must be hold to maturity. The difference between the cash-flow yield and the treasury yield is a *nominal* yield. This spread will include prepayment risk.

The prepayment model that market participants are using is very likely to be different from bank to bank. This means that in a *liquid* market, the market price of an MBS may be different from the internal model price. In order to apply a more marked-to-market approach an additional spread r_{OAS}, the OAS spread, was applied to the interest rates used to discount the cash-flows, such that the market price and model price coincide.

In order to simulate the one-month future interest rates, if $f_t(j)$ is the one-month future interest rate for month t on path j, interest rate paths are collected in the matrix illustrated in Table 4.1. These futures rates are then assumed to be the future realized rates in a Monte Carlo risk management exercise. The same thing is now done for simulating future refinancing mortgage rates. If $r_t(j)$ is the one-month future interest rate for month t on path j, then the refinancing

Table 4.1. Pathway Monte Carlo simulation for future interest rates.

Month	Path					
	1	2	$\cdots$	j	$\cdots$	n
1	$f_1(1)$	$f_1(2)$	$\cdots$	$f_1(j)$	$\cdots$	$f_1(n)$
2	$f_2(1)$	$f_2(2)$	$\cdots$	$f_2(j)$	$\cdots$	$f_2(n)$
$\cdots$	$\cdots$	$\cdots$	$\cdots$	$\cdots$	$\cdots$	$\cdots$
t	$f_t(1)$	$f_t(2)$	$\cdots$	$f_t(j)$	$\cdots$	$f_t(n)$
$\cdots$	$\cdots$	$\cdots$	$\cdots$	$\cdots$	$\cdots$	$\cdots$
$M-1$	$f_{M-1}(1)$	$f_{M-1}(2)$	$\cdots$	$f_{M-1}(j)$	$\cdots$	$f_{M-1}(n)$
M	$f_M(1)$	$f_M(2)$	$\cdots$	$f_M(j)$	$\cdots$	$f_M(n)$

Table 4.2. Pathway Monte Carlo simulation for future mortgage rates.

Month	1	2		j		n
				Path		
1	$r_1(1)$	$r_1(2)$	$\cdots$	$r_1(j)$	$\cdots$	$r_1(n)$
2	$r_2(1)$	$r_2(2)$	$\cdots$	$r_2(j)$	$\cdots$	$r_2(n)$
$\cdots$	$\cdots$	$\cdots$	$\cdots$	$\cdots$	$\cdots$	$\cdots$
t	$r_t(1)$	$r_t(2)$	$\cdots$	$r_t(j)$	$\cdots$	$r_t(n)$
$\cdots$	$\cdots$	$\cdots$	$\cdots$	$\cdots$	$\cdots$	$\cdots$
$M-1$	$r_{M-1}(1)$	$r_{M-1}(2)$	$\cdots$	$r_{M-1}(j)$	$\cdots$	$r_{M-1}(n)$
M	$r_M(1)$	$r_M(2)$	$\cdots$	$r_M(j)$	$\cdots$	$r_M(n)$

Table 4.3. Pathway Monte Carlo simulation for future pool cash-flows.

Month	1	2		j		n
				Path		
1	$C_1(1)$	$C_1(2)$	$\cdots$	$C_1(j)$	$\cdots$	$C_1(n)$
2	$C_2(1)$	$C_2(2)$	$\cdots$	$C_2(j)$	$\cdots$	$C_2(n)$
$\cdots$	$\cdots$	$\cdots$	$\cdots$	$\cdots$	$\cdots$	$\cdots$
t	$C_t(1)$	$C_t(2)$	$\cdots$	$C_t(j)$	$\cdots$	$C_t(n)$
$\cdots$	$\cdots$	$\cdots$	$\cdots$	$\cdots$	$\cdots$	$\cdots$
$M-1$	$C_{M-1}(1)$	$C_{M-1}(2)$	$\cdots$	$C_{M-1}(j)$	$\cdots$	$C_{M-1}(n)$
M	$C_M(1)$	$C_M(2)$	$\cdots$	$C_M(j)$	$\cdots$	$C_M(n)$

rates will correspond pathwise to the simulated monthly future interest rates. This process is depicted in Table 4.2. The refinancing rate can be taken as a fixed spread over a proxy interest rate such as the 10-year rate or as a linear combination between the 2-year and 10-year government spot rates.

Combining the above two facilitates the simulation of future cash-flows for the pool. Denoting by $C_t(j)$ the loan pool cash flow for month t on path j, the future monthly cash-flows generated by the mortgages in the pool are collected in the matrix described in Table 4.3.

The cash-flows are obtained from the schedule of payments and also applying prepayments and defaults from internal models.

Now it becomes straightforward to slice the cashflows according to all tranche specifications. If $NC_t(j)$ is the cash flow arriving to a given tranche (note) for month t on path j then Table 4.4 illustrates the cash-flows along each simulated path. Note that the actual number of future months M may be different for different notes due to different prepayment speeds.

From any term structure of future rates one can derive the spot rates to any month maturity. The spot rate for maturity given by month t on the j-th path is

$$s_t(j) = \left\{ [1 + f_1(j)][1 + f_2(n)] \cdots [1 + f_t(j)] \right\}^{1/t} - 1$$

Table 4.4. Pathway Monte Carlo simulation for future tranche cash-flows.

			Path			
Month	1	2	$\cdots$	j	$\cdots$	n
1	$NC_1(1)$	$NC_1(2)$	$\cdots$	$NC_1(j)$	$\cdots$	$NC_1(n)$
2	$NC_2(1)$	$NC_2(2)$	$\cdots$	$NC_2(j)$	$\cdots$	$NC_2(n)$
$\cdots$	$\cdots$	$\cdots$	$\cdots$	$\cdots$	$\cdots$	$\cdots$
t	$NC_t(1)$	$NC_t(2)$	$\cdots$	$NC_t(j)$	$\cdots$	$NC_t(n)$
$\cdots$	$\cdots$	$\cdots$	$\cdots$	$\cdots$	$\cdots$	$\cdots$
$M-1$	$NC_{M-1}(1)$	$NC_{M-1}(2)$	$\cdots$	$NC_{M-1}(j)$	$\cdots$	$NC_{M-1}(n)$
M	$NC_M(1)$	$NC_M(2)$	$\cdots$	$NC_M(j)$	$\cdots$	$NC_M(n)$

Table 4.5. Pathway Monte Carlo simulation for spot rates on a monthly grid.

			Path			
Month	1	2	$\cdots$	j	$\cdots$	n
1	$s_1(1)$	$s_1(2)$	$\cdots$	$s_1(j)$	$\cdots$	$s_1(n)$
2	$s_2(1)$	$s_2(2)$	$\cdots$	$s_2(j)$	$\cdots$	$s_2(n)$
$\cdots$	$\cdots$	$\cdots$	$\cdots$	$\cdots$	$\cdots$	$\cdots$
t	$s_t(1)$	$s_t(2)$	$\cdots$	$s_t(j)$	$\cdots$	$s_t(n)$
$\cdots$	$\cdots$	$\cdots$	$\cdots$	$\cdots$	$\cdots$	$\cdots$
$M-1$	$s_{M-1}(1)$	$s_{M-1}(2)$	$\cdots$	$s_{M-1}(j)$	$\cdots$	$s_{M-1}(n)$
M	$s_M(1)$	$s_M(2)$	$\cdots$	$s_M(j)$	$\cdots$	$s_M(n)$

This allows the calculation of the present values of all cash-flows

$$PV(NC_t(j)) = \frac{NC_t(j)}{[1 + s_t(j) + r_{OAS}]} \tag{4.4}$$

$$PV[Path(j)] = PV[NC_1(j) + PV[NC_2(j)] + \ldots + PV[NC_M(j)]] \tag{4.5}$$

The theoretical value under OAS spread discounting framework is then calculated as with any Monte Carlo exercise by averaging all present values across all simulated paths

$$\frac{PV(Path(1)) + PV(Path(2)) + \ldots + PV(Path(n))}{n}$$

In order to be able to calculate the present values of future cash-flows one needs to be able to simulate paths of monthly interest spot rates that are the discounting rates. These are collected in a similar matrix or table as shown in 4.5 where $s_t(j)$ is the spot rate up to month t on path j.

With all the above calculated, the OAS risk-adjusted discount factors are calculated using the formula

$$df(t) = \prod_{k=0}^{t-1} exp(-(s_k + r_{OAS})\Delta t) = exp[-\sum_{k=0}^{t-1}(s_k + r_{OAS})\Delta t] \qquad (4.6)$$

The OAS spread is calculated by trial and error until

$$MBS_0 = E\left[\sum df(t)c(t)\right] = \text{market price+accrued interest} \qquad (4.7)$$

4.6 **Balance Guaranteed Swaps**

4.6.1 INDEX AMORTIZING SWAPS

In the US, index amortizing swaps, also called indexed principal swap or index amortizing rate swap (IARS) were introduced specifically to help with amortizing notional. The amortization refers to interest payments on a notional that is declining, and it does not reimburse reductions of notional. One minor but still important observation is that even when the amortization schedule of the notional is known in advance, an IARS does not price on par as shown below. This is quite different from the standard vanilla fixed for floating interest rate swap that is priced on par off the LIBOR curve using a no-arbitrage enforcing principle. The amortization of the notional, however, is not fully known in advance because it is linked to the future paths of interest rates.

Galaif (1993) describes the main characteristics of this financial instrument and discusses the main financial risks. The usual maturity for an IARS is five years and there is a lock-out period of two years during which no amortization applies. This feature is equivalent to a call option where the fixed rate payer has to reduce the portion of the interest rate swap when interest rates decline. This option is similar to but not quite the same as the prepayment option embedded in a mortgage security. In addition, the presence of this optionality for IARS impacts on the convexity of the product which is more relevant when the yield curve experiences nonparallel shifts.

In essence, an IARS can be used as a proxy for MBS in terms of yield provision but it is disconnected from the prepayment/default risk that mortgage products carry inherently. Hence, the credit mortgage risk is somehow circumvented but that may work well in good times when the estimation of the notional of the pool of mortgages is fairly stable. In turbulent times, the discrepancy between the distressed portfolio of mortgages and the scheduled amortization may be quite large. Clearly, model risk is the main concern here particularly given the series of embedded options to reduce the notional when interest rates are in a given range and with nonparallel shifts in mind.

The pricing of an index amortizing swap is very different from the pricing of a standard interest rate swap. One common misunderstanding related to the hedging of MBS notes or bonds paying floating coupons is that the price is not given by the par value.

If $p(0, t_i)$ is the price of a zero coupon bond paying 1 at maturity t_i then this is equivalent to the discount factor for the same maturity. The forward LIBOR rate for the period $[t_{i-1}, t_i]$ is by definition

$$L_i = \frac{1}{\Delta} \left(\frac{p(0, t_{i-1})}{p(0, t_i)} - 1 \right) \tag{4.8}$$

where $\Delta = t_i - t_{i-1}$.

The price of a floating rate note with notional N paying LIBOR L_i is

$$Price_0 = \sum_{i=1}^{n} L_{i-1} \Delta N p(0, t_i) + N p(0, t_n)$$

$$= N \sum_{i=1}^{n} \frac{1}{\Delta} \left(\frac{p(0, t_{i-1})}{p(0, t_i)} - 1 \right) \Delta p(0, t_i) + N p(0, t_n)$$

$$= N \sum_{i=1}^{n} \left(\frac{p(0, t_{i-1}) - p(0, t_i)}{p(0, t_i)} \right) p(0, t_i) + N p(0, t_n)$$

$$= N(1 - p(0, t_n)) + N p(0, t_n) = N$$

This means that, when the notional is constant across periods, a floating rate bond always prices on par.

On the other hand, the price of a floating rate note with *amortizing* notional $\{N_i\}$ paying LIBOR L_i can be calculated as follows

$$Price_0 = \sum_{i=1}^{n} L_{i-1} \Delta N_i p(0, t_i) + N_n p(0, t_n)$$

$$= \sum_{i=1}^{n} N_i \frac{1}{\Delta} \left(\frac{p(0, t_{i-1})}{p(0, t_i)} - 1 \right) \Delta p(0, t_i) + N_n p(0, t_n)$$

$$= \sum_{i=1}^{n} N_i \left(\frac{p(0, t_{i-1}) - p(0, t_i)}{p(0, t_i)} \right) p(0, t_i) + N_n p(0, t_n)$$

$$\neq N$$

Pricing an amortizing swap can be carried out as with a standard swap by equating the present value of the fixed leg with the present value of the floating leg.

4.6.2 CAPS, FLOORS, AND SWAPTIONS

An interest rate cap is a contingent claim whereby the buyer receives payments at the end of each period in which the interest rate exceeds the agreed strike price. An example is an agreement to receive a payment for each month that the LIBOR rate exceeds 4.5%. The interest rate cap is a portfolio of European call options or caplets which exist for each period over the life of the cap. A caplet payoff on a rate L struck at K is $N\Delta \max[L - K, 0]$ where N is the notional and Δ is the day count accrual. For example a caplet on the six month GBP LIBOR rate with an expiry of 1st of February 2009 struck at 4.5% with a notional of 1 million sterling, if the GBP LIBOR rate sets at 5% on 1st of February the payoff is $1m \times 0.5 \times \max(0.05 - 0.045, 0) = 2500$.

Usually the payment is made at the end of the period. An interest rate floor is a portfolio of floorlets on a specified reference rate, usually LIBOR. The buyer of the floor receives money if on the maturity of any of the floorlets, the index rate fixed is below the agreed strike price of the floor.

A is an option to enter into an underlying swap. There are two types of swaption contracts:

- A *payer swaption* gives the owner of the swaption the right to enter into a swap where they pay the fixed leg and receive the floating leg.

- A *receiver swaption* gives the owner of the swaption the right to enter into a swap where they will receive the fixed leg, and pay the floating leg.

A Bermudan swaption is a multiperiod contract, with possibility to exercise at fixed dates. The terms agreed on are: the premium (price) of the swaption, the strike rate (equal to the fixed rate of the underlying swap), length of the option period (which usually ends two business days prior to the start date of the underlying swap), the term of the underlying swap, notional amount, amortization (if any), frequency of settlement of payments on the underlying swap.

A fixed payer swaption is from a cash-flow point of view a generalization of a cap while a fixed receiver swaption is a generalization of a floor.

The Bermudan swaption is *the* instrument in fixed income markets. It allows the buyer at fixed discrete times to enter into a fixed for floating interest rate swap, with pre-specified maturity and with a pre-specified exercise rate. This is an option so there will be a premium to pay upfront. Once the swaption is exercised the holder will be a party in a swap that will take marked-to-market risk. It is difficult to price the swaption since it needs to be calibrated to the volatility.

4.6.3 BALANCE GUARANTEED SWAPS

A balance guaranteed swap enables the counterparties to exchange (fixed or SVR-linked) interest payments on a pool of underlying (collateral) mortgages for LIBOR-based payments. The notional of this type of swap is determined each period by the outstanding balance of the collateral loans, which we shall denote by $\{B_t\}_{t \geq 0}$. Therefore, a loan originator can sell a balance guaranteed swap, where he would receive LIBOR-based payments and pay mortgage coupon payments to his counterparty, thus hedging the interest rate risk introduced by the mismatch between the mortgage coupon payments and LIBOR. What this type of instrument does not hedge against, however, is the stochastic variation of the principal balance of the collateral pool of mortgages, stochasticity stemming from the two risks which are inherent in both residential and commercial mortgages, namely prepayment and default risk.

The balance guaranteed swap (BGS) is a financial contract whereby one party, the seller, will pay the counterparty, the buyer, the total coupons collected on a portfolio of loans and it will receive in exchange LIBOR plus a spread on the same notional. This financial instrument has grown in importance because rating agencies required for securitization process to have in place and there are not viable alternatives to hedge out interest rate risks for non-fixed, i.e. stochastic, balance portfolios. There is also a version for cross currency where the receipts in one currency are swapped against a LIBOR coupon in a different currency.

Here are some of the main characteristics of BGS. The notional is stochastic and it usually decreases (amortizes) but it may also increase. The coupons paid are stochastic because of the varying notional and also because of the mixture in the portfolio (who are the obligors prepaying first?) Since CPR speeds and default rates are unknown *ex ante* it is impossible to completely hedge completely this product. The index LIBOR is problematic as the 3M LIBOR is preferred in the market because this is what investors in MBS usually require. There is basis risk because the mortgage coupons are collected monthly. It is normal in practice to collect monthly coupons on mortgage loans during the entire month; the calculation agent usually has the fixing schedule a few business days before the end of the month.

In general the monthly balance of the pool decreases. It is possible to have humps or jumps back up in balance due to arrears. The time point when the balance goes to zero or becomes immaterial is not known although it is estimated in practice by the WAL. The actual balance calculations from month to month depend on what is written in the contract. LIBOR is known at the beginning of the period whereas the total coupon collected is known at the end of the period. There could be a mismatch between the time accrual within the period for the two legs.

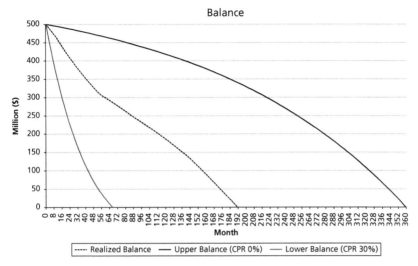

Figure 4.3. The three main curves used in pricing and risk managing balance guaranteed swaps.

Notes: The construction is hypothetical. The values of the amortizing balances depend on the pre-payment model used by the bank to generate future prepayment speeds from given mortgage loan pools.

Figure 4.3 illustrates the three main curves that are used in order to tailor the portfolio of balance guaranteed swaps used by RMBS desks to hedge the amortization risk. There is an upper curve calculated under the assumption that there is 0% CPR and also 0% defaults. The convexity of balance amortization changes from concave to convex as the CPR increases. The area to the left of the 30% CPR curve is indicative for the prepayment (and default) risk that the seller of a balance guaranteed swap will have to take on their book.

Note that the realized curve is assumed to be between the lower and the upper curves. This is the case in most of the situations. Although highly unlikely it is not impossible for the realized curve to move to the left of the lower curve. The lower curve can be moved more to the left or to the right, depending on the risk appetite of the RMBS structurer and the prepayment and default model calculations.

4.6.4 STRUCTURING OF BGS

Pricing BGS with swaptions

When designing the hedging strategy behind a BGS, a trader at an investment bank may use three plus one curves used in practice: an upper curve, a lower curve, a middle curve and the realized or observed curve. The pricing methods are different depending on which of these three reference *ex ante* curves is used. The realized curve is unfolding with time. The main determinant of the amortization profile of the curve is the CPR model, although the default and arrears model are as important.

The dynamics from a pricing point of view is monthly so for pricing purposes the desk will use an *amortizing swap* bundled with some derivatives that will allow monthly compression or inflation of the notional. The standard is to use a series of *receiver Bermudan swaptions* with varying notionals determined by the slicing of the area between the upper and the lower curve. The slicing can be done horizontally or parallel to the upper curve or lower curve. The BGS seller has some maintenance costs related to exercising the Bermudan swaptions.

The idea is that the seller gets a full index amortizing swap for the balance difference between the upper curve, representing the maximum feasible amortizing balance when CPR, defaults and arrears are zero, and the lower amortizing balance that has the fastest likely amortization due to CPR, defaults and arrears. Note that while the upper curve is model free the lower curve is model dependent. The BGS trader knows that, depending on the ebbs and flows of the economy, the realized balance will drop below the upper curve after some time and, if all risk-management calculations are correct, will not fall below the lower curve.[1]

The index amortizing swap on the notional $\{B_t^U - B_t^L\}_{t \geq 0}$ may overhedge the BGS as time goes by. Thus, the BGS trader needs a mechanism to partially offload this hedge. The most used mechanism used by investment banks is provided by a series of Bermudan swaptions that have cash-flows in the opposite direction to the amortizing swap. Hence, these will be Bermudan receiver swaptions that will give the BGS trader the option to enter, whenever they choose to, into a receiver interest swap with amortizing notional representing only fractions of the total portfolio notional at risk. Therefore, the BGS trader will pay a fixed coupon rate c_t^* and receive LIBOR plus a spread y on the index amortizing swap $B_t^U - B_t^L$ and they will receive the same fixed coupon rate c_t^U that is scheduled to be paid on mortgages and pay LIBOR plus y on $\frac{1}{N}[B_t^U - B_t^L]$ on the swap under the Bermudan swaption, once this is exercised. The swaption will be exercised when the realized mortgage portfolio balance drops faster than the scheduled amortization.

There are some problems with the risk management of the Bermudan swaptions used in the hedging portfolio. The first is that once the swaption is exercised the acquired position in the swap carries future counterparty risk, so if there is a fast reversal of interest rates on the market, carrying this swap until

---

[1] If it does then the BGS trader will take that loss on their book since in that region the BGS risk is not hedged. If the BGS trader would like to hedge in full her exposure then the index amortizing swap will have the notional given only by the upper curve.

its maturity may trigger unforeseen costs due to new market conditions and the relative position in the market of the counterparty in that swap. Secondly, the mortgage portfolio balance may jump back if arrears are cleared. Again, the swap resulting from exercising the swaption will reduce the exposure balance and it is impossible to revert things back once the decision to exercise the swaption is taken. The decision of when to exercise the Bermudan swaption is very important for the risk management of the BGS.

The appeal of using the swaptions for risk management in this context is due to the fact that the alternatives, using floors or caps, are more expensive.[2] Other alternatives are to use a cap bundled with an amortizing swap off the upper curve or a floor bundled with an amortizing swap off the lower curve. While these alternative look more expensive because of the upfront premium cost, we advocate that in fact they can provide a viable alternative, without any real downside.

First, consider the BGS with a series of Bermudan swaptions. Table 4.6 presents the cashflows faced by the BGS trader. For simplicity we denote by $\{c_t\}$ the realized coupon series, by $\{B_t\}$ the realized balance series, L_t is the realized LIBOR rates series, and y is the premium charged by the BGS desk.

Assuming that $N = 10$, suppose that the realized balance B_t drops to a level between $B_t^L + \frac{7}{10}[B_t^U - B_t^L]$ and $B_t^L + \frac{8}{10}[B_t^U - B_t^L]$. Then the BGS trader will exercise two or three swaptions, depending on her risk preferences. Consider that three swaptions are exercised. Then, upon exercising the swaptions the overall situation is described in Table 4.7.

Ignoring the outstanding swaptions, the BGS trader will have an overall position given by

$$B_t[c_t - (L_t + y))] + \frac{7}{10}(B_t^U - B_t^L)[(L_t + y) - c_t^U] \tag{4.9}$$

Table 4.6. Cash-flows for the BGS trader of a BGS hedged with an index amortizing swap and Bermudan swaptions.

Position	Cash-flow for BGS trader
Mortgage Pool BGS	$B_t[c_t - (L_t + y)]$
Index Amortizing Swap	$(B_t^U - B_t^L)[(L_t + y) - c_t^U]$
Bermudan Amortizing Swaption	$N \times \frac{1}{N}(B_t^U - B_t^L)[c_t^U - (L_t + y)]$

---

[2] A swaption is always cheaper than a floor or a cap with similar characteristics.

Table 4.7. Cash-flows for the BGS trader of a BGS hedged with an index amortizing swap and Bermudan swaptions assuming $N = 10$ and three swaptions being exercised.

Position	Cash-flow for BGS trader
Mortgage Pool BGS	$B_t[c_t - (L_t + y)]$
Index Amortizing Swap	$(B_t^U - B_t^L)[(L_t + y) - c_t^U]$
Bermudan Amortizing Swaption	$7 \times \frac{1}{N}(B_t^U - B_t^L)[c_t^* - (L_t + y)]$
New Amortizing swap	$\frac{3}{10}(B_t^U - B_t^L)[c_t^U - (L_t + y)]$

Clearly this can be positive or negative depending on the relationship between c_t, c_t^U and $L_t + y$. For example, if $c_t < L_t + y$ the BGS position is positive if and only if

$$\frac{B_t}{\frac{7}{10}(B^U - t - B_t^L)} < \frac{L_t + y - c_t^U}{L_t + y - c_t} \tag{4.10}$$

The spread y over LIBOR can be interpreted as the BGS price. This quantity is difficult to determine analytically given that it depends on the swaptions volatilities and correlations. A Monte Carlo exercise may help the BGS seller determine a fair value for y.

Pricing off the lower curve

We propose using caps instead of Bermudan swaptions. For the BGS seller, the trade including hedges could be organized as described in Table 4.8. Because one does not know how far down the mortgage portfolio balance may fall, the caps should cover the entire area between the upper and lower curve. Then, because the caps do not have a downside, as opposed to the swaps under the swaption, there is no need to divide the balance notional $B_t^U - B_t^L$ into smaller pieces. The strategy is to buy an index amortizing swap with the notional given by the lower curve profile and strike price series $\{c_t^L\}$ determined by association with the lower balance B_t^L and add the caps on top of it. In the BGS deal the

Table 4.8. Cash-flows for the BGS trader of a BGS hedged with an index amortizing swap and amortizing caps.

Position	Cash-flow for BGS trader
Mortgage Pool BGS	$B_t[c_t - (L_t + y)]$
Index Amortizing Swap	$B_t^L[(L_t + y) - c_t^L]$
Amortizing Caps	$(B_t^U - B_t^L)\max[(L_t + y) - c_t^L, 0]$

risk for the seller is that the LIBOR plus a spread that she needs to pay is much larger than the coupon rate harvested from the mortgage pool.

The cap has the same payoff benefits as the swaption but without the downside. Obviously it will be more expensive, only slightly if they are OTM and quite expensive if they are ITM. One big advantage is that there is no maintenance, if ITM then it is exercised in full. The cap is a portfolio of caplets so every period the cash-flows are directly settled.

There are two important scenarios to take into consideration. First assume that $(L_t + y) - c_t^L > 0$. Then the BGS overall position is given by

$$(B_t^U - B_t)(L_t + y) + B_t c_t - B_t^U c_t^L \tag{4.11}$$

which is positive if and only if

$$L_t + y > \frac{B_t^U c_t^L - B_t c_t}{B_t^U - B_t} \tag{4.12}$$

This condition is automatically satisfied if $B_t^U c_t^L - B_t c_t \leq 0$ which is equivalent to $\frac{B_t^U}{B_t} \leq \frac{c_t}{c_t^L}$ and it does not depend on the LIBOR.

Secondly, when $(L_t + y) - c_t^L \leq 0$ the caplets are not exercised and the overall position for the BGS seller is

$$B_t c_t - B_t^L c_t^L - [B_t - B_t^L](L_t + y) \tag{4.13}$$

which can be interpreted as the difference between the excess cash generated by the mortgage pool above the minimum expected lower tail scenario and the excess cash generated if all mortgages would have LIBOR instead of fixed rates. This quantity is positive if and only if

$$L_t + y < \frac{B_t c_t - B_t^L c_t^L}{B_t - B_t^L} \tag{4.14}$$

that is when LIBOR plus the spread is less than the weighted difference of the realized coupon rate c_t and the lower coupon rate c_t^L.

Pricing off the upper curve

The structurer may also decide to follow a top down hedging procedure, using floors. The idea is to start the hedging with an index amortizing swap with the notional given by the scheduled mortgage pool balance and corresponding coupon rates and continue by replacing the swaptions with floors. The overall position, BGS plus hedges, is described in Table 4.9.

Table 4.9. Cash-flows for the BGS trader of a BGS hedged with an index amortizing swap and amortizing floors.

Position	Cash-flow for BGS trader
Mortgage Pool BGS	$B_t[c_t - (L_t + y)]$
Index Amortizing Swap	$(B_t^U - B_t^L)[(L_t + y) - c_t^U]$
Amortizing Floors	$(B_t^U - B_t^L)\max[c_t^U - (L_t + y), 0]$

The floor has the same payoff benefits as the swaption but without the downside. Obviously it will be more expensive, only slightly if it is OTM and quite expensive if it is ITM. One big advantage is that there is no maintenance, if ITM then it is exercised in full. The floor is a portfolio of floorlets so every period the cash-flows are directly settled. Moreover, pricing is much easier than Bermudan swaptions.

As for the strategy with caps there are two important scenarios to take into consideration. First assume that $(L_t + y) < c_t^U$. Then floorlets are in the money and the BGS overall position at time t is given by

$$B_t(c_t - (L_t + y)) \tag{4.15}$$

and this quantity will be positive or negative depending whether $L_t + y < c_t$ as well. However, this scenario is for low LIBOR so it is quite likely that this condition will also be met.

Secondly, if $(L_t + y) \geq c_t^U$ the floors expire worthless and the overall position for the BGS seller is

$$B_t(c_t - (L_t + y)) + (B_t^U - B_t^L)(L_t + y - c_t^U) \tag{4.16}$$

In this situation the BGS seller is at a loss from the BGS but she will recoup the losses from the index amortizing swap. Since the index amortizing swap should in theory offer the needed protection for BGS, most of the time the cash-flow in (4.16) will be positive when LIBOR is very high.

The spread y over LIBOR can incorporate the upfront premium transformed into a running premium rate. In this way the beneficiary of the deal will not have to pay upfront any hedging costs, such as caps or floors premia, and they will pay as they go for their BGS protection.

Pricing off the middle curve

If there is confidence about the internal models for predicting CPR and default rates then it is possible to price the BGS off a middle curve, the amortizing balance curve forecasted $\{B_t^F\}$ representing the reference point. The hedging can be provided by an index amortizing swap with the notional given by $\{B_t^F\}$ and fixed rates given by $\{c_t^F\}$, plus a portfolio of caps and floors. The BGS trader will use amortizing caps with the notional given by $\{B_t^U - B_t^F\}$ and will employ amortizing floors for the region below the middle curve, that is with a notional $\{B_t^F - B_t^L\}$. The two derivatives will provide protection when the realized balance stays closer to the upper curve, that is when prepayments and defaults are low, as well as when the amortization is more aggressive as it is the case when the prepayments and/or defaults and arrears are high.

The structure is described in Table 4.10. One advantage of using this type of hedging structure is that since the floors and the caps have the same strikes vector they will not be in the money at the same time.

There are two possibilities. First, if $L_t + y > c_t^F$ then the caps are ITM while the floors are OTM. The overall position is then given by

$$B_t[c_t - (L_t + y)] + B_t^U(L_t + y - c_t^F) \tag{4.17}$$

This is positive if and only if

$$L_t + y > \frac{B_t^U c_t^F - B_t c_t}{B_t^U - B_t} \tag{4.18}$$

which holds true all the time when $B_t^U c_t^F \le B_t c_t$.

Secondly, if $L_t + y < c_t^F$ the floors are ITM and the caps are OTM. The overall position would then be

$$B_t[c_t - (L_t + y)] + B_t^L(L_t + y - c_t^F) \tag{4.19}$$

This will be positive if and only if

$$L_t + y < \frac{B_t c_t - B_t^L c_t^F}{B_t - B_t^L} \tag{4.20}$$

Table 4.10. Cash-flows for the BGS trader of a BGS hedged with an index amortizing swap and amortizing caps and floors.

Position	Cash-flow for BGS trader
Mortgage Pool BGS	$B_t[c_t - (L_t + y)]$
Index Amortizing Swap	$(B_t^U - B_t^F)[(L_t + y) - c_t^F]$
Amortizing Caps	$(B_t^U - B_t^F)\max[(L_t + y) - c_t^F, 0]$
Amortizing Floors	$(B_t^F - B_t^L)\max[c_t^F - (L_t + y), 0]$

Note that, under the assumption that y is positive, the condition (4.20) is always violated when $B_t c_t < B_t^L c_t^F$.

Other BGS contracts

A similar product is used for situations when the pool of loans pay in one currency but investors are paid in a different currency. A typical situation is a pool of mortgages paying in EUR but a securitized deal paying note holders in GBP. The FX risk is not straightforward to hedge as the notional is unknown *a priori*.

There are even more exotic situations where the loans are paid in local currency but linked to a foreign interest rate, say CHF or EUR, and investors are paid in a third currency, say GBP. Even if the first FX is absorbed by the borrowers, the changes in the local currency interest rate may impact on the dynamics of prepayments and defaults and arrears.

Problems with BGS

The BGS works well for a pool of mortgages paying fixed. Many portfolios contain a mixture of loans with fixed and floating coupons. Even fixed rate mortgage loans have a remainder part of the mortgage life linked to floating rate. The floating rate on the mortgage loans may be linked to a variable rate like the Bank of England Base Rate (BBR), and not necessarily LIBOR. The basis between LIBOR and BBR needs to be hedged as well.

One of the main advantages of using caps and floors for hedging instead of portfolios of Bermudan swaptions is that the subjectivity on exercising these instruments is removed. For caps and floors, as long as they are in the money they are exercised in full. This is not the case with the swaptions. Even if the premia for caps and floors is higher than the premium for swaptions, this can be transformed into a running fixed rate on a given notional (amortizing) and be passed on to the client to be paid on a monthly basis.

If the swaptions, caps and floors are not bought in-house further counter-party credit risk considerations may become relevant.

LIBOR-BBR swap

This instrument should help hedging away the basis risk between BBR and LIBOR. It pays LIBOR - spread on one leg and *average* BBR over the accrual period on the other leg. The BBR leg is similar to LIBOR in an arrears contract. The notional is stochastic again which makes it difficult to price. Because of that the buyer of the swap, the party paying the average BBR, will have the option to decide at the beginning of each period the size of the notional within a pre-specified band.

It has high maintenance costs because of the option to decide on the size of notional on which payments will be made at the end of the period. The seller of the swap will always assume the worst scenario against him. There is another basis risk that may surface due to 3M LIBOR paid monthly, say, and the monthly average BBR. The average BBR is calculated depending on the time accrual before the change and after the change.

4.6.5 RISK MANAGEMENT ISSUES

Interest rate risk can affect an MBS structure in more than one way. Changes in the yield curve, short term in particular, may have a big impact on the portfolio run by an MBS desk.

In Europe RMBS deals usually pay investors a standard floating interest rate such as LIBOR or Euribor. From a cash-flow point of view the mortgage loans provide either fixed or floating interest payments of various types. To add to the complexity of risk managing RMBS positions, the reset dates differ for mortgages most of the time from those of the notes for investors, creating an exposure to interest rate risk. In Europe in particular, currency risk was also present when mortgages were linked to foreign currency interest rates while notes were paid in a domestic currency.

In order to manage these risks, mortgage specialized trading desks employ a variety of swaps, like basis swaps, index amortizing fixed-for-floating swaps, index amortizing currency swaps, and more importantly, balance guaranteed swaps. The BGS can be likened to a misnomer as it is not the balance of the mortgage pool that is guaranteed. It is rather related to guaranteeing the exchange of cash-flows calculated on the mortgage pool balance that will fluctuate due to defaults, prepayments, and curtailments. There is a natural basis introduced by the mismatch in tenors between the monthly cash-flows produced by mortgages and the quarterly or semiannual payments to investors. There could be a mismatch between hedges, such as amortizing swaps, where the reference index rate is usually 6-month LIBOR and the 3-month LIBOR is requested by investors. While BGS may help to mitigate the interest rate hedging, they introduce counterparty credit risk and quite importantly model risk.

A mortgage desk is best placed to underwrite real-estate related risks. Even when mortgages are securitized and taken off the balance sheet of the bank issuing the mortgages, rating agencies require BGS to be put in place. Those BGS contracts are sold to the special purpose vehicle by the mortgage desk but most of the time they will have to manage their short BGS positions post-securitization for the SPV.

A mortgage trading desk can use a strategy to hedge prepayment risk based on a portfolio of receiver swaptions. One other possibility is to hedge the exposure to credit mortgage risks (default, prepayment, and curtailments) dynamically on at least a monthly basis. This can be done by creating a portfolio of interest rate swaps with various maturities and notionals, long and short positions, such that the mortgage exposure and evolution is approximated closely by this portfolio of vanilla swaps. However, there are some hidden dangers with this zero-cost entry hedging strategy. In order to follow dynamically the amortizing balance of the mortgage pool very large swap positions must be entered into. The total notional of the swaps exposure may be several times larger than the total notional of mortgage exposure. Therefore non-parallel shifts of the yield curve may create liquidity pressure at given points in time and being over-hedged or under-hedged during turbulent times when LIBOR rates may experience more volatility may lead to large temporary losses from this hedging portfolio. Hence, the solution using receiver swaptions has been preferred by many mortgage desks.

The subprime-liquidity crisis of 2007–2008 emphasized that it is very difficult to forecast the behaviour of mortgage obligors. Moreover, the interest rate risks manifest themselves through several channels, the interest rate themselves, i.e. the coupons paid to investors versus the mortgage payments received from borrowers, but also the notional on which these payments are calculated in aggregate vis-a-vis a fixed pool of mortgages. The common view before the crisis was that low interest rates imply high prepayment rates and very low default rates. During and in the aftermath of the crisis low interest rates did not lead to high prepayment and low default rates, quite the contrary. The impact of low and high interest rates should be considered in direct linkage with the state of the economy and the available credit. The hedges put in place by a mortgage desk are in essence multi-period products and a great deal of maintenance and decision effort is put in managing the Bermudan swaptions. It is not trivial to make sure that after all payments are made, the mortgage desk – as the seller of BGS to the special purpose vehicle – has no loss occurring. While the borrowers' behaviour cannot be influenced, the decision to exercise the Bermudan swaptions used as a balance compression tool, cannot be undone. The danger here is that while LIBOR rates may look favourable to the whole structure in a particular month, they may swing in the opposite direction subsequently, causing losses to the mortgage desk.

In the next section we show a simulation based methodology that can help taking a more informed decision about the timing of when to exercise the Bermudan swaptions. In addition we compare on various simulated scenarios a less known hedging strategy for BGS products based on caps and floors.

There is a BGS variant designed to cover mortgages that have a floating rate. A floating rate mortgage payment may appear in several ways. The first channel is a floating rate mortgage such as LIBOR plus a spread or a tracker mortgage such as Bank of England Base Rate (BBR) plus a spread. The second way floating rates appear is when the term of the fixed rate mortgages end and they switch to Standard Variable Rates (SVR). A grey area surrounds how SVR rates are determined, legally they are settled by the mortgage issuer without any reference calculation or pre-calculation methodology published.

Some mortgage desks may assume for risk management purposes that future SVR rates are equal to BBR plus a spread or an average of mortgage rates from several different mortgage issuers. Consequently, a second type of BGS swaps exist, with one leg of the swap paying BBR plus a spread while the other leg pays a LIBOR rate, both legs calculated on a stochastic notional given by the total mortgage balance outstanding. Moreover, the party paying coupons determined by the BBR rate has the option to switch notional calculation from the upper curve to a lower curve or vice versa, at the beginning of each month. This decision is difficult to take since it is not clear whether the BBR rate may change suddenly during the month and also what is going to be the short-term evolution of the reference LIBOR rate. On a percentage basis, historically there does not seem to be much difference between the 3-month LIBOR, 6-month LIBOR and the base rate set by the Bank of England, as illustrated in Figure 4.4. However, given the size of the notional involved in MBS deals, even a few basis points difference may cause substantial gains or losses.

Historically the basis between BBR and LIBOR has been small, but during and in the aftermath of the subprime crisis, this basis has experienced wild fluctuation. Not only can the basis between LIBOR rates and BBR reach substantial levels, more than 1% during the subprime crisis period as depicted in Figure 4.5, but it is important to remark that the basis has also occasionally

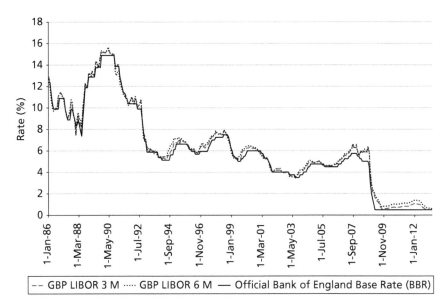

Figure 4.4. Historical evolution of GBP 3-month LIBOR, GBP 6-month LIBOR, and Bank of England Base Rate.

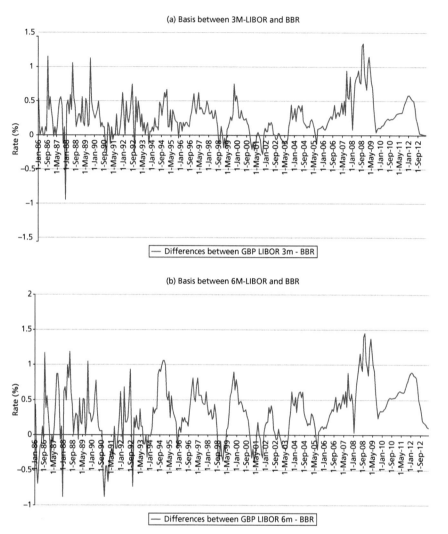

Figure 4.5. Basis between main LIBOR rates and the BoE base rate.

been negative. Both time series appear stationary and mean-reverting. Fitting a mean-reversion model may help in taking a decision of when to exercise the BGS in order to compress the outstanding notional under hedges.

4.6.6 RISK MANAGEMENT WITH BALANCE GUARANTEED SWAPS

Fabozzi et al. (2010) emphasized that hedging the risk inherent in a portfolio of mortgages is a tremendously complex task. The major risks involved are interest rate risk, as well as prepayment and default risk. The cumulative of these risks results in the problem of hedging a pool of mortgages being one of hedging ununcertain exposure to interest rate risk. Due to two of aforementioned risks, the initial balance of the mortgage portfolios varies in a non-deterministic manner: while prepayment risk leads to a (stochastic) reduction in the total amount of interest initially expected to be received, eventual defaults lead to the reduction in both expected notional and interest payments. A number of alternative solutions to this hedging problem have been suggested in Fabozzi et al. (2010) and are exemplified in this section; specifically, we consider below the hedging of a portfolio of mortgages using a structured swap (i.e. balance guaranteed swap), and amortizing swap and swaptions, floors or caps. In our numerical example we shall assume a pool of self amortizing loans, with a total notional of $500,000,000, coupon rate of 6% (payable monthly) and maturity of 30 years (i.e. 360 months).

As explained in Fabozzi et al. (2010) balanced guaranteed swaps and balance guaranteed LIBOR-base rate swaps are two examples of structured swaps used by players in the real-estate market like, for example, the banks who originated the loans to hedge the interest rate risk resultant from the mismatch between the coupons/ interest payments received on the pool of (securitized) mortgages, which are either fixed or given by the standard variable rate (SVR), which in turn is intrinsically linked to the base rate set by the Central Bank, and the LIBOR-based payments that they have to pass onto the investors in the securitized loan. As mentioned above, the notional in the balance guaranteed swap is determined each period by the principal balance of the collateral loans. Figure 4.6 depicts how this balance can vary depending on prepayment rates. More specifically, the different curves depicted represent the potential evolution of the balance based on various assumptions for the conditional prepayment rate (CPR). To (partially) eliminate this uncertain exposure risk given by the stochastic nature of the notional of the balance guaranteed swap one can use a portfolio of a self-amortizing swap, combined with swaptions, floors or caps; we shall discuss each of these three possibilities in turn.

In Figure 4.6 we illustrate various amortizing portfolio balance curves generated under various prepayment assumptions. In practice it is difficult to predict which balance curve will be the realized one. The balances may amortize faster or slower depending on the prepayment and defaults.

Firstly, one would need to determine a region that will contain the realized balance evolution. We set the upper boundary of this region as being the 0% CPR curve (i.e. no prepayments, notional payments made as scheduled for a self-amortizing loan, which underlines the self-amortizing swap), while the lower boundary is represented by the 30% CPR curve (i.e. assuming annual pre-payments of 30% in excess of scheduled notional payments). Subsequently, under the first hedging scenario (i.e. using swaptions), a self-amortizing swap with notional given by the upper curve (i.e. low CPR; notional denoted by u_t) in the above graph is entered into: the seller of the balance guaranteed swap would buy the self-amortizing swap (i.e. pay fixed and receive LIBOR

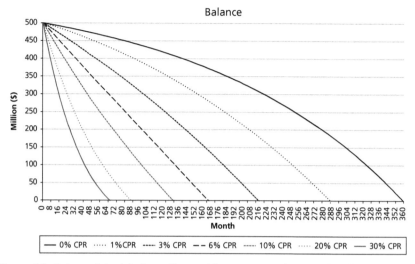

Figure 4.6. Balance Schedule for self-amortizing mortgage loans with different prepayment rates (CPRs).

(+ a spread). As the realized notional balance (i.e. ρ_t, the notional of the balance guaranteed swap) moves away from the low CPR curve (i.e. u_t, the notional of the self-amortizing swap), the hedge is adjusted (i.e. the upper curve is lowered closer to, but not crossing, the realized curve) using a series of Bermudan swaptions. The swap underlying the swaptions can be either a plain vanilla swap, or an amortizing swap.

The results presented below use the amortizing version of the swap underlying the swaptions. More specifically, the way this strategy is implemented is as follows: at each point in time, the difference between the upper and lower balance is divided into a constant number of units n; in our numerical example below we shall use $n = 60$ corresponding to a five year horizon. The notional of the amortizing swap underlying the swaptions will now be given by $w(u_t - l_t)$, with $w = \frac{1}{n}$, and where u_t and l_t represent the time-t balances under the upper (i.e. low CPR) and lower (i.e. high CPR) curves.

For instance, in our numerical example, $u_1 = \$499,502,247$ and $l_1 = \$484,874,059$. Hence, the notional of the swap (from the swaption) at time time t_2, should the swaption be exercised at time t_1 would be equal to $\$243,803$. The time-$(t + 1)$ payoff for this strategy is hence equal to:

$$\rho_t \Delta_t \left(c^{(1)} - L(t, \tau) - s^{(1)} \right) + u_t \Delta_t \left(L(t, \tau) + s^{(2)} - c^{(2)} \right)$$

$$+ I_t w(u_t - l_t) \left(c^{(2)} - s^{(2)} - L(t, \tau) \right) \qquad (4.21)$$

where $\Delta_1 = \frac{1}{12}$, that is one month, $(c^{(1)}, c^{(2)})$ and $(s^{(1)}, s^{(2)})$ are the coupon rates and swap spreads for the balance guaranteed swap and amortizing swap off the upper curve, respectively; $L(t, \tau)$ is the time-t LIBOR with maturity ĬĎ, where (i.e., six months in our numerical application). Thus, $I_t = 0$ if none of the ($n = 60$) Bermudan swaptions are exercised at time-t and it is equal to m if exactly m of the Bermudan swaptions are exercised by time-t. In formula (4.21) the first term is the payoff from the balance guaranteed swap, the second term represents the amortizing swap and the third term is the payoff from a swaption with strike $c^{(2)} - s^{(2)}$.

The second hedging option would again involve the same structured (balance guaranteed) swap as well as the same amortizing swap off the upper curve as before. The swaptions however will now be replaced by a series of floors, with notional equal to the difference between the upper and the lower curves (i.e. $u_t - l_t$) and strike equal to the strike of the swaptions above (i.e. $c^{(2)} - s^{(2)}$). The time-$(t + 1)$ payoff for this strategy is hence equal to:

$$\rho_t \Delta_t \left(c^{(1)} - L(t, \tau) - s^{(1)} \right) + u_t \Delta_t \left(L(t, \tau) + s^{(2)} - c^{(2)} \right)$$
$$+ (u_t - l_t) \left(c^{(2)} - s^{(2)} - L(t, \tau) \right) \tag{4.22}$$

The difference in formula (4.22) compared to (4.21) is the third term, which now is a floorlet with strike $c^{(2)} - s^{(2)}$.

Finally, the third hedging strategy would again include the same balance guaranteed swap as in the previous two cases, but now the amortizing swap will be off the lower curve and the strategy will be completed by a series of caps, with notional equal to the difference between the upper and the lower curves (i.e. the same as the notional of the floors above) and strike equal to the difference between the coupon rate (fixed leg) and the price (swap spread) of the amortizing swap (now of the lower curve). The time-t+1 payoff for this strategy is hence equal to:

$$r_t \Delta_t \left(c^{(1)} - L(t, \tau) - s^{(1)} \right) + l_t \Delta_t \left(L(t, \tau) + s^{(3)} - c^{(3)} \right)$$
$$+ (u_t - l_t) \left(L(t, \tau) - c^{(3)} + s^{(3)} \right) \tag{4.23}$$

where $c^{(3)}$ and $s^{(3)}$ are the fixed leg and the price of the amortizing swap of the lower curve. Note that the second term of formula (4.23) is the payoff of an amortizing swap, similar to formula (4.21) and formula (4.22), but the notional and the fixed rates are different. The third term in formula (4.23) can be recognized as the payoff of a caplet with strike $c^{(3)} - s^{(3)}$.

It is worthwhile noting that if all coupon rates for the structured swap and the two amortizing swaps, off the upper and lower curves, respectively, are constant and equal (i.e. $c^{(1)} = c^{(2)} = c^{(3)}$, and also if the swap spreads for the two amortizing swaps (of the lower and upper curve) are also equal (i.e. $s^{(2)} = s^{(3)}$), then the latter two strategies yield the same results. If however, coupon and/or swap rates are different, then the results obtained with these two strategies will differ. In our numerical example below we assume: $c^{(1)} = c^{(2)} = c^{(3)} = 6\%$; $s^{(1)} = 0.16\%$ and $s^{(2)} = s^{(3)} = 0.20\%$.

Numerical simulations

The LIBOR can be simulated for any maturity, 1-month, 3-month, 6-month, based on a simulated instantaneous short rate, as explained in Appendix 4.8 and using the closed form expression for the term structure.

For example, in panels c and d of Figure 4.7 below, we plot the simulated evolution of 6-month LIBOR vs. that of 1-month and 3-month LIBOR, respectively, using the CIR model, over a period of five years (60 months). We notice that, like in the Vasicek case, the shorter maturity rates are more volatile and also that the longer maturity rate can be both above and below the shorter maturity rate.

We now turn to the implementation of the three hedging strategies described above i.e. using swaptions, floors, or caps based on the realized curve and simulated paths for the 6-month LIBOR, using the Vasicek and CIR models, as described above. Also, we assume monthly payments, a maturity of 30 years (i.e. 360 months), n =60 (i.e. 60 Bermudan amortizing swaptions), as well as all coupon rates (for the structured swap as well as the two amortizing swaps, off the upper and lower curve) constant and equal to 6.

In Figure 4.8 we plot the evolution of the hedge using swaptions, for one of the simulated LIBOR path, using the Vasicek model.

If we calculate the total payoff (ignoring the timing of cash flows and hence time-value of money effects) for the two strategies, first with swaptions then with floors) we can conclude, that for this particular scenario, the hedge with floors (caps) appears to be superior: while the total payoff for the swaptions hedge is equal to $4,177,466, the value obtained for the floors (caps) hedge is $81,781,850. However, since this staggering difference was obtained for one particular simulated path for the 6-month LIBOR, we repeated the simulation 1,000 times and also varied the assumed model; the average payoffs across all simulations are reported in Table 4.11.

4.6.7 BACKTESTING WITH HISTORICAL LIBOR DATA

If we now repeat the same exercise as before but instead of relying on simulated interest rates, we use historical (BBA) LIBOR monthly data, from January 1986 to January 2013. The evolution of the hedges with swaptions and floors (caps)

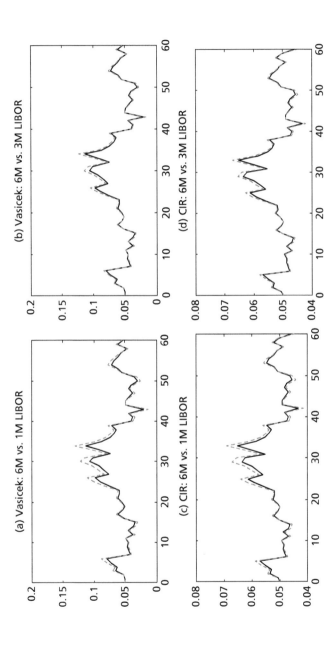

Figure 4.7. Simulated paths for 6-month LIBOR (solid lines) versus 1-month and 3-month LIBOR (dashed lines). Simulations are performed assuming Vasicek and CIR dynamics, respectively.

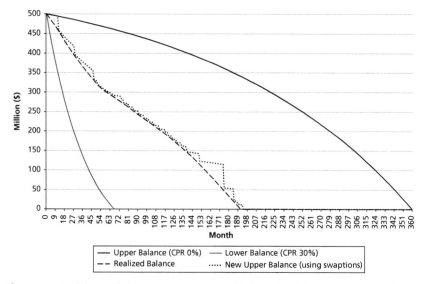

Figure 4.8. Hedging with (amortizing) swaptions Vasicek simulated 6-month LIBOR.

Table 4.11. Average Payoffs over 100 simulations.

Hedging strategy	Vasicek LIBOR model	CIR LIBOR model
Swaptions	$3,151,330	$1,134,259
Floors	$90,396,660	$26,680,327

is depicted in Figure 4.9. While the payoff is still greater for the hedge with floors (65,204,874 *vs.* 52,894,96), the difference between the two approaches is no longer so large in percentage terms.

While real-estate risk is notoriously difficult to hedge, with the advancement of property derivatives such as futures traded on exchanges and total-return swaps, traded over-the-counter, it becomes easier to control the magnitude of this risk. At the same time, interest rate risk is still the main risk that must be managed pro-actively by this type of market participant. As opposed to other asset classes, interest rate risk is also affected by the stochastic evolution of the notional involved, which may change according to the behaviour of mortgage borrowers. Hence, once a portfolio of hedges is put in place versus a portfolio of mortgages it is quite easy to be under-hedged or over-hedged at the wrong time when interest rates move against you.

The standard procedure in mortgage markets is to use amortizing Bermudan swaptions to allow total mortgage balance compression when needed. However, once a swaption is exercised the resulting swap may be counter-beneficial later on. This makes is very difficult as a decision process since every

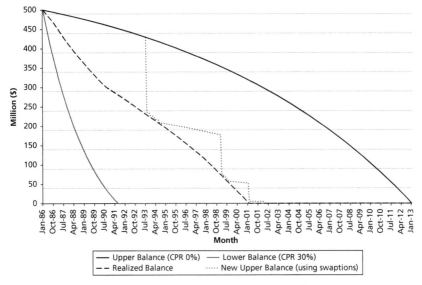

Figure 4.9. Hedging using swaptions: Historical BBA 6-month LIBOR, January 1986–January 2013.

month the owner of such swaptions would need to make a decision based only on current market conditions. We propose an alternative solution based on caps or floors that would eliminate this problem from the risk management process since caplets/floorlets do not have any downside and are exercisable every month. Although caps and floors are more expensive than Bermudan swaptions we illustrate that this difference is offset by the excess cash obtained when exercising the caps and floors for the entire notional covering the risk region, since there is no compression of notional as such.

4.7 **Summary Points and Further Reading**

Securitization of mortgages is more or less back to the level seen before the eruption of the subprime crisis. Some interesting readings on the role played by real-estate products in the subprime crisis can be found in Shiller (2008c), Gorton (2009), Lybeck (2011). The relationship between structured finance and the subprime crisis is analysed in Coval et al. (2009).

The concept of OAS has been specific to mortgage markets. A discussion on the source of this innovation including various interpretations is provided in Kupiec and Kah (1999). Some caution is in order here, since all issues that differentiate mortgage loans from other types of loan are squeezed into one number. This could be very dangerous, particularly since mortgage contracts are multi-period and risk management may not be restricted to the monitoring of one quantity, the OAS rate in this case.

The index amortizing swap is a financial contract that is very easy to understand and utilize but it may be more difficult to price and hedge. A valuation procedure under the worst-case scenario has been proposed by Epstein and Wilmott (2002). Some interesting practical insights in the valuation of caps, floors and swaptions are discussed in Albota and Tunaru (2012). The valuations of these instruments is complex model risk may be of some concern for these instruments. Furthermore, negative interest rates are adding a new dimension to modelling in this area.

Balance guaranteed swaps are derivatives covering real-estate risk coming out of mortgages. These products helped transferring prepayment and default risk bundled with interest rate risk to investors. More discussion on the applications of balance guaranteed swaps in European real-estate markets are described in Fabozzi et al. (2010).

In this chapter, we unveiled some of the mechanics of this type of derivatives and analysed them from the point of view of a market-maker in RMBS. We showed that it is possible to organize different types of hedging structures, based on the traditional swaptions but also on caps and floors, or a combination of both, all being applied to an amortizing notional.

There is a clear advantage of using options such as caps or floors rather than swaptions when hedging the balance guaranteed swaps. They may be more expensive upfront but when interest rates move such that the hedging portfolio is in the money, a larger balance is used for actual calculation. Thus, over time some of the high premium is very likely to be recouped. In addition, when swaptions are exercised an interest rate swap position is added to the trading book and this swap can have inflows as well as outflows.

It is not possible to hedge exactly the risk associated with BGS because of the evolving nature of the exposure with time. The only possibility at this moment in time is to manage the risk in a dynamic fashion, looking forward on how interest rates, prepayments, and defaults may evolve and taking a decision looking at simulations.

Further interesting readings in this area are Campolongo et al. (2013), Gorton (2009), and Raynes and Rutledge (2003).

4.8 Appendix: Simulating Interest Rate Paths

One simple way to simulate the future evolution of LIBOR is to employ well-known interest rate continuous time models such as Vasicek and CIR short rate models. The CIR model guarantees by construction positive interest rates while the Vasicek model allows negative rates to occur. Given the evolution of interest rates post subprime crisis with several rates entering negative territory, it seems wise to use both models when generating paths of future interest rates. The simulated LIBOR paths will be considered as "realized" rates. Then we calculate and compare the performance of the different hedges, i.e. with swaptions, floors, or caps.

Vasicek model

The first continuous-time interest rate model used is the celebrated Vasicek model for short rates, described by the following equation

$$dr_t = k(\mu - r_t)dt + \sigma dW_t \tag{4.24}$$

The LIBOR rates $L_t(\tau)$ with maturity τ are spot rates and the short rate can be interpreted as $r_t = \lim_{\tau \to 0} L_t(\tau)$. The analytics of the Vasicek model give a closed-formula for $L_t(\tau)$ once the model parameters are estimated. Thus

$$L_t(\tau) = L(\infty) + (r_t - L(\infty))\frac{1 - e^{-k\tau}}{k\tau} + \frac{\sigma^2}{4k^3\tau}(1 - e^{-k\tau})^2 \tag{4.25}$$

with $L(\infty) \equiv \lim_{\tau \to \infty} L_t(\tau)$ and $L(\infty) = \mu - \frac{\sigma^2}{2k^2}$.

Using stochastic calculus one can solve the equation 4.24. However, for simulation purposes, all that we need to know is the fact that the short rate r_t is a Gaussian random variable with the conditional mean and variance given by

$$E(r_t|r_s) \equiv \mu_r(s, t) = e^{-k(t-s)}r_s + \mu\left(1 - e^{-k(t-s)}\right) \tag{4.26}$$

$$var(r_t|r_s) \equiv \sigma_r^2(s, t) = \frac{\sigma^2}{2k}\left(1 - 2^{-2k(t-s)}\right) \tag{4.27}$$

Interest rate paths should be simulated on a monthly grid defined by the time points $0 = t_0 < t_1 < \ldots < t_n$. The simulation can be done recursively using the formula

$$r_{t_{i+1}} = \mu_r(t_i, t_{i+1}) + \sigma_r(t_i, t_{i+1})Z_{i+1} \tag{4.28}$$

starting from a rate r_0 and using independent draws Z_i from a standard Gaussian distribution.

Another possibility would be to use the Euler-Maruyama discretization of the Vasicek continuous-time process

$$r_{t_{i+1}} = r_{t_i} + k(\mu - r_{t_i})(t_{i+1} - t_i) + \sigma\sqrt{t_{i+1} - t_i}Z_{i+1} \tag{4.29}$$

Using the discretization in (4.29) is not advisable given that there is a good alternative as described in (4.28). The Vasicek model has been criticized for a long time because it may lead to negative rates. From a practical perspective the model was used in risk management by simply discarding those paths that entered the negative territory. However, in the aftermath of the subprime-liquidity crisis some major economies operate with negative rates. This may put the Vasicek model back into focus.

CIR model

The CIR model of Cox et al. (1985) gained popularity due to the fact that it guaranteed positive interest rates. It is also a continuous time model for the short rate

$$dr_t = k(\mu - r_t)dt + \sigma \sqrt{r_t} dW_t \tag{4.30}$$

The LIBOR rate $L_t(\tau)$ can be calculated again in closed form

$$L_t(\tau) = -\frac{2k\mu}{\sigma^2 \tau} \ln(A(\tau)) + \frac{r_t}{\tau} B(\tau) \tag{4.31}$$

where

$$A(\tau) = \lambda(\tau)\gamma e^{\frac{(k+\gamma)\tau}{2}}, \quad B(\tau) = \lambda(\tau)(e^{\gamma\tau} - 1)$$

and

$$\lambda(\tau) = \frac{2}{(k+\gamma)(e^{\gamma\tau} - 1) + 2\gamma}, \quad \gamma = \sqrt{k^2 + 2\sigma^2}$$

The probability density function of the short rate r_t under CIR dynamics is known in closed form but involves cumbersome formulae. For simulation purposes, one may work with the Euler-Maruyama discretization of the continuous-time CIR process

$$r_{t_{i+1}} = r_{t_i} + k(\mu - r_{t_i})(t_{i+1} - t_i) + \sigma\sqrt{(t_{i+1} - t_i)r_{t_i}}Z_{i+1} \tag{4.32}$$

5 Real-Estate Derivative Instruments

5.1 Introduction

Financial derivatives can be traded on exchanges and in the over-the-counter (OTC) market. In spite of a long campaign by Nobel laureate Robert Shiller for the introduction of financial derivatives contracts capable of reflecting and distributing real-estate risk to investors, the truth is that even now, after the subprime crisis of 2007–2009, the real-estate derivatives market is very much in its infancy. As we will highlight in this chapter there are instruments available for trading real-estate risk on both exchanges and over the counter. However, when compared to the spot real-estate market it is evident that real-estate derivatives are only in an embryonic stage.

We will cover here total return swaps, the instrument of choice OTC for real-estate hedging, forwards which are also traded OTC, futures traded on exchanges and also a very interesting new derivative type of contract called MacroShare that is the brainchild of Robert Shiller and Karl Case.

Without loss of generality we shall use the IPD index for any index in the IPD family of indices. The introduction of futures contracts on the IPD index on EUREX has marked an important milestone in the development of real-estate derivatives for commercial real-estate. Likewise, the Case-Shiller futures contracts are the first exchange traded instruments covering housing real-estate risk.

The main activity on real-estate derivatives has been in the US and the UK although important single deals have been reported also in Europe, particularly in France and Germany. Between 2005 and 2015, the total notional for property total return swaps and property futures combined reached about £26 billion in the UK the volumes being smaller in US, Europe and Asia.

Far East Asia may present the biggest growth opportunities for real-estate derivatives, given the know-how hubs like Hong Kong and Singapore and the immediate vicinity of China. Sun Hung Kai Financial and ABN AMRO did the first property derivative in that part of the world (Baum and Hartzell, 2012). The deal covered a Hong Kong residential property and the derivative contract was designed such that ABN AMRO receives a return from the change in the University of Hong Kong's Hong Kong Island Residential Price Index (HKU-HRPI) while Sun Hung Kai Financial will receive a coupon linked to an interest rate.

This chapter is dedicated to the innovation of real-estate derivatives, with a focus on vanilla products such as forwards/futures, total return swaps, European call and put options. We described the mechanics behind these instruments and the range of applications.

5.2 Over-the-Counter Products

5.2.1 TOTAL RETURN SWAPS

The main contract traded over-the-counter (OTC) is the total return swap (TRS). This contract, which is referred to as a contract for difference, involves the two counterparties swapping a total return index[1] for a reference interest rate that could be fixed or floating. No principal is exchanged. TRSs maturities are typically in the one to five year range.

TRSs for commercial real-estate were first offered in the United States by Credit Suisse First Bonds in 2005 based on the National Council of Real Estate Investment Fiduciaries Property Index discussed in Chapter 2. The NCREIF property index is the underlying for two types of swaps that were traded to date. One is the total-return swap that allows an investor to synthetically reproduce the economic gains of the index return. The other is an instrument used to swap different NCREIF property sectors. In June 2008, the NCREIF Property Index Total Return Swaps changed from a quarterly to an annual payment schedule, all contracts paying at the end of the fourth quarter. Since June 2008, there are two new TRS indices traded; the 4-year and 5-year NCREIF National.

In 2005, a TRS engineered by Deutsche Bank and Eurohypo was done on the IPD index (UK) while Prudential and British Land did a commercial property swap. In the same year, Quintain and Barclays did a £15 million notional swap. The first property swap on the IPD France Offices Annual Index Dec was finalized in 2006 between Merrill Lynch and AXA Real Estate Investment Managers.

TRS trades are implemented with reference to the International Swaps and Derivatives Association (ISDA) standardized documentation. Two ISDA agreements must be completed and this may take time. The first agreement, the ISDA Master Agreement between the investor and a bank, covers general terms and conditions including the details as to what happens in the event of default or termination. This document contains no specific details about the actual trade. The second document is the trade confirmation where all details of the actual trade are specified, such as notional, maturity, and reference index.

---

[1] Examples of such reference indexes are IPD index or Halifax HPI in United Kingdom or NCREIF index or RPX in United States.

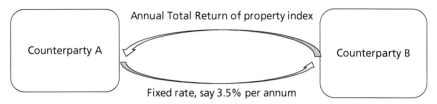

Figure 5.1. The structure of a total return swap between two counterparties.

The typical structure of a total return swap is depicted in Figure 5.1. The swap can also be structured with a monthly or quarterly tenor on the property index leg and cash-flow payments can be made quarterly rather than the standard annually. Investors would clearly like a more frequent payment of cash flows, which is one of the reasons why the IPD UK Total Return Index has been calculated on a quarterly tenor following the purchase of the IPD indexes by MSCI.

When the TRS was first introduced into the market in the United Kingdom, the TRS on IPD was quoted as 3-month LIBOR plus or minus a spread (in basis points). The IPD index leg accrued over a calendar year and settled on the last business day of the March following the year end; the LIBOR leg paid and reset on a quarterly tenor corresponding to the last business day of March, June, September, and December. However, the academic community insisted that to be consistent with contract conventions in other markets, the TRS should be priced on par LIBOR, meaning that the spread was zero. Investors in the IPD index market were unwilling to accept a zero spread and consequently the quotation on TRS changed to a simplified annual contract with a fixed interest rate.

An example of a TRS on IPD index with a floating rate payment is illustrated in Figure 5.2. The swap starting date is 1 January 2007, the maturity is 31 December 2008. The long party will receive the IPD Total Return while the short party will receive quarterly floating-rate payments linked to the 3-month LIBOR plus a spread of 42 basis point (bps). Notice that the floating-rate payments are made every quarter, at the end of the period based on the 3-month LIBOR settled at the beginning of the period. The IPD index leg makes annual payments at the end of March based on calculations on an end of December to end of December roll. Therefore, there are two basis risks present in this contract design, one due to the mismatch in the frequency of payments on the two legs and the other attributable to the one quarter shift on the IPD index leg.

The two panels in Table 5.1 illustrate the old floating quoting convention and the new fixed quoting convention. Notice that the day count convention has also changed from actual/365 (i.e. Act/365) for the floating convention to 30/360 for the new fixed convention. The main reason for making this

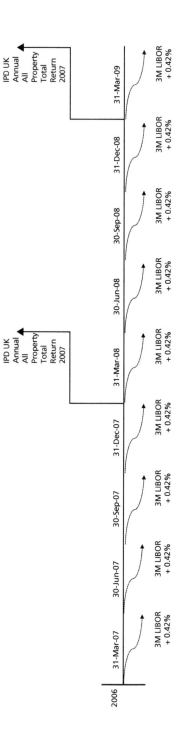

Figure 5.2. Illustration of a 2-year total return swap on the IPD index with a floating reference rate.

Table 5.1. Illustration of the Old and New Quotation Convention for Total Return Swaps on IPD index.

Old floating quotation convention: Day count convention of Act/365, modified following, accrual unadjusted, settlement adjusted			
Floating Leg		IPD leg	
Period	Time payment	Period	Time payment
Nov 07–Mar 08	31 Mar 2008	Dec 07–Nov 07	31 Mar 2008
Mar 08–Jun 08	30 Jun 2008	Dec 08–Dec 07	31 Mar 2009
Jun 08–Sep 08	30 Sep 2008	Dec 09–Dec 08	31 Mar 2010
Sep 08–Dec 08	31 Dec 2008		
Dec 08–Mar 09	31 Mar 2009		
Mar 09–Jun 09	30 Jun 2009		
Jun 09–Sep 09	30 Jun 2009		
Sep 09–Dec 09	31 Dec 2009		

New fixed quotation convention Day count convention is 30/360, modified following, accrual unadjusted, settlement adjusted			
Fixed Leg		IPD leg	
Period	Time payment	Period	Time payment
Dec 06–Dec 07	31 Mar 2008	Dec 07–Dec 06	31 Mar 2008
Dec 07–Dec 08	31 Mar 2009	Dec 08–Dec 07	31 Mar 2009
Dec 08–Dec 09	31 Mar 2010	Dec 07–Dec 06	31 Mar 2010

change in the quotation mechanism was twofold: (1) the absence of a swap pricing model that was widely accepted in the market and (2) the fact that a mechanism involving LIBOR $+/-$ spread exposed investors in real-estate markets to interest rate risk.

5.2.2 FORWARD CONTRACTS

TRSs are usually traded for commercial real-estate indices while forwards are preferred for residential real-estate indices. There are other hybrid formats of the TRS concept that may sometimes be encountered. For example, a swap plus a deposit are traded as a funded note. A real-estate or property forward is an OTC contract whereby one party will pay (or receive) the difference between a property index at maturity and the forward price.

Example 5.1. *Considering the generic forward contract depicted in Figure 5.3 assume as an example that the forward is on Halifax HPI with a 5-year maturity and is quoted as 130%. This means that in five years time, if the Halifax HPI return over a five year period is larger than 30% vis-à-vis the initial value of the index when the contract was started, then the long party will receive the excess over the 30% return. If the return is only 10%, for example, then the short party will receive 30%–10%=20% times the notional.*

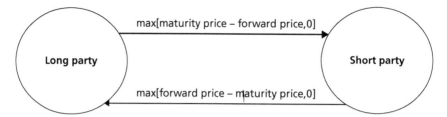

Figure 5.3. Description of a forward contract on a residential property index.

The real-estate forward on the Halifax HPI is a contract for difference. The forward on HHPI has been changed on 1st May 2009 from an annual contract month to month[2] calendar roll to a December to December calendar roll in order to improve liquidity and allow clients to match trades against each other. Furthermore this is helpful when taking into consideration that the IPD derivatives are contracted on a December roll. Hence, a real-estate desk will find it easier to monitor and aggregate risk positions across residential (HHPI) and commercial (IPD) exposures. The old style contract has prices based off the last published index so for example the 10/05/2007 contract trades are from April to April such that the one year here measures the Apr07–Apr08 growth, the two year forward measures growth for the period Apr07–Apr09, and so on. All the payments are then settled the following month end (after the end index date).

The new style contract measures the returns based out of the December base. For example, on 02/05/2009, the measurement for the HHPI forward curve is for 1Y covering the period Dec08–Dec09, for 2Y the period Dec08–Dec10, and so on. The starting index here rolls forward when the starting Dec index is published. For example on 07/01/2010 the index measurement is now covering 1Y = Dec09–Dec10, 2Y = Dec09–Dec11, and so on, and all the settlements/payments are made 31 Jan the following year.

The forwards on HHPI measures the increase in the index from start to finish with no coupon paid in between. The calculation for measuring the index growth is simply

$$\frac{HHPI_T}{HHPI_0} - 1.$$

Royal Bank of Scotland (RBS) was an important market-maker on HHPI forwards, trading forward curves with annual maturities rolling from one year to fifteen years ahead, and also 20, 25, and 30 year maturities. This was a great

---

[2] This means January to January for all contracts traded in January, February to February for all contracts traded in February, and so on.

initiative and perhaps in the near future this contract will move to one of the exchanges.

Example 5.2. *For example if we take the 5Y contract as of today such that the measurement period is Dec09 - Dec14 and assume that the price is equal to 109. This means that the Dec14 index will be 109% of the Dec09 index or you can think of this as 9% growth. Suppose that an investor bought a 2Y contract Dec09 - Dec11 at 101.5% for a notional of 5 million. Let's say the index reaches 105% in Jan12. So the HHPI index here would be Dec11 = 568.365 and*

$$\frac{\text{Dec11}}{\text{Dec09}} = \frac{568.365}{541.30} = 105\%$$

The growth is then equal to 105%–100% = 5% which gives $\sqrt{(1 + 5\%)} - 1 = 2.47\%$ per annum.

The investor bought the HHPI forward at 101.5%, so then she would receive a payment from your counterparty on 31 Jan 12 equal to

$$105\% - 101.5\% = 3.5\%$$

so the actual payment to the long HHPI forward party is equal to

$$3.5\% \times 5{,}000{,}000 = 175{,}000.$$

To understand better how the forward on HHPI works, we present in Figure 5.4 the forward curves with mid prices on three different days, 8 March 2007, 30 October 2007, and 3 April 2009. One can see that as the subprime crisis started to emerge the shape of the forward curve was more or less identical but the level was falling in an almost parallel fashion. The 5 year contract on 8 Mar 2007 had a mid price of 1.12625, implying an expected growth of 12.645% over the next five years. The basis for this contract was February to February so all contracts on that day were considering February to February contracts.

By contrast, on 3 April 2009 the five year forward mid price was 0.78, implying an expected fall of 22% over the next five years. Since the basis here is March to March, the market was expecting a fall to March 2014 of almost a quarter of the house prices in UK. In the aftermath of the subprime crisis, one may understand *ex post* this negative risk outlook. The three curves also hint that the 10 year maturity contract is the elbow point beyond which investors expect a rapid increase in house prices. This is in stark contradiction with the mean-reverting effects one may expect to occur over time and to the negative autocorrelations documented in Chapter 2. Investment banks could take advantage of their expertise and they could organize a trade that may be profitable for them and also help to stabilize the markets. By going long to 10 years and short for

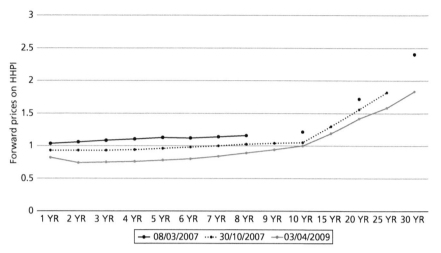

Figure 5.4. The term structure of forward mid prices for the Halifax HPI index on three different days.

Table 5.2. The summary statistics of the mid prices for the Halifax HPI forward contract between 23 May 2006 and 30 April 2009.

Maturity (Year)	1	2	3	4	5	6	7
Mean	0.8970	0.8468	0.8700	0.8802	0.9242	0.9052	0.9665
Std	0.0833	0.1231	0.1507	0.1498	0.1521	0.1173	0.1221
Max	1.0375	1.1000	1.0925	1.1225	1.1500	1.1425	1.1750
Min	0.7800	0.6500	0.6500	0.6500	0.6700	0.7350	0.7900
No. Obs	522	519	569	545	607	475	543

Maturity (Year)	8	9	10	15	20	25	30
Mean	0.9730	0.9953	1.0827	1.2346	1.5048	1.8614	2.1534
Std	0.0843	0.0650	0.0991	0.0703	0.0848	0.0873	0.2523
Max	1.1600	1.1738	1.2550	1.3750	1.7588	1.9250	2.4050
Min	0.8500	0.9000	0.9500	1.1500	1.3500	1.5850	1.8350
No. Obs	456	438	590	438	496	400	50

Notes: The data is daily and the contract specification is using full yearly contracts on a roll, with a basis given by the calendar month before the month of the current date of the observation.
Source of the data: RBS in London.

longer maturities, investment banks are able to be counterparties in aggregate to individual house holders looking to hedge the value of their properties and hence be short in the forward contracts up to ten years. Furthermore, by going short longer maturities they will act as deflators to speculative effects on the long term.

Table 5.2 contains the summary statistics for the mid prices constructed from the bid-ask prices on the forwards on HHPI, daily between 23 May 2006 and 30 April 2009. For this period the forward contracts had yearly specifications with maturities month given by the preceding month of the date of the observations. The average mid price values show an upward trending curve. For example, the 5 year maturity average mid price suggests a drop of 8.58% over the next five years whereas the 10 year contract on average over this period of the analysis implies a growth of 8.27% over the decade ahead. Interestingly, the mid price forward curve suggests a return to positive growth only after ten years. Looking back now in July 2016, we can see that the derivatives market implied a more subdued evolution of the house prices in UK than the realized price evolution to 2016. This may suggest that, *once again* the market sentiment pushed the prices on an upward spiral that may have bad consequences later on. The average house buyer in the UK is not sophisticated enough to consider information embedded in the Halifax HP forwards. Furthermore, these contracts are traded OTC and they are not in the pubic domain. This lack of information for the house buyers can be managed a lot better if the forwards were futures, that is if the real-estate housing derivatives are traded on an exchange. That in itself would contribute to increased stability in real-estate markets.

An investor may use this information to trade the curve by going long the 10 year contract and shorting the five year contract. The positive slope of the curve between the five year and 10 year tenor should provide a good return, if the direction of this trade is proven correct.

The liquidity of the HHPI forward contract can be gauged from the summary statistics information on the bid-ask spread presented in Table 5.3. The analysis covers the period between 23 May 2006 and 30 April 2009, daily and the contract specification is using full yearly contracts on a roll, with a basis given by the calendar month before the month of the current date of the observation. The number of observations indicate where interest was in the residential real-estate forward contract on HHPI and the five and 10 year maturities are clearly the contracts with most interest. On the other hand the mean bid-ask spread is indicative for the efficiency of this contract and the contracts with the narrowest spreads were one year and four year and from the long end of the term the 10 year. The largest bid-ask spread was 0.85 for 30 year forward contracts and the smallest was 0.005 for the one year contract, as expected.

This type of market quotation seems to have been adopted on other residential property markets, most notably in Asia in Hong Kong. The forward contract on the Hong Kong Real Estate Index Series (HKU-REIS) has changed quotation from a spread over Hibor to a % forward of the current spot index level. Hence, a one year residential property forward quoted at 110%/130% bid-offer means that the buyer of the contract would receive at maturity the

Table 5.3. The summary statistics of the bid-ask spread for the Halifax HPI forward contract between 23 May 2006 and 30 April 2009.

Maturity (Year)	1	2	3	4	5	6	7
Mean	0.0547	0.0733	0.0707	0.0686	0.0734	0.0816	0.0769
Std	0.0316	0.0231	0.0210	0.0234	0.0232	0.0208	0.0224
Max	0.1000	0.1400	0.1050	0.1000	0.1150	0.1300	0.1200
Min	0.0050	0.0300	0.0200	0.0200	0.0200	0.0325	0.0150
No. Obs	522	519	569	545	607	475	543

Maturity (Year)	8	9	10	15	20	25	30
Mean	0.0923	0.0919	0.0887	0.1641	0.1747	0.1791	0.5700
Std	0.0276	0.0304	0.0303	0.0332	0.0567	0.0801	0.2663
Max	0.1500	0.1500	0.1500	0.2000	0.3200	0.4000	0.8500
Min	0.0500	0.0450	0.0100	0.1000	0.0300	0.1400	0.1900
No. Obs	456	438	590	438	496	400	50

Notes: The data is daily and the contract specification is using full yearly contracts on a roll, with a basis given by the calendar month before the month of the current date of the observation.
Source of the data: RBS in London.

HKU-REIS return over 30%. The investor that believes the property in Hong Kong will not appreciate more than 10% in one year may shorten the contract. Then, at maturity if the HKU-REIS return is less than 10%, say 6% only, the investor will receive the 4% differential. Notice that the short party does not necessarily bet on a market downturn, but on a slower rate of growth of the real-estate index.

In the United Kingdom, residential real-estate derivatives were traded over-the-counter on a house price index such as Halifax or Nationwide, the most common being the Halifax (HPI) UK index (as capital only) described in Chapter 2. The market for options and forwards on the Halifax housing price index reached a cumulative notional volume of almost £2 billion before the subprime crisis eruption. In United Kingdom, options on the IPD index have also been traded over-the-counter. The first option on an IPD index outside the UK was based on the German IPD / DIX Index as an underlying and it was brokered by Goldman Sachs in January 2007.

Trading on total return swaps contingent on the RPX index began in September 2007 in the US but RPX forward contracts subsequently began trading in May 2008 and have since become the most liquid contracts based on the RPX index.

The pricing of real-estate derivatives such as TRS and forwards is not as trivial as presented in some sources and will be covered in Chapter 7. In my opinion it is wrong to price property forward contracts as if they are equity forwards.

Linking TRS curves to forward curves

It is important to understand how a portfolio of TRSs can be used to reverse engineer implied forward rates. This would allow an investor to look for arbitrage opportunities in this market. The market rates illustrated in Table 5.4 indicate that on the 23 December 2008 the nearest maturity contract will most likely settle for a decline of 20.50% for the period December 2007 to December 2008. Likewise, for the period December 2007 to December 2009, the representative economic agent on the IPD index market infers a similar total return decline over the two year period of 19.75%. This also shows a possible stabilization of the decline since the value is almost the same as the previous year. The next period, December 2007 to 2010 shows a reduced decline of only 14.25% and the next three maturities, December 2011, 2012, and 2013 indicate a soft landing. However, the term structure of TRS rates is not directly interpretable since each rate is applied multi-period wise and for increasing periods.

On the commercial real-estate OTC the TRS contract seems to be preferred, hence one may ask the question whether we can derive the equivalent term structure of one-year forward rates that are directly interpretable and suggest a future evolution of this real-estate market. Given the importance of real-estate risk for stress testing in banking and also as a part of financial stability analysis by central banks we believe that the real-estate markets offer a viable tool for risk management and also financial stability.

The TRS rates are paid as in any swap contract on a multi-period basis, whereas the forward rates cover a single period. Using the TRS rates in Table 5.4 that reflected the market conditions on IPD UK All Property Total Return as of 23 December 2008 we can derive the implied forward rates for future one-year periods. Denoting the TRS rate on a given contract by S, the total return on IPD paid in a given year by R and the corresponding discount rates for the same periods by r, the implied forward rates are given by those R rates satisfying a recursive system of equations. Bootstrapping the forward rates from the TRSs is done as follows, assuming for simplicity that the discount rate is $r = 5\%$ per annum for all maturities. First consider the December 2008 maturity. For this the TRS rate will equal the forward rate because

$$\frac{S_1}{1 + r_1} = \frac{R_1}{1 + r_1}$$

Hence $R_1 = -20.50\%$. The implied forward rate for the year December 2008 to December 2009 is R_2 that is calculated from the equation

$$\frac{S_1}{1 + r_1} + \frac{S_2}{(1 + r_2)^2} = \frac{R_1}{1 + r_1} + \frac{R_2}{(1 + r_2)^2}$$

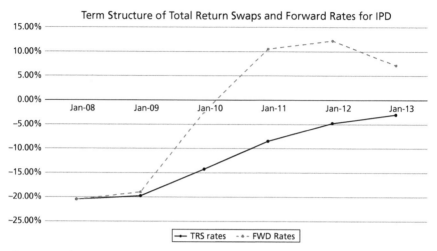

Figure 5.5. The term structure of total return swaps mid prices and implied forward rates for the IPD UK All Property Total Return for 23 December 2008.

From Table 5.4 we can see that S_2 is equal to -19.75% and solving the above equation for R_2 gives the solution -18.96%. Next iteration for R_3 is based on the equation

$$\frac{S_1}{1+r_1} + \frac{S_2}{(1+r_2)^2} + \frac{S_3}{(1+r_3)^3} = \frac{R_1}{1+r_1} + \frac{R_2}{(1+r_2)^2} + \frac{R_3}{(1+r_3)^3}$$

and again the only unknown here is R_3. Solving the linear equation gives 2.41% as the solution. Figure 5.5 illustrates both term structures TRS rates and implied forward rates. It is evident that the implied forward curve is much steeper than the market TRS curve. The implied forward curve shows a return to the positive range much sooner, beginning 2010, as compared to the TRS curve that misleadingly may suggest positive returns only from 2012. Further-more the difference between the two curves appears quite large, particularly over the year 2011. However, bear in mind that these calculations are from the point of view of 23 December 2008 and the implied forward rates are not neces-sarily the future realized rates. On the other hand, the implied forward curves may provide investors and regulators with a market forward-looking view, possibly anticipating market downturns and potentially even market crashes.

5.2.3 TRADING PLATFORMS AND EXCHANGE TRADED INSTRUMENTS

The first evidence of property derivatives traded on an exchange comes from Australia. In 2002 the Australian Stock Exchange offered the ASX

Table 5.4. Total return swaps bid, offer and mid prices for the IPD UK All Property Total Return index on 23 December 2008.

Maturity end of month	Maturity in years	Bid (%)	Offer (%)	Mid (%)
December 2008	1	−21.00	−20.00	−20.50
December 2009	2	−20.25	−19.25	−19.75
December 2010	3	−15.00	−13.50	−14.25
December 2011	4	−9.25	−7.75	−8.50
December 2012	5	−5.25	−4.25	−4.75
December 2013	6	−3.75	−2.25	−3.00

Note: The calculation year in all total return swaps is December 2007.

Property-Trust futures on the S&P/ASX200 Listed Property-Trust index. The underlying index in this futures contract had 23 constituents and a market capitalization of 77 billion AUD. This was followed in 2005 by the Sydney Futures Exchange that also offered futures on the Dow Jones Australia Listed Property-Trust index. The underlying index for this futures contract had 15 constituents, all liquid trusts.

Eurex began trading property futures on February 9, 2009. These Eurex IPD futures contracts are annual contracts based on the total returns of the IPD index[3] for individual calendar years. With the introduction of this futures contract, Eurex seeks to eliminate counterparty risk, to improve liquidity to the commercial property sector of the real-estate property market, and to attract a complete range of potential participants in this asset class. Additional futures contracts have been launched by Eurex on IPD property indices, such as the UK sector indices (Offices, Retail, Industrial) and other European indices (initially France and Germany) on a demand-led basis.

EUREX IPD futures

The IPD futures contract will be settled upon the total returns of the index for an individual year. A particular feature of this contract, as opposed to other futures contracts in other asset classes such as equity, foreign exchange, or commodity, is that the calculations period is end of December to end of December, while the actual expiry maturity is end of March to end of March. This is done in order to allow the publication of the index after the end period in December. The Eurex property IPD index futures have no counterparty risk, carry no VAT, stamp duty, agents, and legal fees.

---

[3] The IPD UK Annual Property Total Return Index is value-weighted and it measures un-geared total returns to direct UK property investments using time-weighted methodology based on monthly returns compounded for the purposes of the annual index construction. Each property covered contributes proportionally to its capital employed.

Example 5.3. *For example, the IPD futures contract for maturity December 2009 will expire on 31 March 2010 since the last day in March is a trading day. Each day there are five successive annual contracts available on a December calendar roll maturity.*

Each contract is cash settled on the first exchange day after the last trading day, calculated to two decimal places and rounded to the nearest 0.05. The IPD futures contract has a nominal size of £50,000 and a par value of 100, with a minimum price change of 0.05 that represents £25. Usual transactions are between £1m and £25m.

The transaction costs for trading a futures contract via Eurex vary between 0.1% and 0.5%, depending whether brokers are employed or not. If similar trades are conducted in the spot market the transaction costs may reach 7% (PDIG, 2015).

The final settlement index IPD futures contracts price formula is given by

$$100 \times \frac{TRI_t}{TRI_{t-1}} \tag{5.1}$$

where TRI_t is the total returns index value at the end of the annual index calculation period, while TRI_{t-1} is the total returns index value at the beginning of the annual index calculation period. Interestingly, the final settlement price will be calculated to three decimal places and rounded to the nearest 0.005 or 0.01.

Example 5.4. *For example, the final settlement price for the 31st December 2009 maturity IPD index futures was equal to 85.50 because the IPD index at 31st December 2008 was 1178.0732 and the IPD index at 31st December 2009 was 1007.2526.*

One of the great advantages of being able to trade futures on the IPD index is the possibility to implement trades along the curve. For example, an investor may go long the five years IPD index futures and short the two years IPD index futures. This combined trades effectively give no exposure to commercial real-estate risk in the UK for the first two years and it implies that this sector will start increasing again thereafter. This trading strategy would have been very beneficial in the aftermath of the subprime crisis.

In Figure 5.6 we illustrate the evolution of the indexIPD futures contracts! futures curves for the IPD index traded on Eurex in London. The contracts seem to experience a stationary almost flat evolution for the back end maturities while there seems to be more activity for the near end maturity. This is in line with the Samuelson effect.[4]

---

[4] The Samuelson effect claims that the volatility of futures prices increases as the contract delivery date approaches.

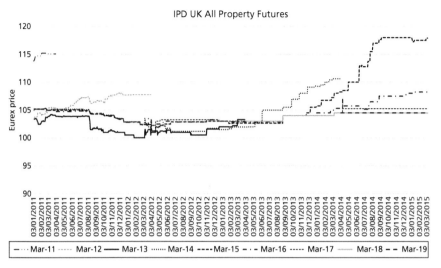

Figure 5.6. The IPD index futures settlement prices, daily between 3 Jan 2011 and 5 Mar 2015.

Notes: The contracts are traded with fixed maturities March 2011, March 2012, March 2013, March 2014, March 2015, March 2016, March 2017 and March 2018.
Source of data: Eurex, London

Table 5.5. Summary statistics of the IPD index futures settlement prices, daily between 3 Jan 2011 and 5 Mar 2015.

	2011–03	2012–03	2013–03	2014–03	2015–03	2016–03	2017–03	2018–03	2019–03
Mean	114.96	106.51	101.89	104.16	106.33	104.32	103.97	104.05	104.50
Median	115.10	106.70	101.50	104.10	104.00	104.00	104.00	104.50	104.50
Mode	115.10	107.75	101.00	101.20	102.65	102.90	105.25	104.50	104.50
std	0.34	1.25	1.29	2.59	5.20	1.69	0.95	0.58	0.00
Kurtosis	2.92	−0.92	−1.12	0.05	0.51	−0.13	−1.48	−0.55	
Skewness	−1.72	−0.58	0.51	0.88	1.43	0.98	0.34	−1.00	
Minimum	113.80	103.75	100.00	101.10	101.25	102.25	102.25	103.00	104.50
Maximum	115.25	108.05	104.20	110.62	118.00	108.25	106.10	104.50	104.50
Count	64.00	322.00	574.00	828.00	1063.00	999.00	741.00	489.00	235.00

Notes: The contracts are traded with fixed maturities March 2011, March 2012, March 2013, March 2014, March 2015, March 2016, March 2017, and March 2018.
Source of data: Eurex, London.

The summary statistics described in Table 5.5 convey a more informed view. The March 2015 maturity contract has had the largest interquartile range of 17.75. The overall view offered by the values summarized in the table indicate a moderate optimism reflected by small growth in the commercial property sector in the UK. The absolute maximum growth implied from the futures on IPD over the January 2011 to March 2015 was the 18% growth in the March 2015 contract. The longer maturity contracts have very small standard deviations in general.

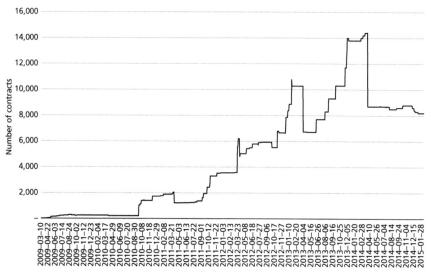

Figure 5.7. The IPD UK Annual All Property futures open interest, daily between 10 March 2009 and 11 February 2015.

Source of Data: Eurex, London.

Figure 5.7 shows the evolution of open interest for IPD UK. All Property futures traded on Eurex. There is a clear increasing trend but when compared with the spot real-estate market there is a lot more trading that needs to be done.

S&P/Case-Shiller Index Futures

In May 2006, CME introduced housing futures and options contracts based on the S&P/Case-Shiller indices to enable hedging and speculation in US residential real-estate. As of 2009, there are futures contracts with maturities extending 18 months into the future, listed on a quarterly cycle of February, May, August, and November; futures contracts with maturities extending 19 to 36 months into the future, listed on a bi-annual schedule May and November; and futures contracts with maturities going from 37 months to 60 months into the future, listed on an annual schedule with November maturity. The futures contracts trade at $250 times the index with a tick of $50, while the options trade on one futures contract with a tick of $10, for a range of strikes at five index point intervals from the previous day close price of the futures on the Case-Shiller Index. There are futures for 10 US cities (Boston, Chicago, Denver, Las Vegas, Los Angeles, Miami, New York City, San Diego, San Francisco and Washington D.C.), in addition to the composite index containing all 10 cities. On CME over-the-counter bespoke contracts are also traded, with major Wall Street dealers trading on platforms such as TFS. More details can be found about the CME CS at www.cme.com. Options such as call and put are also traded on the Case-Shiller Index but with a one-year maturity.

5.2.4 RPX FUTURES

On the brink of the subprime crisis a real-estate contract based on the 28-day version of the RPX index family started trading in September of 2007. Initially both a total return swap (TRS) and a simple forward agreement were traded. Since the TRS implied a periodic cash flow exchange with the floating leg receiver getting paid market return on the index, it was difficult to agree on pricing models. Hence, after September 2008, the RPX market covered only forward contracts, which are settled at each year-end based on the Radar Logic index published for five preceding consecutive business days. The RPX market is traded up to five years forward for the composite index and only up to three years for local indices from the same family. As with the Case-Shiller index derivatives, the RPX derivatives are covered by major Wall Street dealers via trading platforms such as ICAP.

Levin (2009) remarked that because in 2008 the bid-ask spread on RPX derivatives reached 2 or more percentage points, government agencies or large loan insurers could not operate on this market because of lack of liquidity. RPX forwards are used by MBS investors or home builders for hedging purposes and by speculators who are willing to take directional bets. Both the Case-Shiller index and the RPX forwards trades are generated by credit protection buyers and incorporate a large risk premium. Hence, Levin (2009) pointed out that these forward prices are likely to be lower than real-world expectations.

5.2.5 OTHER FUTURES AND OPTIONS

Just before the subprime crisis started, CBOT launched a futures contract on the Dow Jones US Real Estate Index. This index covers primarily REITs. The contract has a quarterly expiry and is cash-settled. The tick size is $10. For many years investment banks were trading options contingent on EPRA Euro Zone index. Two futures contracts on FTSE EPRA/NAREIT Europe and FTSE EPRA/NAREIT Euro Zone indices started being traded in October 2007 on LIFFE. The contracts have a quarterly expiry, are settled in cash, trade in units of €10 per index point, and have a tick size of €5.

5.3 **MacroShares**

5.3.1 MECHANICS OF THE MACROSHARES IN REAL-ESTATE MARKETS

MacroSharesTM (also called Macros, Macro Securities and Proxy Assets) are new instruments that will allow the management of a much broader array of economic risks than are currently available in the financial market.

MacroShares are a patented product of MacroMarkets LLC, and are the brain innovations of Allan N. Weiss and Robert J. Shiller.

This new financial instrument is a cash security tracking the S&P/Case-Shiller Composite-(10 City) Home Price Index that gives investors and house-holders the opportunity to express either a bullish view on future home prices by purchasing an Up MacroMarket (UMM) security or a bearish view on future home prices by purchasing a Down MacroMarket (DMM) security. Moreover, the DMM lets an investor express a bearish view similar to shorting the market, without a margin account. There is no counterparty risk because the trusts are fully secured by US. Treasury securities and cash. Upon issuance, UMMs and DMMs will trade separately in the NYSE.

These new securities started[5] trading in June 2009 on NYSE. The new Home Price Macros (UMM and DMM) are issued with a par value of $25, and $50 for a pair consisting of one share of UMM and one share of DMM. For calculations of the index, a leverage factor of 2 is applied.[6] The macro-hedge index (which equals $25 times the underlying value in the UMM until stop-out) is defined in terms of a reference value equal to the last S&P/Case-Shiller Composite (10-City) Home Price Index when the securities are issued. Payments to each of the two security accounts are updated each month when a new index value is announced at 9:00 Eastern Standard Time on the last Tuesday of the month, transfers being made between the UMM trust and the DMM trust so that the UMM trust always has a dollar amount equal to the index, with an obvious limit of $50. Because of the transfer mechanism and the fact that the index cannot drop more than 100% from the initial value, the contract has a trigger such that when the index hits 50, the trust balances are refunded to UMM so that the DMM receives nothing.

Each share in the UMM and in DMM attract payments similar to dividends at periodic payment dates, with cash being moved freely from one account to another such that the sum of the pair should stay close to the initial proceeds of the sale. The shares trade individually on a daily basis and the traded values will coincide with the calculated values only at maturity T or immediately after termination if contracts are abruptly terminated because of index appreciation hitting the barrier of 2, in which case the UMM share doubles in value while the DMM goes to zero. The initial MacroShares prospectus stipulates a leverage factor of 3 so returns on UMM and DMM accounts were magnified three times. However, since it is difficult to conceptualize a loss of more than 100% of the house value, a leverage factor of 2 was subsequently introduced

---

[5] The first MacroShares were issued by MacroMarkets LLC on November 30, 2006, but on the price of one barrel of oil so for a different market.

[6] The initial design suggested that the "Up" Major Metro MacroShare (NYSE:UMM) could have been leveraged three times the return of a five year investment in the a S&P/Case-Shiller real-estate 10-city composite index.

and therefore the house price index should evolve stochastically within the boudnaries $0.5H_0 \leq H_t \leq 1.5H_0$.

The Housing MacroShares is a claim on the evolution of the real-estate index that is traded as a security on a stock-exchange. There are no daily settlement or margin accounts. The MacroShares payment system is similar to an extent to dividends and individuals who would like to use them for hedging the value of their house and do not need special approval to trade them. They are also default free since by design the contract stops when the DMM trust is emptied.

On the 21 December 2009 MacroShares Housing Depositor announced the liquidation of the MacroShares Major Metro Housing UMM and DMM due to assets on deposit becoming inferior to $50 million. The UMM and DMM continued trading on NYSE Arca until the closing day of trading on 28 December 2009. A final distribution payment was made on 6 January 2010 and MacroShares Housing Depositor calculated early termination expenses in the range of $85-$90 per share relative to 430,000 shares outstanding in each of the two trusts.

5.3.2 PRICING OF MACROSHARES

The issuance and redemption of this contract is done as a pair, one UMM share and one DMM share, together for $50. Since the money will move from one account to its twin account mirroring the total return increase or decrease of the real-estate reference index, it is only necessary to price the UMM. The DMM price is just $50 minus the UMM price. At the end, or at the termination trigger, the investor gets the macro shares index as reflected in the account of the share she bought, UMM or DMM. The price of the UMM share or DMM share at one point in time may differ from the money existing in that trust account, depending on the market expectation of future real-estate index levels. For example, after a series of house-price increases, an external shock to the economy occurs that makes the representative market agent believe that until the maturity of the MacroShares the real-estate price levels will drop significantly. Therefore, the DMM account looks more likely to be in the money at the maturity of the contract and therefore, in spite of the low levels in the DMM account, this may trigger a spike in the DMM price. To differentiate between the two we shall denote by $\widetilde{UMM_t}$ and $\widetilde{DMM_t}$ the price of the UMM share and DMM share respectively, and by UMM_t and DMM_t the money levels in those accounts.

The levels of the UMM and DMM accounts evolve with reference to the house price index $\{H_t\}_{t\geq0}$ as follows

$$UMM_t = UMM_0 \left(1 + 2\frac{H_t - H_0}{H_0}\right) \tag{5.2}$$

$$DMM_t = DMM_0 \left(1 - 2\frac{H_t - H_0}{H_0} \right) \tag{5.3}$$

where the calculations are recalibrated monthly.[7] These formulae show that the macro shares implied levels of house price index $\widetilde{H}_t$ could be reverse-engineered as follows

$$\widehat{H}_t = H_0 \left(1 + \frac{1}{2} \frac{UMM_t - UMM_0}{UMM_0} \right) \tag{5.4}$$

$$\widehat{H}_t = H_0 \left(1 - \frac{1}{2} \frac{DMM_t - DMM_0}{DMM_0} \right) \tag{5.5}$$

Note that $UMM_0 = DMM_0 = \$25$ and a 1% increment in UMM_t should reflect a 0.5% increase of the Case-Shiller real-estate composite 10-city index. Likewise, a 1% increase in the DMM_t should be equivalent to a decrease of 0.5% of the real-estate index.

For valuation purposes we shall focus only on the UMM security, the price of the DMM being easily calculated as 50 minus the price of the paired UMM, as mentioned above. A simple model for pricing the Housing MacroShare proposed by Shiller (2008b) assumes a constant risk-free rate r and a series of futures prices with maturities matching the coupon date on the MacroShare contract. The risk is eliminated if one constructs a portfolio of short positions in r futures contracts for all maturities $i = \{1, \ldots, T_1\}$ and one short position in the futures contract with the final maturity. The Housing UMM MacroShare and this portfolio together should offset each other so the net present value is zero.

This gives the formula

$$\widetilde{UMM_0} = \frac{rH_0}{1+r} + \frac{rf_i}{(1+r)^2} + \ldots \frac{rf_{T-1}}{(1+r)^T} + \frac{f_T}{(1+r)^T} \tag{5.6}$$

where $f_i = UMM_0 \left[1 + 2 \times E\left(\frac{H_i - H_0}{H_0} \right) \right]$. The price of UMM in this simplified model is a weighted average of futures prices. This is a no-arbitrage model that will connect the market on the real-estate index futures, which is not easily accessible to the individual investor and to house owners. More advanced pricing models are described in Shiller (2008b).

Example 5.5. *This example refers to the values in the initial prospectus when the real-estate index was at 186.06. The pricing of a Housing MacroShare issued on 10 June 2008 is considered and the pricing is done based*

---

[7] Note that prices of UMM and DMM evolve daily.

on the Case-Shiller futures curve on 10 June 2008 with five yearly out maturities

$$F = (-9.6\%, \ -19.4\%, \ -18.6\%, \ -18.7\%, \ -19.1\%)$$

The risk-free rate is taken as the 5-year Treasury note yield at 3.78% and evidently, $UMM_0 = 25$. Using formula (5.6)

$$f_i = UMM_0(1 + 2 \times F(i))$$

so one gets

$$f_1 = \$20.20, \ f_2 = \$15.30, \ f_3 = \$15.70, \ f_4 = \$15.65, \ f_5 = \$15.45$$

Using formula (5.6) leads to a price for UMM equal to $15.97 while the pair security DMM will be priced at $34.03. The pricing indicates a high likelihood of a down market.

5.4 Other Products: Options and Structured Products

5.4.1 PICs, PIFs, AND PINs

Just three years after the failure of the FOX contracts, Barclays began issuing its Property Index-Certificates (PICs) in 1994 and its PIFs in 1996 on the capital component of the index, with the index comprising UK commercial property only. In 1999, Barclays offered the Property Index Notes (PINs). These were notes paying the current yield of the annual IPD index and having a redemption value determined by the changes in the capital component of the IPD index after issuance.

PICs are structured products designed as Eurobonds with annual coupon payments linked to IPD index income return, and a capital redemption value defined by the IPD index capital gain over the life of the certificate. In essence this product is bought at par and then it replicates IPD index returns (less any dealing fees and spreads) for the bond holder. There could be fees and spreads for the structure and any exit from this instrument before maturity may be affected by tracking error. The attraction of this instrument is that it gives a low entry cost in commercial real-estate as an investment while at the same time it is not that useful as a hedging tool.

Because it is considered a debt instrument, a PIC may be more useful than a TRS to investors who are not authorized to trade derivatives. Since 2004 more than £900 million worth of PICs have been traded. The issuer of a PIC will receive the capital and will pay in exchange the yield on the index until redemption of the certificate at par issuance plus or minus changes in the capital value of the index. For the PIFs the underlying variable determining the return was the change in the IPD index rather than the aggregated index, but the payments were done at the end of the year, thus introducing a basis. PINs were structured more like a fixed income instrument with returns paid on a quarterly tenor.

5.4.2 MORE EXOTIC PRODUCTS

In 2003, Goldman Sachs issued the first series of a range of covered warrants based on the Halifax All-Houses All-Buyers seasonally-adjusted index on the London Stock Exchange (LSE). The first option on an IPD index outside the United Kingdom was referenced to the German IPD/ DIX Index and was traded in January 2007 with Goldman Sachs acting as a broker. In August 2007, Morgan Stanley agreed on an exotic swap on Halifax House Price Index with an undisclosed counterparty. This is the UK's first residential property derivative trade that included an embedded exotic option, a "knock-in put" option allowing the counterparty to gain if the index rises, subject to a maximum payout. The investor's capital is protected unless the index falls below an initially specified value.

City Index introduced spread betting on house prices in UK. The bets were calculated based on Land Registry figures, simple averages of all property transactions done in the previous quarter. The underlying house price averages were not adjusted for their mix and they exhibited seasonality. Due to the lack of smoothing there was a difference between the market sentiment of house prices and the observed prices. City Index ceased to offer these spread bets. IG index also initiated spread bets on the Halifax family of house price indices covering the entire UK and also 12 regional subindices. Surprisingly, the broker was forced to cease trading from September 2004 to April 2005 following a significant increase in the volume of spread betting in the direction of an imminent decline of house prices in August 2004. Another interesting aspect was that the spread betting was tax-exempt. This may explain the reopening of property spread betting markets in the United Kingdom, the most notable example being the Cantor Index that launched spread betting on UK home prices (www.spreadfair.com). This activity was mirrored in United States by HedgeStreet, a US online broker, who designed a contract called Hedgelets by analogy with the spread bets in the United Kingdom. These started traded in October 2004 and covered six metropolitan areas with prices determined by the Median Sales-Prices of Existing Single-Family Homes, which were updated quarterly. These contracts were aimed at consumers, each contract was a $10 bet on the direction of home prices. The technology for Hedgelets seem to be the predecessor of RPX derivatives technology. Shiller (2008a) points out that the founder John Nafeh believed that the hedgelets would help ordinary citizens to immunize themselves against house price crashes. The idea did not progress as hoped and the trading has since been shut down. In February 2006, the Zurich Cantonal Bank issued two structured products on the residential index ZWEX, that were traded by both institutional and retail investors.

A forward starting total return swap on RPX is reported in a newsletter by ICAP (2007). For example a company may decide that is exposed to real-estate risk only two years from now, for a period of five years. Then the company may decide to enter a two-year forward start five-year swap. Another very interesting product that has been investigated mainly in academic circles is the perpetual futures contract proposed by Shiller (1993) and analysed by Thomas (1996). The idea is to consider first a perpetuity contract that pays a yield determined by an index of income on property. This is similar to the Barclays PICs contract, with the difference that there is no maturity. The perpetual futures are contracts written on this perpetuity.

5.5 **CMBS Total Return Swaps**

Total return swaps have been also successfully traded on various CMBS indexes, an excellent review is given in Goodman and Fabozzi (2005). The real-estate indices tracking the US commercial property prices introduced in 2006 by Real Capital Analytics and MIT were designed specifically for derivative trading, motivated by the fact that CMBS swaps were traded over-the-counter based on the Bank of America CMBS indices. In the commercial mortgage-backed securities (CMBS) market several dealers have offered swaps on various CMBS indices and their subsectors. Goodman and Fabozzi (2005) provide an insight into the mechanics and the economic rationale of the total return swaps issued on these indices. They also explain the attraction to those who want to get exposure to a CMBS in a synthetic way.

As is well known, a total return swap is a bilateral contract in which one party advances the total return, including all additional cash-flows paid plus capital appreciation or depreciation, realized on a reference asset in exchange for an interest rate payment such as LIBOR plus a spread. The party receiving the total return is the swap receiver and it is long the asset. For a CMBS total return swap (CMBS TR) the reference asset is a CMBS index, say Bank of America Index. The total return on the underlying CMBS index is calculated from the income on the CMBS index and the capital appreciation or depreciation on the CMBS index. The tenor of the swap is monthly and the maturity is usually six months because the main users are commercial loan lenders who are employing this financial instrument in order to hedge their exposure to any economic shocks while they warehouse the commercial loans in preparation for securitization.

5.6 Summary Points and Further Reading

Robert Shiller argued over the last three decades for the introduction of real-estate derivatives in order to manage one of the most important and dangerous financial risks; the risk of a property price crash. In spite of thousands of pages of financial economic analysis highlighting the advantages to society of introducing such instruments, as can be seen from the evidence in this chapter, the real-estate derivatives market is very much in its infancy.

Efforts in the right direction have been made but overall the pace of financial innovation is very slow in this area. This is highly surprising given the size of the real-estate markets in developed economies. The special issues on real-estate in the Journal of Portfolio Management published every other year are a valuable source of keeping up to date with the latest developments regarding products being discussed, as well as the problems related to these instruments.

The main vanilla instruments are present and they are traded in both OTC and on the exchanges but without great participation from any major market players. It is difficult to understand how large investment banks, mutual funds, pension funds can say they are widely diversified if they do not hold positions in real estate.

An important reference for the theoretical development of real-estate derivatives is Case and Shiller (1987). Other relevant readings in this area are Shiller (2008a), Shiller (2014), Lecomte and McIntosh (2005), Lecomte and McIntosh (2006), Levin (2009) and Syz et al. (2008), each reading opening up new directions for research into real-estate derivatives contracts.

Mitchell and Bond (2009) pointed out that the information implied by real-estate derivatives are generally more accurate in terms of forecasting future property return outcomes than the values put forward by the IPF consensus forecast. The difference is more significant for the near term outcomes, as expected, but during periods like autumn 2007 and autumn 2008, the real-estate derivatives adjusted much quicker than the IPF Consensus. Furthermore, it appears that in 2006, the IPF Consensus forecast for 2006 was too conservative, whilst the opposite was true for their forecast for 2007. In addition, Mitchell and Bond (2009) argue that changes in the real-estate derivatives market can be useful to predict price changes in the listed sector.

6 Financial Applications of Real-Estate Derivatives

6.1 Introduction

The most likely users of property derivatives are investment banks for proprietary trading and hedging operations; insurance companies for portfolio diversification and long-term investment; pension funds for sector allocation and portfolio diversification; property companies for getting exposure to sectors and trade directional trends in property markets or relative value trades; and funds, hedge funds, mortgage lenders for hedging real-estate risk in general.

Real-estate derivatives allow investors to take on property price risk without actually buying a spot asset. In this way, transactional, legal, and tax costs may be circumvented and the execution, in and out, of exposure to property risk is more efficient. Investors can use real-estate derivatives for making strategic decisions. For example, a finance house may decide to invest in real-estate in the United States while being sceptical about the prices in the United Kingdom at the same time. Operating with physical assets is problematic due to increased friction costs.

Using property derivatives allows the finance house to get positions in both markets simultaneously and, depending on market evolution, they may also exit either of the two property markets a lot more easily. Likewise, investors may want to benefit from the alpha of their current portfolio while diversifying the property risk geographically.

This chapter shows some applications of real-estate derivatives. These include trading strategies and also an extensive arbitrage detection analysis. The linkages between the over-the-counter markets in real-estate derivatives and the similar markets on exchanges is likely to play a crucial role in the future.

6.2 Strategies Based on Property Derivatives

Property derivatives allow investors to perform a fast, low-cost and more dynamic execution of investment strategies in real-estate that would not be possible otherwise. Property fund managers may use property derivatives to

Figure 6.1. Country property index total return swap.

Notes: Example of a real-estate total return swap across two countries. The returns on each country property index are swapped directly.

reduce tracking error, lock-in future property returns, reduce risk at total port-folio level and switch between various real-estate sectors.

6.2.1 COUNTRY SWAP

The investors in the country swap deal illustrated in Figure 6.1 will enter this deal based on their expertise in the domestic market. The advantage of this property derivative trade is that the investors will preserve the alpha on their usual portfolio and they will obtain beta diversification in the other foreign market.

6.2.2 CHANGING EXPOSURE

Property derivatives can be used to implement arbitrage strategies related to geographical opportunities or a lack of synchronization between major and less major real-estate markets. Relative value strategies can also be searched with the help of real-estate derivatives, allowing investors to aim at divergence or convergence trades. The investors can also use property derivatives to lower financing costs. In spite of liquidity problems, derivatives contracts with a large exposure of notional can be executed very fast, in contrast with direct investment in spot property markets where completing trades can take several months.

The deal illustrated in Figure 6.2 is beneficial for all parties since both par-ties only get a synthetic portion of portfolios in other sectors, hence they do not invest in physical assets and are saving transaction costs and the deal is executed much faster. The broker is only exposed to counterparty credit risk for which they will charge each party a fee reflecting the default risk of each counterparty. The fee could be structured as a lump sum paid at the inception of the trade or as a pay as you go annuity premium.

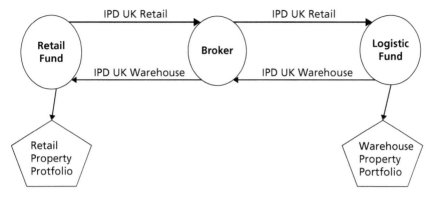

Figure 6.2. A cross-sector real-estate total return swap.

Notes: The cross-sector TRS between between a fund managing a portfolio of warehouses in the UK and a property fund managing a large portfolio of retail properties. Both funds are interested in diversifying their property portfolios. The broker takes positions in two cross-sector swaps with offsetting cash-flows.

Pension funds are typically interested in changing the nature of their portfolio and also have a well-diversified portfolio. Given the large size of spot real-estate markets in well developed countries, no pension fund can claim they are fully diversified without being exposed to real-estate risk. Hedge funds may also be interested in property derivatives to achieve synthetic exposure to a very interesting asset class. At the other end of the spectrum, real-estate companies are interested in using property derivatives for hedging current portfolios of properties or future property developments.

Real-estate derivatives, futures in particular, can be used to get market beta when investment portfolios are rebalanced following recent information. They can be also used to ramp up portfolios when a new line of business involving real-estate is opened. Another interesting application is the protection or virtual sale of a building development, locking the value prior to construction. Alpha Beta Fund Management, an open-end investment company based in Ireland, does not get direct exposure to physical property assets but instead seeks more efficient means of harvesting real-estate index returns. The firm targets pension funds and other investors that are considering access to British housing by dealing in an over-the-counter property derivatives market which tracks the Halifax House Price Index (HHPI).

Another very interesting use of property derivatives is to extract the market view expectations on the future level of property across the next five years. This information should, in theory, be at least more reliable than the similar type of information extracted from the REIT market where expectations can be skewed due to portfolio composition effects. The information extracted from IPD futures for example can be used as part of an analysis of the stability of a financial system and hence provide a great tool for policy makers, regulators and central bankers. Depending on the jurisdiction in question, another possible advantage of employing real-estate derivatives is a more favourable tax treatment. There are no transaction costs other than the usual bid-ask spread. Compared to investing directly on the spot market, using property derivatives can save approximately 6.75% of the purchase price in stamp duty, legal costs, agency fees and sale costs in the United Kingdom.

Furthermore, the main usage of derivatives is to create synthetic trading positions. Thus, through derivatives, investors may be able to get exposure well above their capacity, they can get negative net exposure to the market and benefit from a possible market downturn. In addition, investors using TRSs employ a form of leverage exposure to property. They initially require only a margin of 5–10% of the notional size of the swap. Other advantages include the possibility of achieving a high level of diversification, low transaction costs, low volume entry, and quick entry into markets that may be opaque in their spot markets.

The example illustrated in Figure 6.3 shows how a real-estate derivative (RED) can be used to manage exposure to real-estate from different perspectives. Suppose that an investor in UK commercial real-estate (office, warehouses, retail) has a portfolio of properties but for various reasons (tax, risk management, future tactical decisions) she/he would like to reduce the exposure to real-estate but without effectively going into an actual sale that may take a long time to execute and also cost some fees. A market broker knows that at the same time another investor such as a pension fund would like to get exposure to real-estate but once again they would not go into a real buy of properties.

The deal put together by the broker, two total return swaps, illustrated in Figure 6.3 shows that the buyer will pay a fixed rate interest rate to the broker and receive in exchange the IPD Total Return (income and capital); likewise

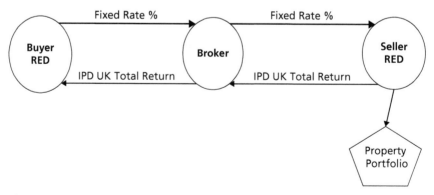

Figure 6.3. Managing real-estate exposure using a real-estate derivative (RED) contingent on a real-estate index such as IPD UK All Property Total Return.

the seller will transfer the IPD Total Return to the broker and receive a fixed rate, obviously smaller, from the broker. The seller will keep its alpha, the buyer will get exposure to a different asset class at a low cost and the broker only faces counterparty risk on both sides of the deal.

Example 6.1. *As an example, consider that a housing building company starts a new building complex in New York and therefore is exposed to housing price risk in that area. They decide to hedge with a 3-year RPX forward trading at 4% annualized rate. For the sake of explanation assume that the forward is 88.69. Then the seller of the contract will pay the difference between the observed RPX and 88.69, if positive, at maturity. Likewise, the seller of the contract will receive the difference between 88.69 and the observed RPX at maturity. Suppose now that RPX falls somehow such that at the end of the three years it ends up at 91.39. Then the seller of the contract will pay 2.70% times the notional. If the RPX ends up at the level of 86.07 then the seller of the contract will receive 2.62% times the notional at maturity.*

There are also some disadvantages of using property derivatives. When trading is done over the counter, counterparty risk is still an issue, and this coupled with the intrinsic illiquidity of the market may result in significant risk management problems at particular points in time associated with market downturns. Marking-to-market is still very difficult since property derivatives are still in their infancy and there is no generally accepted framework to price these products. Last but not least, the derivatives contracts in real-estate markets can only be as good as the indices they are written on. The IPD index is an appraisal index and therefore is based on the subjective beliefs of appraisers. Other disadvantages include insufficient liquidity, lack of data available for model calibration, as very little is known on the risk management side.

6.2.3 REBALANCING A DIRECT PROPERTY PORTFOLIO

Here we illustrate how the IPD futures traded on EUREX can be used to reduce tracking error and rebalance the portfolio for the 2017 horizon. The example below uses fictitious numbers not real market numbers.

Suppose that a UK property fund is benchmarked to the total return performance of the MSCI IPD Quarterly UK All Property Index. Based on this benchmark index assume that in June 2016 the fund has an underweight position of £100 m to the UK Shopping Centre and an overweight position of £100 m to the UK Retail Warehousing. The manager of the fund aims to rebalance his overall position to reduce tracking error and boost his overall portfolio return for 2017, expecting Shopping Centre to do better than the retail warehouses by 6% (12%–6%). Rebalancing the property portfolio in the spot market will attract high transaction costs and may take a long period of

Table 6.1. Rebalancing strategy first trade June 2016: long 2017 IPD UK Quarterly Shopping Centre Index.

	Year 2017
Manager forecast Shopping Centre Total Return	12.0%
Less Futures IPD UK Shopping Centre	8.75%
Less Liquidity Risk Premium	0.0%
Less Transaction Cost	0.25%
Expected Return	3.00%

Table 6.2. Rebalancing strategy first trade June 2016: long 2017 IPD UK Quarterly Retail Warehouse Index.

	Year 2017
Less Manager forecast UK Retail Warehouse	6.0%
Futures IPD UK Retail Warehouse	8.0%
Less Liquidity Risk Premium	0.0%
Less Transaction Cost	0.25%
Expected Return	1.75%

time. Alternatively, the fund manager could enter long futures on IPD UK Quarterly Shopping Centre for a £100 m notional and maturity 2017 and simultaneously enter short futures on IPD UK Quarterly retail Warehouse for a £100 m notional and 2017 maturity.

The strategy is described in Tables 6.1 and 6.2. If the manager's forecasts prove to be correct this strategy would then also produce 4.75% returns on £100 m notional.

6.3 **Forward-Futures Arbitrage**

With a functional IPD futures market and a viable OTC market in TRS on IPD, is it possible to somehow compare the two, given that both contracts offer protection against the same risk, commercial property price risk? It is not straightforward to compare futures contracts with swap-like contracts, the latter being multi-period instruments. However, as we have shown previously in this chapter it is possible to reverse engineer from a term structure of TRS rates the implied equivalent term structure of forward rates, and then compare those with the futures prices for the same maturities. Large differences should be indicative of arbitrage opportunities or misalignments between the investors in the two markets.

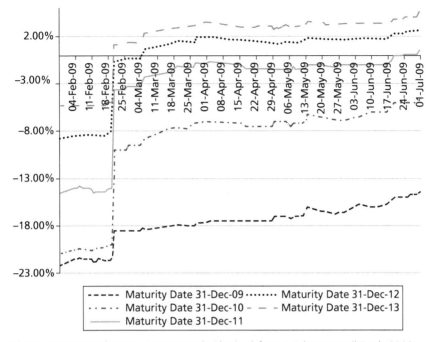

Figure 6.4. IPD Total Return Swap Rates (mid prices) from 4 February until 7 July 2009.

Notes: The IPD Total Return Swap Rates (mid prices) for the five maturity dates fixed in the market calendar, for the period of study. The total return swap rates are given as a fixed rate and not as a spread over LIBOR. A negative total return swap rate implies that the underlying commercial property market will depreciate over the period to the horizon indicated by the maturity of the contract.

This idea has been explored in Stanescu et al. (2014), who analysed the differences between the forward and futures prices on the IPD UK property index. Here we revisit that analysis and focus mainly on whether the observed difference between the forward and futures prices is statistically different from zero for n = 5 different maturities and N = 71 daily observations for each maturity. The data needed to replicate this study includes the IPD property futures prices, TRS rates, the IPD index itself, and also the GBP discount rates. Futures prices were gathered courtesy of Eurex-Deutsche Borse in London, the property TRS data has been obtained courtesy of Tradition Group, a major dealer on this market. The IPD index and the GBP discount rates can be downloaded from Datastream or Bloomberg. Due to the availability of the property futures and TRS data, the sample period used by Stanescu et al. (2014) was daily from 4 February 2009 until 7 July 2009, giving 71 property futures daily curves and 71 sets of TRS rates with up to five years maturity (the first maturity date is 31 December 2009, the second maturity date is 31 December 2010, the third maturity date is 31 December 2011, the fourth maturity date is 31 December 2012, and the fifth maturity date is 31 December 2013).

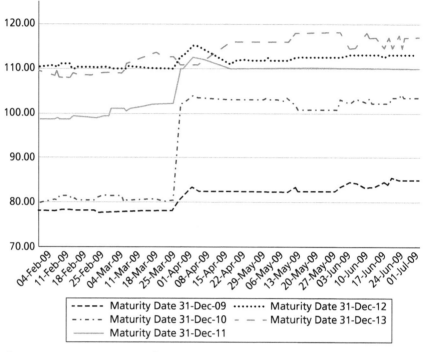

- - - - - Maturity Date 31-Dec-09	········· Maturity Date 31-Dec-12
- · - · - Maturity Date 31-Dec-10	- — - Maturity Date 31-Dec-13
——— Maturity Date 31-Dec-11	

Figure 6.5. Eurex Futures Prices from 4 February until 7 July 2009.

Notes: Eurex Futures Prices for the five maturity dates fixed in the market calendar. Futures prices are given on a total return basis so a futures price of 110 for December 2012 implies that the market expects a 10% appreciation of the commercial property in the UK at this horizon.

The TRS curves constructed from market prices used for this analysis are depicted in Figure 6.4. These curves reveal that, for the time period of the investigation, the IPD TRS rates are negative for the first, second, and third maturity contracts while for the remaining maturity contracts the TRS rates are mostly positive. The extreme value at the end of February 2009 may be explained as being caused by the rollover off the futures contracts in March combined with the publication of the IPD index for the year ending in December 2008.

In order to search for arbitrage, one would also need the corresponding property futures prices for the same maturity contracts over the same time period. The IPD futures curves are illustrated in Figure 6.5. However, futures prices are not directly comparable with TRS prices.

One can succeed in having an apples for apples comparison by reconstructing the implied forward prices from the TRS prices, under the no-arbitrage principle. Then the pairs of implied forward prices and futures prices, on the same property index and with the same maturity, can be scrutinized for arbitrage. The implied fair forward prices obtained by bootstrapping from the

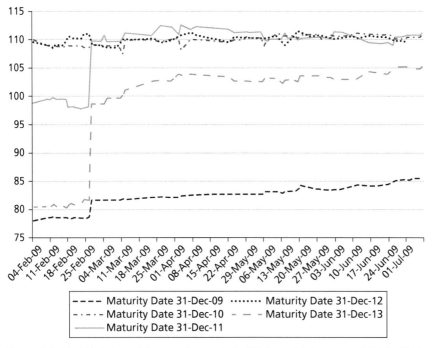

Figure 6.6. The Fair Prices of Property Forwards for IPD from 4 February until 7 July 2009.

Notes: The Fair Prices of Property Forwards for the five maturity dates fixed in the market calendar, for the period of study. The fair property forward prices are reversed engineered from the corresponding portfolio of total return swaps.

TRS curves in the analysis conducted by Stanescu et al. (2014) are shown in Figure 6.6.

Table 6.3 reports the descriptive statistics of the three series in the arbitrage analysis. The mean values for TRS rates are mostly negative and increase with maturity. For the period of study the mean values for the forward-futures differences are consistently positive. However, this observation may be due to random variation and therefore needs to be formally tested before an investor embarks on an evident trading strategy.

In order to test whether the time series of the differences between implied forward and futures prices is significantly different from zero, first one has to test for stationarity for both the forward and futures price series. This is done using the well-known Augmented Dickey-Fuller test. Based on the results presented in Table 6.4 one should conclude that the forward series for the first, second, third, and fifth maturity dates are non-stationary while the forward series for the fourth maturity date is stationary at 5% significance level. The testing also indicates that the futures series is non-stationarity for all maturity

Table 6.3. Descriptive Statistics for total return swap rates, Eurex futures prices and the forward-futures differences.

	Maturity Dates				
	31-Dec-09	31-Dec-10	31-Dec-11	31-Dec-12	31-Dec-13
	Total Return Swaps				
Mean	−0.178	−0.0971	−0.0389	−0.0056	0.0138
standard deviation	0.0217	0.0548	0.0521	0.0401	0.0336
Skewness	−0.6925	−1.3581	−1.4446	−1.4177	−1.3889
Kurtosis	−0.5131	0.1383	0.2633	0.2135	0.1585
	Futures Prices				
Mean	81.1982	94.275	106.1732	111.7035	113.5915
standard deviation	2.6558	10.6358	5.1369	1.2792	3.7762
Skewness	−0.0992	−0.4889	−0.5411	0.164	−0.2771
Kurtosis	−1.5313	−1.7844	−1.6426	−0.6302	−1.6544
	Forward-Futures Prices				
Mean	1.1018	4.2432	2.0765	−1.599	−3.7103
Standard Deviation	1.3846	7.2574	3.7344	1.0573	3.0863
Kurtosis	0.3093	0.9912	0.8006	0.0824	−1.6454
Skewness	1.2702	1.6562	1.5582	0.3179	0.2274

Notes: The descriptive statistics are of the total return swap rates, futures prices and forward-futures differences on IPD UK All Property index. Daily mid prices are used for calculation for the period 4 February 2009 to 7 July 2009 for the five market calendar maturities, namely December 2009, December 2010, December 2011, December 2012, and December 2013.

Table 6.4. ADF test for the forward and future prices for the IPD UK index.

	Forward		Futures	
Maturity Date	Level	First Differences	Level	First Differences
31 December 2009	−1.3453	−8.3646***	−0.8098	−5.1662***
31 December 2010	−1.9185	−8.4575***	−1.3019	−8.3168***
31 December 2011	−2.0106	−8.6799***	−1.3278	−4.3724***
31 December 2012	−3.4368**	−5.4320***	−2.3581	−5.9891***
31 December 2013	−0.9618	−6.4863***	−1.2087	−12.1882***

Notes: The test is performed for both the data in levels as well as for the first differenced data. The optimum number of lags used in the ADF test equation is based on the Akaike Information Criterion (AIC). *, **, and *** denote significance at the 10%, 5%, and 1% level, respectively. The data is from 4 February until 7 July 2009 for the five maturity dates given in the first column.

contracts. In addition, the forward and futures series for all maturity dates are stationary in the first differences.

The main aim is to test whether the forward-futures differences are statistically significantly different from zero. The simplest way to conduct this test is to employ a regression model fitted for each maturity date T_i, $i \in \{1, 2, 3, 4, 5\}$:

$$F(t, T_i) = \alpha_{0i} + \beta_{0i} f(t, T_i) + \varepsilon_{ti} \tag{6.1}$$

The null hypothesis in this case is $H_0 : \alpha_{0i} = 0$ and $\beta_{0i} = 1$ and if this hypothesis is rejected then there is evidence that the difference between forward and futures prices is significant. The data in this investigation combines the term structures of futures and implied forwards. Thus, the statistical analysis is focused on panel data. This is important because it will allow a larger number of degrees of freedom. Consequently, a reduction in the collinearity among explanatory variables can be achieved, which in turn improves the efficiency of the estimation. Real-estate data is different from other time series encountered in finance. Statistical analysis may be more difficult in these circumstances. Employing panel data analysis is also helpful because we can achieve a technical solution to model identification and omitted variable problems.

The regression equation in (6.1) is rewritten for our panel data as:

$$F(t, T_i) = \alpha_0 + \beta_0 f(t, T_i) + \varepsilon_{ti} \tag{6.2}$$

with $i \in \{1, 2, 3, 4, 5\}$ and $t \in \{1, 2, \ldots, 71\}$. One can design various panel regression models, with fixed effects, time effects, random effects and combinations of those. The simplest panel data model can be assembled by the pooled regression, described above in (6.2). Then the model can be estimated rapidly by simply stacking all the data together, for both the explained and explanatory variables.

A slightly more complex model is the fixed effects model described by the equation:

$$F(t, T_i) = \alpha_0 + \beta_0 f(t, T_i) + \alpha_i + \nu_{ti} \tag{6.3}$$

where i varies cross-sectionally (i.e. in our case it is different for each maturity date T_i), but not over time.

The next model in level of complexity is the time-fixed effects model given by the equation

$$F(t, T_i) = \alpha_0 + \beta_0 f(t, T_i) + \lambda_t + \nu_{ti} \tag{6.4}$$

where t varies over time, but not cross-sectionally. Stanescu et al. (2014) employed the fixed effects model and the time-fixed effects model for their analysis, as well as a model with both fixed effects and the time-fixed effects. It is useful to test whether the fixed effects are needed, using the redundant fixed effects LR test.

An important panel data model is the panel data random effects model, that increases the level of complexity in the following way:

$$F(t, T_i) = \alpha_0 + \beta_0 f(t, T_i) + \varepsilon_i + v_{ti} \tag{6.5}$$

where ε_i is now assumed to be random, with zero mean and constant variance σ_ε^2, independent of v_{it} and $f(t, T_i)$. Furthermore, this model can be slightly modified to include random time-effects models that will be fitted using the regression specification:

$$F(t, T_i) = \alpha_0 + \beta_0 f(t, T_i) + \varepsilon_t + v_{ti} \tag{6.6}$$

The random effects, random time-effects models and the two-way model which allows for both random effects and random time-effects are estimated and then the null hypothesis, that the random effects are uncorrelated with the regressors, is tested.

Before carrying out the tests we need to consider the stationarity of the time series involved. The preliminary ADF tests indicated that the IPD forwards and futures data were non-stationary in levels and stationary in the first differences, so the analysis will continue on the first differenced data. The results reported in Table 6.5 depict the outcome of testing the null hypothesis $H_0 : \alpha_{0i} = 0$ and $\beta_{0i} = 1$ vs. $H_1 : \alpha_{0i} \neq 0$ or $\beta_{0i} \neq 1$ is tested using an F-test. The results in Table 6.5 imply that the difference between forward and futures is not just noise.

The outcome of the testing described in Table 6.6 implies that the significance of the forward-futures difference is also not driven by the month of

Table 6.5. 3 F-Test and Durbin Watson statistic results for the property forward and futures data.

Maturity Date	F-test	Durbin-Watson Statistic
31 December 2009	83.5072***	1.9905
31 December 2010	49.4309***	2.0595
31 December 2011	23.8320***	2.0613
31 December 2012	31.1717***	2.2589
31 December 2013	158.2534***	2.7247

Notes: The analysis covers the period 4 February to 7 July 2009 for the five maturity dates given in the first column. For the F-test, the null hypothesis is that the difference between the forward and futures prices is just noise (i.e. 0i = 0 and 0i =1). *, **, and *** denote significance at the 10%, 5%, and 1% level, respectively.

Table 6.6. The values of the t-test are computed for the differences between forward and futures prices on the IPD UK index.

t-statistic	Maturity Dates				
	31-Dec-09	31-Dec-10	31-Dec-11	31-Dec-12	31-Dec-13
4 Feb 7 Jul 2009	6.7060***	4.9265***	4.6852***	−12.741***	10.1291***
2 Apr 7 Jul 2009	6.695***	6.826***	4.612***	−20.003***	−20.261***

Notes: The analysis covers data from 4 February until 7 July 2009 and from 2 April to 7 July, respectively, for the five maturity dates given in the second row. *, **, and *** denote significance at the 10%, 5%, and 1% level, respectively.

abnormally high differences. The difference between forward and futures is still significant when a shorter sample period, 2 April to 7 July 2009, is considered, excluding the abnormal sub-period from end of February 2009 to the end of March 2009.

One may improve the analysis by further considering Levin and Lin (1993), Levin, Lin, and Chu (2002), Im, Pesaran, and Shin (1997) and Maddala and Wu (1999) unit root tests for panel data, these tests being collected in Table 6.7. As in the case of time series data, the panel data is non-stationary in the levels but it is first differenced stationary.

To see whether the fixed effects are necessary, it is useful to employ the redundant fixed effects LR test. The outcomes of this test are reported in Table 6.8.

The results shown in Table 6.8 reveal that a model with fixed time effects only has the most empirical evidence in this study. However, a random effects model may also be appropriate and this can be tested with the Hausman test. The outcome results given in Table 6.8 indicate that the random effect model is preferred for our application. The analysis is completed with an F-test statistic for multiple coefficient hypotheses computed using the panel regression

Table 6.7. Panel Unit Root Tests of Levin, Lin, and Chu (2002) and Im, Pesaran, and Shin (2003) for forward and futures price data on the UK IPD commercial property index.

Method	Forward		Futures	
	Level	First Differences	Level	First Differences
Levin, Lin & Chu t*	−1.8292	−6.7737***	−0.7206	−4.0345***
Im, Pesaran & Shin W-stat	−1.1578	−10.4686***	0.3880	−8.3918***

Notes: The analysis covers the period from 4 February until 7 July 2009 for five maturity months, namely December 2009, December 2010, December 2011, December 2012 and December 2013. *, **, and *** denote significance at the 10%, 5%, and 1% level, respectively.

Table 6.8. Tests for determining the most suitable panel regression model.

Test	Value
Redundant Fixed Effects Test	
Cross-section F	1.09
Cross-section Chi-square	5.52
Period F	2.21***
Period Chi-square	154.19***
Cross-Section/Period F	2.14***
Cross-Section/Period Chi-square	157.74***
Hansen Test	
Cross-section random	3.0341*
Period random	0.0003
Cross-section and period random	0.1690

Notes: The redundant fixed cross-section effects test has a panel regression with fixed time (period) effects only under the null. Both the F and the chi-square version of the test are reported. The redundant fixed time (period) effects have a panel regression with fixed cross-section effects only under the null. For the random effects test (i.e. Hansen test) the null hypothesis in this case is that the random effect is uncorrelated with the explanatory variables. The panel data are from 4 February until 7 July 2009 for five maturities, namely December 2009, December 2010, December 2011, December 2012, and December 2013. *, **, and *** denote significance at the 10%, 5%, and 1% level, respectively.

random effect specification. The testing results give an F-statistic equal to 237.3960 which is significant at the 1% level. This shows that, at 1% level, the null hypothesis $H_0 : \alpha_0 = 0$ and $\beta_0 = 1$ can be strongly rejected and therefore the differences between forward and futures are not just noise in the panel data. In addition, the value of the Durbin-Watson test 2.1419 shows that there is no autocorrelation in the panel regression errors.

Overall there is significant empirical evidence indicating that the time series of differences between forwards and futures was different from zero in the period of investigation. This is equivalent to saying that there were arbitrage opportunities between the TRS market on IPD, that is OTC, and the futures on IPD traded on Eurex.

6.4 Other Applications of Real-Estate Derivatives

Real-estate derivatives may spread out to include trades with specific portfolios rather than indices as the underlying in the contract. In 2007 an Australian property company sold the returns of a portfolio of shopping centres to a Dutch pension fund. Sectoral trades may become more popular in the future, in spite of lack of liquidity experienced in the aftermath of the subprime crisis.

Forum (2008) contains four impressive case studies using property derivatives. Grosvenor Group Limited used property derivatives to manage exposure to property market returns (beta). The trade was the first in Australia in May 2007 with ABN Amro as counterparty. DTZ Corporate Finance & Protego Real Estate Investors considered a hypothetical trade involving the optimal use of IPD swaps in hedging the performance of a UK Property Portfolio until December 2008. Scottish Widows Investment Partnership used a funded note to increase their unit linked property fund allocation to property. Standard Investments considered a scenario for their Select Fund in 2007 targeting a performance of CPI + 5%, and using a derivative based on the IPD French Office Index as being optimal for their problem.

6.5 Summary Points and Further Reading

Real-estate derivatives are not only instruments for hedging property price risk. They can be used to circumvent large friction costs imposed by taking positions on the spot real-estate markets. They can be seen as financial products allowing investors to extract the financial economics from various real-estate markets without being physically involved in those markets. The range of applications highlighted in this chapter can be only the tip of the iceberg, more educated and sophisticated investors in the future may introduce more derivatives useful for taming the real-estate risk. More applications are described in Syz (2008). Baum and Hartzell (2012) contains some interesting examples involving derivatives in the commercial property area.

It is also important to realize that the coexistence of various real-estate derivatives, on the exchanges and OTC, may occasionally lead to arbitrage as discussed in more detail by Stanescu et al. (2014). The flexibility in trading real-estate contracts as paper based with cash delivery means that investors can spot those arbitrage opportunities and take positions such that arbitrage opportunities will disappear relatively quickly.

Real-estate derivatives can be very useful to policy makers as a compass where the market is navigating to and as early signals of potential market crashes. Futures and forwards contracts for example can be very useful to short the real-estate markets, both commercial and residential. Since shorting cannot be done in spot real-estate markets, the derivatives for this asset class are vital to break the self-fulfilling prophecy cycle leading to herding and irrational exuberance in property markets. The relationship between real-estate prices and inventory has not been fully investigated. A starting point in this direction could be Geman and Tunaru (2012).

7 Real-Estate Derivatives Models

7.1 Introduction

An MIT survey asked a pool of usual derivatives and real-estate traders and investors why they thought real-estate derivatives are not used more frequently. The majority listed as the main obstacle the lack of flexible models that they can trust in this area.

Traditionally derivatives have been used for all asset classes except real-estate. Given the huge size of the spot real-estate markets there is an opportunity for a large market to be established.

In this chapter we describe some of the best models proposed in relation to real-estate derivatives. They range from equilibrium models such as Geltner-Fisher and Cao-Wei, to no-arbitrage models such as Bjork-Clapham, BFSP and Fabozzi-Shiller-Tunaru. Shiller-Weiss and Syz models are also discussed given their large appeal in terms of simplicity and the important role they have played in the development of real-estate derivatives.

7.2 Equilibrium Models

In this section we shall present some equilibrium models developed for pricing contingent claims on a real-estate index.

7.2.1 GELTNER-FISHER MODEL

Geltner and Fisher (2007) developed an equilibrium model for pricing property swaps on an appraisal real-estate index. Their equilibrium model insists that there is a difference between the expected return on a property portfolio in an equilibrium state $E(r_P|\Xi)$ and the LIBOR rate considered as representative of risk-free rate LIBOR. The difference between the two is the risk premium for the property portfolio q_P so one can write

$$E(r_P|\Xi) = \text{LIBOR} + q_P. \tag{7.1}$$

When the property portfolio is perfectly tracked by the property index X_t, the expected return on the index r_X *in the long run* is given by

$$E(r_X) = \text{LIBOR} + q_P \qquad (7.2)$$

Here we detail the version of the Geltner-Fisher equilibrium model for the total return swap reworked by Lizieri et al. (2010), rather than the capital return swap described by Geltner and Fisher (2007). The former may have more applications in financial markets.

Because of lagging and smoothing effects, the real-estate index is likely to be lower than the actual market value of the property portfolio. This implies that the equilibrium total return risk premium in the real-estate index q_X would be lower than the corresponding one of the portfolio q_P.[1] Hence

$$E(r_X|\Xi) = \text{LIBOR} + q_X < \text{LIBOR} + q_P = E(r_P) = E(r_X). \qquad (7.3)$$

The lag effects can be quantified as the difference between the expected return on the index in the current state of the economy and the expected return on the index in equilibrium

$$L = E(r_X) - E(r_X|\Xi). \qquad (7.4)$$

Using the above formulae

$$L = q_P - r_X + m$$

where the term m is defined by Geltner and Fisher (2007) as a momentum effect.

The long position will face the following constraint on their trade

$$s \leq \text{LIBOR} + L + B^{Long}$$

where s is the interest rate to be paid on the swap, B^{Long} accounts for the long party beliefs about a possible abnormal return. If $L = B^{Long} = 0$ then $s = \text{LIBOR}$.

Likewise, the short party position faces the following constraint

$$s \geq \text{LIBOR} + L - \alpha + B^{Short}$$

---

[1] One observation we have here is that we do not know what a long run means in terms of years. Furthermore, the equilibrium state is not applicable during a long crisis like the subprime crisis.

where α is the short investors belief that her portfolio will earn abnormal return and B^{Short} is her expectation of abnormal negative growth in the returns index. Again, if $L = \alpha = B^{Short} = 0$ then s =LIBOR.

Combining the two conditions leads to

$$\text{LIBOR} + L - \alpha + B^{Short} \leq s \leq \text{LIBOR} + L + B^{Long}. \qquad (7.5)$$

If the party that has invested in the real-estate has no expectation of alpha and there are no differences in expectation of abnormal growth, then the interest rate for the short leg will be given by the risk free rate plus the lag or smoothing effect.

Geltner and Fisher (2007) also considered the impact of bid-ask spreads and the asymmetry of the investors' willingness to occasionally pay larger spreads. This imbalance in supply and demand may impact the final price. The observed margins are taken to be equal to the mid-point trading prices

$$s^* = s + (Ask - Bid)/2.$$

7.2.2 CAO-WEI MODEL

Cao and Wei (2010) generalized the well-known Lucas discrete model for a pure exchange economy with a financial market by considering a continuous-time economy with two markets, one financial and one dedicated to housing. In this economy each individual economic agent can trade a single risky stock, pure discount bonds and a finite number of other contingent claims written on the risky stock, the pure discount bond or on the price of the house. The risky stock is represented by the market portfolio and its dividend stream $\{\delta_t\}$ is the aggregate dividend in the economy. The calculations are normalized such that the total supply of the market portfolio is one share. The risk-free bond and contingent claims are all in zero net supply.

At time zero the market representative agent has one share of the market portfolio and one house. The agent is assumed to have a fixed working life up to time T and a post-retirement life span of up to $T^* > T$. The agent receives a constant salary y per unit of time.

The aim of this equilibrium model is to optimize the present value of the agent's expected utility from the pre-retirement consumption and the post-retirement wealth. Cao and Wei (2010) assume that the agent will not sell the house until her retirement at time T.

Some further notations are needed for this model. Denoting by H_t the housing value at time t, it is assumed that $\{\delta_t\}$ and $\{H_t\}$ are exogenous Markov processes, and hence, the information flow that the agent is exposed to is generated by these two processes. If the financial asset prices at time t are denoted by X_t and the dividends they generate by q_t, the cum-dividend vector of dividends is defined by $D_t \equiv \int_0^t q_u du$. The agent will finance consumption using the income from her salary and a continuous trading strategy $\{\theta_t\}_{t \geq 0}$ where $\theta_t = (\theta_t^s, \theta_t^B, \theta_t^{x'})$ denotes the market portfolio, the discount bond and other contingent claims.

Since the agent cannot sell the house before retirement it seems natural to assume that the utility function can be separated over time and between housing consumption and other consumption. Cao and Wei (2010) also assume that the non-housing service is independent of the market value of the home.

Under all these assumption the optimization problem can be formulated as follows

$$\max_{(c_t, \theta_t)} E \left[\int_0^T e^{-\phi t} U(c_t) dt + e^{-\phi T} U(W_T) \right]$$

subject to

$$\begin{cases} H_t + \theta_t X_t + \int_0^t (c_u - y_u) du = \theta_0 X_0 + H_0 + \int_0^t \theta_u dD_u + \int_0^t \theta_u dX_u, \\ W_T = H_T + \theta_T X_T \end{cases}$$

where ϕ is the rate of time preference.

Cao and Wei (2010) show that the solution to this problem by the Euler equation is

$$X_t = \frac{e^{-\phi(T-t)}}{U_c(\delta_t)} E \left(\int_t^T U_c(\delta_u) dD_u \right) \tag{7.6}$$

for any $t \in (0, T)$.

In this economy, the value of a forward contract contingent on the value of the house H_t with forward price K at maturity $T \geq t$ is given, upon direct application of (7.6), by

$$f_t(H_t, K, T) = e^{-\phi(T-t)} E_t \left(\frac{U_c(\delta_T)}{U_c(\delta_t)} (H_T - K) \right)$$

Standard calculations determine K at initial trade time by assuming that $f_t(H_t, K, T) = 0$. Thus, the forward price $F_t(H_t, T)$ is given by

$$F_t(H_t, T) = \frac{E_t(U_c(\delta_T) H_T)}{U_c(\delta_t)} \tag{7.7}$$

The equilibrium European call and put option prices for maturity T and strike price K are determined similarly as

$$c_t(H_t, K, T) = e^{-\phi(T-t)} E_t \left(\frac{U_c(\delta_T)}{U_c(\delta_t)} \max(H_T - K, 0) \right) \qquad (7.8)$$

$$p_t(H_t, K, T) = e^{-\phi(T-t)} E_t \left(\frac{U_c(\delta_T)}{U_c(\delta_t)} \max(K - H_T, 0) \right) \qquad (7.9)$$

This solution is too general to be applied to practical problems. In order to obtain closed-form solutions, three more assumptions were made. First, the utility function employed is assumed to be the CRRA function $U(c_t) = \frac{c_t^{1-\gamma}}{(1-\gamma)}$. Secondly, the aggregate dividend process follows the geometric mean-reverting process

$$d\delta_t = (\mu_\delta - a_\delta \ln \delta_t) \delta_t dt + \sigma_\delta \delta_t dZ_t^\delta \qquad (7.10)$$

Thirdly, the housing index process follows a geometric Brownian motion

$$dH_t = \mu_H H_t dt + \sigma_H H_t dZ_t^H \qquad (7.11)$$

The noise Wiener process Z^H and Z^δ are correlated with the correlation coefficient ρ.

With these added assumptions, Cao and Wei (2010) derived closed form solutions for the equilibrium price of a zero coupon bond

$$B_t(T) = e^{-\phi(T-t) E_t \left(\frac{U_c(\delta_T)}{U_c(\delta_t)} \right)}$$

Furthermore, they derived closed-formulae for the yield-to-maturity and the instantaneous risk-free rate

$$R(t, T) = \phi - \frac{1}{2} \gamma^2 \sigma_\delta^2 \frac{1 - e^{-2a_\delta(T-t)}}{2a_\delta(T-t)}$$

$$+ \gamma \left(\mu_\delta - \frac{1}{2} \sigma_\delta^2 - a_\delta \ln \delta_t \right) \frac{1 - e^{-a_\delta(T-t)}}{a_\delta(T-t)} \qquad (7.12)$$

$$r_t = \phi - \frac{1}{2} \gamma^2 \sigma_\delta^2 + \gamma \left(\mu_\delta - \frac{1}{2} \sigma_\delta^2 - a_\delta \ln \delta_t \right) \qquad (7.13)$$

One major obstacle to using this model is the fact that the aggregate dividend process and the risk-aversion parameter of the representative agent are not observable. Cao and Wei (2010) insist that r_t is observable[2] and given the linear

---

[2] We do not agree that the instantaneous risk-free rate can be observable, given that it is an infinitesimal quantity.

relationship between $\ln \delta_t$ and the endogenized interest rate r_t, they infer the parameters for the aggregate dividend process from the observed interest rates. Denoting for simplicity

$$dr_t = a_r(b_r - r_t)dt + \sigma_r dZ_t^r \qquad (7.14)$$

by identification with the corresponding quantities in (7.12) we have that

$$a_r = a_\delta, b_r = \phi - \frac{1}{2}\left(\frac{\sigma_r}{a_r}\right)^2, \sigma_r = \gamma a_\delta \sigma_\delta, \rho_{rH} = -\rho$$

and

$$R(t, T) = b_r + \frac{1}{2}\left(\frac{\sigma_r}{a_r}\right)^2\left[1 - \frac{1 - e^{-2a_r(T-t)}}{2a_r(T-t)}\right] + (r_t - b_r)\frac{1 - e^{-a_r(T-t)}}{a_r(T-t)})$$
$$(7.15)$$

Given the modelling assumptions above we can observe that for European contingent claims the final distribution is known in closed form. Cao and Wei (2010) apply this to derive the equilibrium prices of the forward contract, and European call and put options as follows

$$F_t(H_t, T) = H_t \exp\left(\mu_H(T-t) + \rho_{rH}\sigma_H\frac{\sigma_r}{a_r^2}(1 - e^{-a_r(T-t)})\right) \qquad (7.16)$$

$$c_t(H_t, K, T) = C_{BS}(F_t(H_t, T), T - t, K; R(t, T), R(t, T), \sigma_H) \qquad (7.17)$$

$$p_t(H_t, K, T) = P_{BS}(F_t(H_t, T), T - t, K; R(t, T), R(t, T), \sigma_H) \qquad (7.18)$$

where $C_{BS}(S_t, \tau, K; r, q, \sigma) = S_t e^{-q^T}N(d_1) - Ke^{-r\tau}N(d_2)$ is the usual Black-Scholes formula, likewise for P_{BS}.

The problem is that this market is inherently incomplete and therefore the pricing measure for contingent claims on the housing price H_t may not be unique. Furthermore, the economy may not always be in a state of equilibrium. For practical purposes, the equations describing the model need to be risk-neutralized. The equilibrium price of a zero-coupon bond is given by the equation

$$dB_t = [r_t + \gamma^2\sigma_\delta^2(1 - e^{-a_\delta(T-t)})]B_t dt + \gamma\sigma_\delta(1 - e^{-a_\delta(T-t)})b_T dZ_t^\delta$$

Then the risk-neutral version of this equation[3] is

$$dB_t = r_t b_t dt + \gamma\sigma_\delta(1 - e^{-a_\delta(T-t)})b_T dZ_t^{\delta,q}$$

---

[3] That is the equation in continuous time under a risk-neutral measure Q associated with the transformation $Z_t^{\delta,Q} = \gamma\sigma_\delta t + Z_t^\delta$.

Then the risk-neutral process for the risk-free rate is

$$dr_t = a_r\left[b_r + \left(\frac{\sigma_r}{a_r}\right)^2 - r_t\right]dt + \sigma_r dZ_t^{r,Q} \tag{7.19}$$

Cao and Wei (2010) observed that the only difference between the equilibrium process and the risk-neutral process in their model relates to the long-run mean. Moreover, they proved that the yield-to-maturity in the risk-neutral world is the same as its equilibrium version.

The risk-neutral process for the house index is considered to be

$$dH_t^Q = r_t H_t^Q + \sigma_H dZ_t^{H,Q} \tag{7.20}$$

This results from the assumption that the housing index is considered to be a traded[4] asset.

In this risk-neutral world, Cao and Wei (2010) derive the housing index derivatives prices to be

$$F_t^Q(H_t, T) = H_t e^{R(t,T)(T-t)}$$

$$c_t^Q(H_t, K, T) = C_{BS}(H_t, T-t, K; R(t,T),,\sigma_H^*)$$

$$p_t^Q(H_t, K, T) = C_{BS}(H_t, T-t, K; R(t,T),,\sigma_H^*)$$

$$\sigma_H^* = \sqrt{\sigma_H^2 + 2\rho_{rH}\sigma_H\frac{\sigma_r}{a_r}\left(1 - \frac{1-e^{-a_r(T-t)}}{a_r(T-t)}\right) + \frac{\sigma_r^2}{a_r^2}\left(1 - 2\frac{1-e^{-a_r(T-t)}}{a_r(T-t)} + \frac{1-e^{-2a_r(T-t)}}{2a_r(T-t)}\right)}$$

Example 7.1. *Here we show how to price a forward contract and an ATM European call and put options on the housing index with the Cao and Wei (2010). The calculation is done as of December 2007 for one year maturity contracts. The composite housing price index for December 2007 was reported as 200.77 and the short rate at the time was calculated as r = 0.2478%. The parameters are estimated by maximum likelihood as in Cao and Wei (2010) using the data between January 1998 and December 2007 and are described in Table 7.1.*

Following the calculations the equilibrium forward price on the housing index is $219.68 while the risk-neutral price is $202.06; the equilibrium price of the European call on the housing index is $48.70 while the risk-neutral price is $13.73.

---

[4] We have difficulties accepting this assumption since this is in contradiction with the earlier assumption that the representative market agent has one house and he cannot sell the house until T! The only way this will work is if the retirement time is earlier than the trading time of the option.

Table 7.1. This table presents the estimated parameters in Table IV from Cao and Wei (2010) for the composite housing index H_t and the interest rate r_t processes.

parameter	μ_H	σ_H	a_r	b_r	σ_r	ρ_{rH}
ML estimate	0.05587	0.02524	0.468	0.0428	0.002	0.084
s.e.	0.544	0.113	0.249	0.010	0.000	0.066

Notes: H_t and r_t are specified as $dH_t = \mu_H H_t dt + \sigma_H H_t dZ_t^H$ and $dr_t = a_r(b_r - r_t)dt + \sigma_r dZ_t^r$, where μ_H and σ_H are the expected return and volatility for the housing index, a_r, b_r, and s_r are the mean-reversion speed, long-run mean, and volatility for the interest rate. The correlation between dZ^H and dZ^r is ρ_{rH}. The monthly composite housing index is retrieved from www2.standardpoors.com, whereas the three-month T-bill rates are downloaded from the Federal Reserve Board website. All parameters are estimated using the Maximum-Likelihood Method over the period Jan 1987– Dec 2007. The numbers in parentheses are standard errors.

Table 7.2. Calculations of risk-neutral and equilibrium forward and European vanilla options prices using the formulae in Cao and Wei (2010). All options are at the money. Calculations are made as of December 2007 and $r = 0.2478\%$.

Maturity	Forward Risk-Neutral	Forward Equilibrium	Call Risk-Neutral	Call Equilibrium	Put Risk-Neutral	Put Equilibrium
1	212.1996	212.3070	10.8392	10.9388	0.0252	0.0232
2	208.5641	224.5067	7.7212	22.8514	0.2185	0.0017
3	206.5110	237.4072	6.6708	35.6188	1.0894	0.000137

Note first that the prices reported in our Table 7.3 do not coincide with the prices reported in Cao and Wei (2010). One possible explanation is that the results are very sensitive to the input r_t which is not specified in Cao and Wei (2010). The risk-neutral prices decrease with maturity here while the equilibrium prices increase with maturity. The reason for that is that the yield to maturity decreases with maturity because $r_t < b_r$ in our example. Furthermore, one can easily check that the put-call parity is verified for the risk-neutral prices while the equilibrium prices do not obey the put-call parity. Moreover, the put-call parity discrepancy increases with maturity.

The decrease of derivatives with respect to increase in maturity is unusual or at least counterintuitive. We have recalculated the real-estate derivatives prices using $r_t = 4.44\%$, which is greater than the long run mean of short rates $b_r = 0.0428$.

In this case, the risk-neutral forward and call prices increase with maturity (puts decrease with maturity). The equilibrium forward prices do not depend on the short rate r_t, while the equilibrium call and put do.

The fact that the equilibrium prices for the European call and put do not verify the put-call parity is not only a numerical peculiarity for the parameter estimates utilized in the example. The formulae (7.17) and (7.18) imply that

Table 7.3. Calculations of risk-neutral and equilibrium forward and European vanilla options prices using the formulae in Cao and Wei (2010). All options are at the money. Calculations are made as of December 2007 and $r = 4.44\%$.

Maturity	Forward Risk-Neutral	Forward Equilibrium	Call Risk-Neutral	Call Equilibrium	Put Risk-Neutral	Put Equilibrium
1	209.2127	212.3070	8.2109	11.0949	0.1088	0.0235
2	218.9753	224.5067	16.1254	21.7649	−0.5663	0.0017
3	229.0908	237.4072	22.8772	32.1081	−1.9425	0.000123

$$c_t(H_t, K, T) - p_t(H_t, K, T) = e^{-R(t,T)(T-t)}[F_t(H_t, T) - K]$$

Then, in order for the put-call parity to be verified for the equilibrium call and put prices given by the formulae in Cao and Wei (2010), the following identity must be true

$$e^{-R(t,T)(T-t)}[F_t(H_t, T) - K] = H_t - Ke^{-R(t,T)(T-t)}$$

leading to

$$F_t(H_t, T) = H_t e^{R(t,T)(T-t)} \tag{7.21}$$

Combining this formula with formula (7.16) implies that

$$R(t, T) = \mu_H(T - t) + \rho_{rH}\sigma_H \frac{\sigma_r}{a_r^2}(1 - e^{-a_r(T-t)})$$

which is in contradiction with the yield-to-maturity formula (7.15). Hence, the equilibrium prices for European call and put derived in Cao and Wei (2010) cannot verify the put-call parity.

7.3 No-Arbitrage Models

The no-arbitrage valuation principle is fundamental to financial markets. Not surprisingly, no-arbitrage models were sought for pricing real-estate derivatives. There is however, an important obstacle in achieving true arbitrage-free models. The real-estate markets are intrinsically incomplete. Thus, one should complete the market first and only then try to identify a pricing measure under which all real-estate derivatives can be priced.

7.3.1 SYZ'S MODEL

One of the simplest models proposed for forward property prices is the model described in Syz (2008). The forward at time t on a property index S_t for maturity T is given by

$$F_t(T) = S_t e^{(r+\rho_T)(T-t)} \tag{7.22}$$

where r is the constant risk-free rate for the period $(t, T]$ and ρ_T is a "property spread" whose role is to make up the difference between the stock-style no-arbitrage forward formula $S_t e^{r(T-t)}$ and the actual observed/traded forward price. Most importantly, t is the date of the most recent index update and T is the date of the last relevant index update before or at maturity. Hence, if the update is done annually, as it was in the case for the IPD index in the UK for example for many years, the model works more as an approximation rather than at any moment in time.

The model is constructed by analogy to some commodity models built on the concept of convenience yield. Syz recognizes some important features of the forward property contract:

- real-estate cannot be easily traded and sold short
- the forward property price cannot be a simple a function of the level of the underlying index and the risk-free rate
- the property spread ρ_T depends on the maturity T

Tacitly, Syz's 2008 formula is based on a Black-Scholes model for the under-lying leading to a formulation for the price process of the forward price F on the (untraded) property index S given by

$$\frac{dF_t}{F_t} = \sigma dW_t \tag{7.23}$$

which will lead according to Syz to a Black-type formula[5] for options on the forward contracts

$$C(F_t, t) = e^{-r(T-t)}[F_t \Phi(d_1) - K \Phi(d_2)] \tag{7.24}$$

$$d_1 = \frac{\ln(F_t/K) + \frac{\sigma^2}{2}(T-t)}{\sigma\sqrt{T-t}} \quad d_2 = d_1 - \sigma\sqrt{T-t} \tag{7.25}$$

---

[5] We have corrected a few typos in the formulae here.

By direct replacement of (7.22) into (7.24) the proposed formula for pricing options on property prices, using the "stochastic property spread", is

$$C(F_t, t) = e^{-\rho_T(T-t)} S_t \Phi(d_1) - e^{-r(T-t)} K \Phi(d_2)] \tag{7.26}$$

$$d_1 = \frac{\ln(S_t/K) + [r + \rho_T + \frac{\sigma^2}{2}](T-t)}{\sigma\sqrt{T-t}} \quad d_2 = d_1 - \sigma\sqrt{T-t} \tag{7.27}$$

We believe that Syz's model is an adapted version of Black-Scholes which does not properly account for the incomplete character of the market. In particular, it is not clear how a pricing martingale measure is selected.

7.3.2 BJORK-CLAPHAM'S MODEL FOR CREILS

Buttimer et al. (1997) argued that the value of a commercial real-estate index-linked swap (CREILS) is not zero. Bjork and Clapham (2002) rejected this view and proposed a no-arbitrage continuous-time modelling framework for pricing CREILS. They argued that their arbitrage-free theoretical value is always zero. In this section we review the modelling approach presented in Bjork and Clapham (2002).

A CREILS makes payments at pre-specified time points $t_0 < t_1 < \ldots < t_n$, one leg paying coupons derived from a real-estate index I_t that will generate some (possibly stochastic) income, while the other leg is associated with a market interest rate such as LIBOR. At the end of any period $[t_{k-1}, t_k]$ the CREILS payer will have a cash outflow determined by the appreciation of the index plus all income generated by the index during that period and a cash inflow determined by the LIBOR plus a spread rate δ. The swap cash payments are made on a given notional. The calculation of the swap price is typically done at time $t \leq t_0$. Buttimer et al. (1997) gave an example where $\delta = 0.00125\%$ while Bjork and Clapham (2002) argued on theoretical grounds that $\delta \equiv 0$.

The framework proposed by Bjork and Clapham (2002) is very general, covering any dynamics of the index, of the income process or the interest rate, but it is also restricted by the strong assumption that "the real-estate index process be treated as the price process of a traded asset with a certain associated dividend (income) process". Whether or not one can replicate the real-estate index through continuous trading in a frictionless market is without question no. The main reason for that is the impossibility of short selling. However, this approach may become useful once futures contracts contingent on real-estate indexes are introduced. The framework is based on the usual no-arbitrage idea for swaps. For each period $[t_{k-1}, t_k]$, at time t_{k-1} the investor will buy $I_{t_{k-1}}$ by borrowing that amount in cash at the LIBOR $L_{(k-1,k)}$. All income provided by the index over the period is deposited in the bank account. At the end of the period, the index is sold for I_{t_k}. The loan is repaid for $(t_k - t_{k-1}) \times L_{(k-1,k)} \times I_{t_{k-1}}$. This strategy will give $I_{t_k} - I_{t_{k-1}} +$ $Income - (t_k - t_{k-1}) \times L_{(k-1,k)} \times I_{t_{k-1}}$, which is the cash flow for the receiver of CREILS. The no-arbitrage idea is that since the initial set-up cost is zero, the value of the strategy should also be zero. This is equivalent to saying that $\delta = 0$.

The Bjork-Clapham model is based on the assumption that there is a financial market given by $(\Omega, \mathcal{F}, \mathbf{F}, P)$ where the filtration $\mathbf{F} = \{\mathcal{F}_t\}_{t \geq 0}$ captures the evolution of information that economic agents have over time. Specific assumptions of the model include that the real-estate index process I_t is ex dividend, the income process is described by a cum-dividend process $\{D_t\}_{t \geq 0}$, the interest rate is represented by a short rate process $\{r_t\}_{t \geq 0}$ defining the money market account process B_t via $dB_t = r_t B_t dt$ and also by a liquid bond market for all maturities, with the price at time t of a ZCB maturing at T being equal to $p(t, T)$. The tenor of the swap is given by $\Delta = t_k - t_{k-1}$.

Asset pricing theory, see Bjork (2009), requires contingent claim pricing to be done under an equivalent martingale measure Q that is equivalent to the historical measure P. Taking the position of the receiver in a CREILS the no-arbitrage value at time t of the CREILS, denoted by $S(t, CREILS)$, is given by

$$S(t, CREILS) = \sum_{k=1}^{n} S(t, X_k)$$

where X_k marks the net payments at payment times t_k, and where

$$S(t, X_k) = E^Q \left[e^{-\int_t^T r_s ds} X_k | \mathcal{F}_t \right]$$

From the mechanics of the CREILS

$$X_k = I_{t_k} - I_{t_{k-1}} + \int_{t_{k-1}}^{t_k} e^{\int_s^{t_k} r_s du} dD_s - \Delta L_{(k-1,k)} I_{t_{k-1}} \qquad (7.28)$$

In formula (7.28) the first difference accounts for the appreciation/depreciation of the index, the second integral term covers cash generated by dividends paid over the period $[t_{k-1}, t_k]$, including their accrual to time t_k in the money account, and the last term is the payment made to the counterparty in the contract. Since by no-arbitrage $L_{(k-1,k)} I_{t_{k-1}} = \frac{1}{\Delta} \left[\frac{1}{p(t_{k-1}, t_k)} - 1 \right]$, replacing this in (7.28) gives

$$X_k = I_{t_k} - I_{t_{k-1}} + \int_{t_{k-1}}^{t_k} e^{\int_s^{t_k} r_s du} dD_s - \left[\frac{1}{p(t_{k-1}, t_k)} - 1 \right] I_{t_{k-1}}$$

$$= I_{t_k} - \frac{I_{t_{k-1}}}{p(t_{k-1}, t_k)} + \int_{t_{k-1}}^{t_k} e^{\int_s^{t_k} r_s du} dD_s$$

Therefore

$$S(t, X_k) = E^Q \left[e^{-\int_t^{tk} r_s ds} I_{t_k} | \mathcal{F}_t \right] - E^Q \left[e^{-\int_t^{tk} r_s ds} \frac{I_{t_{k-1}}}{p(t_{k-1}, t_k)} | \mathcal{F}_t \right]$$

$$+ E^Q \left[e^{-\int_t^{tk} r_s ds} \int_{t_{k-1}}^{tk} e^{\int_s^{tk} r_u du} dD_s | \mathcal{F}_t \right]$$

The variables $I_{t_{k-1}}, p(t_{k-1}, t_k), e^{-\int_t^{t_{k-1}}}$ are all known at time t_{k-1}, so by iterated conditional expectations

$$E^Q \left[e^{-\int_t^{tk} r_s ds} \frac{I_{t_{k-1}}}{p(t_{k-1}, t_k)} | \mathcal{F}_t \right]$$

$$= E^Q \left[E^Q \left[e^{-\int_t^{tk} r_s ds} \frac{I_{t_{k-1}}}{p(t_{k-1}, t_k)} | \mathcal{F}_{t_{k-1}} | \mathcal{F}_t \right] \right]$$

A little calculus shows that

$$E^Q \left[e^{-\int_t^{tk} r_s ds} \frac{I_{t_{k-1}}}{p(t_{k-1}, t_k)} | \mathcal{F}_{t_{k-1}} \right] = e^{-\int_t^{t_{k-1}} r_s ds} I_{t_{k-1}}$$

and

$$E^Q \left[e^{-\int_t^{tk} r_s ds} \int_{t_{k-1}}^{tk} e^{\int_s^{tk} r_u du} dD_s | \mathcal{F}_t \right] = E^Q \left[\int_{t_{k-1}}^{tk} e^{-\int_t^s r_u du} dD_s | \mathcal{F}_t \right]$$

Thus, Bjork and Clapham (2002) collect the results to obtain

$$S(t, X_k) = E^Q \left[e^{-\int_t^{tk} r_s ds} I_{t_k} | \mathcal{F}_t \right] - E^Q \left[e^{-\int_t^{t_{k-1}} r_s ds} I_{t_{k-1}} | \mathcal{F}_t \right]$$

$$+ E^Q \left[\int_{t_{k-1}}^{tk} e^{-\int_t^s r_u du} dD_s | \mathcal{F}_t \right]$$

$$= B_t E^Q \left[\frac{I_{t_k}}{B_{t_k}} - \frac{I_{t_{k-1}}}{B_{t_{k-1}}} + \int_{t_{k-1}}^{tk} \frac{1}{B_s} dD_s | \mathcal{F}_t \right]$$

$$= B_t E^Q \left[G_{t_k}^B - G_{t_{k-1}}^B | \mathcal{F}_t \right]$$

$$= 0$$

The last equality follows from Bjork (2009) with $G_t^B = \frac{I_t}{B_t} + \int_0^t \frac{1}{B_s} dD_s$ the normalized gains process, which is a martingale under the equivalent martingale measure Q.

This proves that the Bjork-Clapham framework always has the no-arbitrage value of a CREILS equal to zero at any time $t \leq t_0$. The same argument, under the same assumptions, should work in a discrete-time set-up, which is more realistic in financial markets. The non-zero spread reported in Buttimer et al. (1997) is explained in Bjork and Clapham (2002) by the fact that simple interest and dividend rates are approximated by continuous rates. This highlights an important issue related to model risk. When using a discrete-time model the prices produced under Bjork-Clapham methodology are arbitrage free but they are not necessarily arbitrage free with respect to the continuous time model.

7.4 Econometric and Mathematical Based Models

Real-estate prices exhibit empirical features that makes this asset class quite different from other financial asset classes such as equity, foreign exchange or bonds. Serial correlation is one of the most important features of real-estate indices as discussed in Chapter 2. Thus, it is not surprising that recent modelling efforts of real-estate dynamics are moving towards econometric specifications rather than financial engineering specifications. Hence, next we will revise some of the models that provide some of the best intuition for real-estate indices evolution.

7.4.1 SHILLER-WEISS LOGNORMAL MODEL

One of the very first models on pricing real-estate derivatives was proposed by Shiller and Weiss (1999) in their paper on home equity insurance. Their model for the observed real-estate log returns $\Delta \ln(H_t)$ is a standard AR(1) process

$$\Delta \ln(H_t) = c + \rho \Delta \ln(H_{t-1}) + \varepsilon_t \qquad (7.29)$$

This model is clearly in the opposite direction of a random walk, implying that price changes tend to continue through time leading to price inertia. The unconditional mean of the annual log price change is $\frac{c}{1-\rho}$. The model can be rewritten equivalently in moving-average form

$$\Delta \ln(H_t) - \frac{c}{1 - \rho} = \varepsilon_t + \rho \varepsilon_{t-1} + \rho^2 \varepsilon_{t-2} + \dots \qquad (7.30)$$

Using this model, the conditional returns and volatilities can be determined analytically.

Because the errors in (7.30) are serially uncorrelated the variance of $\Delta \ln(P_t)$ is the sum of variances of the terms on the right side. Simple algebra gives

$$E_t[\ln(H_{t+n})] - E_{t-1}[\ln(H_{t+n})] = \frac{1 - \rho^n}{1 - \rho}\varepsilon_t$$

Hence, the innovation proportionality to ε_t is larger the higher the n. Therefore, the Shiller-Weiss model indicates an advantage of hedging real-estate risk with long-term contracts.

To price real-estate futures and options Shiller and Weiss (1999) use the model (7.29) and realize that the terminal distribution of the log prices is Gaussian. This assumption was considered sufficient and relates to options pricing literature before the Black-Scholes model was published in 1973. Denoting by H the value of the real-estate index, by μ the expected change in the log real-estate price index between today and T periods from today and by σ^2 the variance of the change in the log real-estate price index between today and T periods from today, standard econometric calculations lead to

$$var(\Delta \ln(H_t)) = \frac{\rho^2}{(1 - \rho^2)}$$

Note that since the model (7.29) assumes autocorrelation of consecutive returns the variance of logarithmic returns at different horizons will have to be calculated individually.

For practical implementation it is important to calculate the mean and variance at time t of the future value H_T of the real-estate index. Taking advantage of the lognormally model the following propositions are useful here.

Proposition 7.1.

$$E_t(\ln H_T - \ln H_t) = (T - t)c + (T - t - 1)\rho c + \rho\frac{1 - \rho^{T-t}}{1 - \rho}\Delta \ln H_t \quad (7.31)$$

where $\Delta \ln H_t = \ln H_t - \ln H_{t-1}$.

Proposition 7.2.

$$var_t(\ln H_T - \ln H_t) = \frac{\sigma_\varepsilon^2}{1 - \rho^2}\left[(T - t) - \rho^2\frac{1 - \rho^{2(T-t)}}{1 - \rho^2} + 2\sum_{1 \le i < j \le T-t}(\rho^{j-i} - \rho^{j+i})\right] \quad (7.32)$$

Shiller and Weiss (1999) price only European derivatives on residential real-estate. Thus, we can assume without loss of generality that all quantities in the model refer to a given maturity T. In essence this means that the total return $R = \frac{H_T}{H_t}$ is lognormally distributed with mean μ and variance σ^2. The following known results are useful for option pricing.

Proposition 7.3. *If U and V are two random variables and $U = aV$, with a being a real number different from zero then[6] $f_U(u) = \frac{1}{a} f_V(u/a)$.*

Proposition 7.4. *If $\ln(R) \sim N(\mu, \sigma^2)$ then the cumulative distribution function of random variable R is $F_R(x) = N\left(\frac{\ln(x) - \mu}{\sigma}\right)$. Moreover,*

$$\int_K^\infty u f_R(u)du = e^{\mu + \frac{\sigma^2}{2}} N\left[\frac{\mu - \ln(K)}{\sigma} + \sigma\right]$$

and

$$\int_0^K f_R(u)du = N\left(\frac{\ln(K) - \mu}{\sigma}\right)$$

In addition, if H_t is a constant, $H_T = H_t R$ is lognormally distributed with parameters $\mu + \ln H_t$ and variance σ^2.

For pricing a put option the calculations go as follows, where T is the time to maturity from today t and $H_T = R H_t$,

$$Put(H_t, K, T, \mu, \sigma, r) = e^{-r(T-t)} E[\max(K - H_T, 0)] = e^{-rT} \int_0^K (K - H_T)f(H_T)dH_T$$

$$= e^{-r(T-t)} \left\{\int_0^K f(H_T)dH_T - \int_0^K H_T f(H_T)dH_T\right\}$$

$$= e^{-r(T-t)} \left\{KN\left[\frac{\ln(K) - \mu - \ln(H_t)}{\sigma}\right] - e^{\mu + \ln(H_t) + \sigma^2/2} N\left[\frac{\ln(K/H_t) - \mu}{\sigma} - \sigma\right]\right\}$$

$$= e^{-r(T-t)} \left\{KN\left[\frac{\ln(K/H_t) - \mu}{\sigma}\right] - H_t e^{\mu + \sigma^2/2} N\left[\frac{\ln(K/H_t) - \mu}{\sigma} - \sigma\right]\right\}$$

The Shiller-Weiss formula for a European put option on the real-estate index with strike price X and maturity T is

$$Put(H_t, K, T, \mu, \sigma, r) = Ke^{-r(T-t)} N\left[\frac{\ln(K/H_t) - \mu}{\sigma}\right]$$

$$- H_t e^{\mu + \frac{\sigma^2}{2} - r(T-t)} N\left[\frac{\ln(K/H_t) - \mu}{\sigma} - \sigma\right] \qquad (7.33)$$

Thus, what Shiller and Weiss do is replace the risk-free rate of return r with the expected real-world return μ and the implied volatility with the estimated value from the AR(1) model. Their model falls onto the Black-Scholes model only when $\mu = rT - \sigma_{BS}^2 T/2$ and $\sigma^2 = \sigma_{BS}^2 T$. It also falls onto the McDonald

---

[6] f denotes generically here the probability density function of the corresponding variable.

and Siegel (1984) pricing formula for options whose underlying asset earns a below-equilibrium rate of return if their equilibrium rate of return equals the risk-free rate.

One can easily derive under the Shiller-Weiss model the price for a European call option with strike price K and maturity T. This is

$$Call(H_t, K, T, \mu, \sigma, r) = H_t e^{\mu + \frac{\sigma^2}{2} - rT} N \left[\frac{\ln(H_t/K) + \mu}{\sigma} + \sigma \right]$$

$$- Ke^{-rT} N \left[\frac{\ln(H_t/K) + \mu}{\sigma} \right] \qquad (7.34)$$

In addition, the formula for the real-estate forwards is the same as the call with strike $K = 0$, so

$$Fwd(H_t, T, \mu, \sigma, r) = H_t e^{\mu + \frac{\sigma^2}{2}} \qquad (7.35)$$

In addition, the Shiller-Weiss formulae for forwards, call and puts verify the put-call parity.

This model has the advantage that it starts from a realistic econometrical behaviour of a real-estate index, capturing the serial correlations that are well documented in real-estate literature. One criticism that has been brought to light by some authors is that the pricing of real-estate derivatives is not done under a risk-neutral measure. In order for someone to apply this model they need to estimate the investor-required rate of return driven by the parameter μ. This shortcoming was solved later on with a more advanced derivatives pricing framework.

Example 7.2. *Assume that an investor is looking to trade forwards and Euro-pean put and call options with various maturities on the IPD UK Monthly Index using the Shiller-Weiss model.*

The trading date is 2 March 2015 and there are five annual maturities starting with March 2015 up to March 2019. The forward contracts are standard over-the-counter forwards contracts with linear payoff.[7] The risk-free rate is 0.5% and the estimation of the model parameters from the historical time-series of the IPD UK monthly index gives $c = 0.00070688$, $\rho = 0.9028$; $\Delta \ln H_t = 0.0129$; $\sigma_\varepsilon^2 = 0.000022053$. Applying the formulae (7.31) and (7.32) allows the investor to calculate the forward prices using formula (7.35) and the European call and put options prices with formulae (7.34) and (7.33), respectively. The results for $K = H_t$, that is at-the-money options, are described in Table 7.4.

Example 7.3. *Consider now the example of a house owner in UK who would like to hedge the value of her house against a possible market crash. Her house is*

---

[7] This should not be confused with the EUREX futures prices.

Table 7.4. Calculation of forwards, European call and put options prices on IPD UK Monthly index using Shiller-Weiss model.

Maturity	μ	σ^2	Forward	Call	Put
March 2015	0.0123	2.2053e-05	1179.61	14.43	0.0072
March 2016	0.1049	0.0080	1299.25	131.29	5.5991
March 2017	0.1435	0.0286	1364.27	193.48	17.7239
March 2018	0.1662	0.0543	1413.65	234.77	28.2100
March 2019	0.1843	0.0816	1459.22	265.77	35.5700

valued at 210,000 GBP in February 2016 and she is looking to use either the Halifax House Price Index or the Nationwide House Price Index for buying put options up to five years ahead. First, the historical time series monthly and seasonally adjusted for the two main real-estate residential UK indices are used to calibrate the Shiller-Weiss model parameters. Then, put option prices are calculated and hedge ratios applied to see how much it would cost the house owner to get the protection via the real-estate put options on those two indices. A heuristic analysis reveals that for the Halifax Index the hedging ratio for a property with value X is given by 1000/3 given that $X_t \approx H_t \times \frac{1000}{3}$ so she would need to buy roughly 333 put options written on the Halifax index in order to be hedged in full for her house of 210,000 GBP. Likewise, for Nationwide the hedging ratio is roughly 1000/2 so 500 options need to be bought. The risk-free rate is considered to be 0.5%, which is equal to the Bank of England Base rate for February 2016.

The results in Table 7.5 show some interesting findings. The price of puts first increases with maturity and then decreases. This is a feature of the autoregressive model specification. Secondly, the hedging costs for the house owner are annual so the monthly hedging costs are quite manageable. Furthermore, the crash costs, calculated from the put options with a strike price equal to 70% of the current value of the real-estate index are effectively zero, for both indices. Thus, the Shiller-Weiss model implies that a property crash in the UK is unlikely in the next five years. The hedging costs seem smaller for the Nationwide index. There are significant differences between the two major UK residential indices as explained in Chapter 2 and therefore there is a degree of model risk involved. In addition, these calculations are also dependable on the goodness-of-fit of the AR(1) model to the Halifax and Nationwide log-return indices.

7.4.2 BFSP MODEL

The model developed by van Bragt et al. (2009) and van Bragt et al. (2015), (BFSP thereafter), is set-up in discrete-time within a risk-neutral valuation framework. The model starts by specifying the dynamics of the underlying

Table 7.5. House price hedging in UK in February 2016 for a property valued at 210,000 GBP.

	Halifax				Nationwide	
c	0.002936			0.002763		
ρ	0.207390			0.367081		
σ	0.011942			0.009613		
			Hedging costs for puts			
Maturity	Put	Hedging cost	Crash Cost	Put	Hedging cost	Crash Cost
March 2016	3.2035	1067.85	1.82e-194	0.81	404.95	0.0000
March 2017	4.0928	1364.26	4.00e-11	1.72	860.13	4.20e-12
March 2018	2.7987	932.89	2.83e-06	1.18	591.82	8.36e-07
March 2019	1.8446	614.86	1.14e-04	0.76	381.23	4.18e-05
March 2020	1.2059	401.97	6.39e-04	0.48	241.65	0.00025

Notes: Full hedging costs is based on ATM put options and hedging the value of the house in full. Crash cost means that only losses larger than 30% of the value of the house are relevant so the put options is OTM by 30% moneyness.

efficient market price of real-estate $\{Y_t\}_{t=1,2,...}$ and then the observed index value $\{X_t\}_{t=1,2,...}$ is derived following a price update rule suggested by Blundell and Ward. (1987)

$$H_t = kY_t + (1-k)H_{t-1} \tag{7.36}$$

where $k \in [0,1]$ is a parameter indicating how much emphasis to put on the most recent market information versus the past price information. The dynamics implied by the price update rule described in (7.36) is useful to model appraisal smoothing in some real-estate indices as well as accounting for serial autocorrelation in transaction based indices.

Applying iterative substitution the model (7.36) can be equivalently rewritten as

$$H_t = k\sum_{i=1}^{m}(1-k)^{i-1}Y_{t-i+1} + (1-k)^m H_{t-m} \tag{7.37}$$

where $1 \le m \le 1$. This is an exponentially weighted moving average (EWMA). If $m = t$ the weight of X_0 is $(1-k)^t$.

One disadvantage of the BSFP model is that the previous value H_{t-1} is not accrued and that automatically implies a systematic undervaluation of the real-estate index.

van Bragt et al. (2009) change the update rule into

$$H_t = kY_t + (1-k)(1+\eta)H_{t-1} \tag{7.38}$$

by adjusting for the accrual in the past real-estate index with the expected annualized return rate η. The revised EWMA formulation of this adjusted model becomes

$$H_t = k \sum_{i=1}^{m}(1-k)^{i-1}Y^*_{t-i+1} + (1-k)^m H^*_{t-m} \tag{7.39}$$

where $1 \le m \le t$ and

$$H^*_{t-m} = H_{t-m}(1+\eta)^m$$

$$Y^*_{t-i+1} = Y_{t-i+1}(1+\eta)^{i-1}$$

Denoting by $r^H_t = \frac{H_t - H_{t-1}}{H_{t-1}}$ the index percentage return and by $r^Y_t = \frac{Y_t - Y_{t-1}}{Y_{t-1}}$ the unobserved return, with annual compounding, one can re-arrange the calculations and derive the dynamics of the annual percentage returns as

$$r^H_t = k\frac{Y_{t-1}}{H_{t-1}}r^Y_t + (1-k)\frac{H_{t-2}}{H_{t-1}}(1+\eta)r^H_{t-1} \tag{7.40}$$

Similar calculations can be applied with logarithmic returns rather than percentage returns. Thus, denoting with R the logarithmic returns van Bragt et al. (2009) provide the equations for continuous compounding returns

$$R^H_t = k^* R^Y_t + (1-k^*)R^H_{t-1} \tag{7.41}$$

or

$$R^Y_t = \frac{1}{k^*}R^H_t - \frac{1-k^*}{k^*}R^H_{t-1} \tag{7.42}$$

Then van Bragt et al. (2009) assume that the underlying market returns follow a random walk process with drift

$$R^Y_t = \eta + \varepsilon_t \tag{7.43}$$

where ε is a normally-distributed, serially-uncorrelated noise term with zero mean and variance σ_e^2.

Combining (7.41) with (7.43) gives

$$R^H_t = k^*\eta + (1-k^*)R^H_{t-1} + k^*\varepsilon_t \tag{7.44}$$

which is an AR(1) process that permits the estimation of the parameter k^*, that can be interpreted as 1 minus the first-order autocorrelation of the index returns. Note that (7.44) is similar to (7.29).

Observing that $Y_{t-1} \approx H_{t-1}$ and $\frac{H_{t-2}}{H_{t-1}} \approx \frac{1}{1+\eta}$ van Bragt et al. (2009) conclude that in practice one can assume that $k = k^*$.

Risk-neutralizing the process

In order to risk-neutralize the process describing the dynamics of the real-estate index, van Bragt et al. (2009) first select the one-factor Hull-White model for the short rate process[8] $\rho_t \geq 0$

$$d\rho_t = \kappa \left(\frac{\theta(t)}{\kappa} - \rho_t \right) dt + \sigma_1 dZ_t \tag{7.45}$$

This model is specified as a continuous-time model and it is a generalization of the Vasicek model with a long-run mean level that is time-dependent and deterministic. Other model specifications are possible, see van Bragt et al. (2009). The bank account $\{B_t\}_{t \geq 0}$ is defined by $B_t = B(0) \exp \int_0^t \rho_u du$.

The second step in risk-neutralizing the process describing the evolution of the real-estate index is to assume that

$$\eta_t \equiv \exp \left(\int_{t-1}^t \rho_u du \right) \exp(-q) \tag{7.46}$$

The term $\exp(-q)$ is a correction factor for the type of return q associated with real-estate investment, such that when $q = 0$ one works with total returns. Then van Bragt et al. (2009) change (7.38) into

$$H_t = kY_t + (1-k)\eta_t H_{t-1} \tag{7.47}$$

By iterative substitutions one can get

$$H_t = k \sum_{i=1}^m (1-k)^{i-1} Y^*_{t-i+1} + (1-k)^m H^*_{t-m} \tag{7.48}$$

---

[8] We have slightly changed the notation here for the short rate so that there is no confusion with the returns rate defined earlier in this section.

$$H^*_{t-m} \equiv H_{t-m} \exp\left(\int_{t-m}^{t} \rho_u du\right) \exp(-qm) \tag{7.49}$$

$$Y^*_{t-i+1} \equiv H_{t-i+1} \exp\left(\int_{t-i+1}^{t} \rho_u du\right) \exp(-q(i-1)) \tag{7.50}$$

The underlying efficient market price is specified by van Bragt et al. (2009) as a geometric continuous time mean-reverting process

$$dY_t = (\rho_t - q)\, Y_t dt + \sigma_2 Y_t dW_t \tag{7.51}$$

with σ_2 a constant and W a Wiener process. Applying Ito's lemma we can see that it is easier to work on the log space

$$d\ln(Y_t) = \left(\rho_t - q - \frac{\sigma_2^2}{2}\right) dt + \sigma_2 dW_t \tag{7.52}$$

If the underlying real-estate index of the property derivative is a total return index $q = 0$ then, under the pricing measure Q the martingale condition:

$$E_t^Q \left[\frac{Y_T}{B_T}\right] = \frac{Y_t}{B_t}$$

If $q > 0$, that is we are not working with a total return index,

$$E_t^Q \left[\frac{Y_T}{B_T}\right] = E_t^Q \left[\frac{Y_t \exp\left(\int_t^T \rho_u du - \sigma_2^2(T-t)/2 - q(T-t) + \sigma_2 W_{T-t}\right)}{B_t \exp \int_t^T \rho_u du}\right]$$

$$= \frac{Y_t}{B_t} \exp\left(-\sigma_2^2(T-t)/2 - q(T-t)\right) E_t^Q[\exp(\sigma_2 W_{T-t})]$$

$$= \frac{Y_t}{B_t} \exp\left(-q(T-t)\right)$$

Thus, the martingale condition for discounted asset prices is not satisfied when $q \neq 0$ so a price index cannot be a tradable asset if direct returns are paid out. Moreover, van Bragt et al. (2009) prove that

$$E_t^Q \left[\frac{H_T}{B_T}\right] = \frac{\exp(-q(T-t))}{B_t}[Y_t(1 - \alpha_{k,T}) + H_t \alpha_{k,T}] \tag{7.53}$$

where $\alpha_{k,T} \equiv (1-k)^{T-t}$. Therefore, the martingale condition is satisfied if $H_t = Y_t$ and $q = 0$. This means that the model given by (7.47) does not represent the risk-neutral process of a tradable asset when $k < 1$, and therefore this model allows for arbitrage opportunities in the case of a complete market with derivatives contingent on an autocorrelated real-estate index.

Pricing real estate derivatives with the BFSP model

The BSFP model is flexible enough to allow closed-form pricing formulae for forwards, swaps and European vanilla call and put options. The value of a short forward on a real-estate index that will pay at maturity T a specified forward price $F_t(T)$ is equal to f_t at time t and it is equal to $f_T = F_t(T) - H_T$. Under the risk-neutral world determined by pricing measure Q, $\{f_t/B_t\}_{t \geq 0}$ should be a martingale and therefore

$$\frac{f_t}{B_t} = E_t^Q \left[\frac{F_t(T) - H_T}{B_T} \right] \tag{7.54}$$

Using (7.53) it follows that

$$f_t = D(t, T)F_t(T) - \exp(-q(T-t))[Y_t(1 - \alpha_{k,T}(t)) + H_t\alpha_{k,T}(t)] \tag{7.55}$$

where $\alpha_{k,T}(t) = (1-k)^{T-t}$ and $D(t, T)$ is the discount factor at time t for maturity T. By requiring that $f_t = 0$ and solving for $F_t(T)$ the forward price closed-formula derived by van Bragt et al. (2009) is

$$F_t(T) = \frac{\exp(-q(T-t))}{D(t, T)}[Y_t(1 - \alpha_{k,T}(t)) + H_t\alpha_{k,T}(t)] \tag{7.56}$$

If $H_t = Y_t$, that is the observed market real-estate index is equal to the true real-estate index then

$$F_t(T) = \frac{\exp(-q(T-t))}{D(t, T)}H_t \tag{7.57}$$

Having a closed-form solution for forwards is beneficial because one can delta hedge movements of the underlying efficient market price Y_t. The delta can be also calculated analytically by a simple derivation of (7.56) with respect to Y_t

$$\frac{\partial F_t(T)}{\partial Y_t} = \frac{\exp(-q(T-t))}{D(t, T)}[1 - \alpha_{k,T}(t) + k\alpha_{k,T}(t)] \tag{7.58}$$

It is well known that one cannot trade continuously in the underlying efficient market index due to limited liquidity and high transaction costs, but the forwards effectively complete the market and allow the traded to replicate via delta hedging the payoffs of other more complicated real-estate derivatives.

Pricing a swap on a real-estate index starting at time T_0 and ending at time $T_n > T_0$ can be done initially following the no-arbitrage framework described in Bjork and Clapham (2002). To be explicit consider a receiver swap that will annually pay a floating rate such as LIBOR spot and receive the price return of the real-estate index.[9] The price of a single swaplet associated with the period $[T_{k-1}, T_k]$ is

$$S(t, H_k) = LB_t E_t^Q \left[\frac{H_{T_k}}{B_{T_k}} - \frac{H_{T_{k-1}}}{B_{T_{k-1}}} \right] \tag{7.59}$$

where L is a scaling parameter used to determine the right level of the notional following appreciation or depreciation of the real-estate index. The total value of the swap is then determined by collecting all the terms of the swaplets

$$S(t) = \sum_{k=1}^n S(t, H_k) = LB_t E_t^Q \left[\frac{H_{T_n}}{B_{T_n}} - \frac{H_{T_0}}{B_{T_0}} \right] \tag{7.60}$$

Applying the martingale condition given by (7.53) again we find

$$S(t) = L \exp(-q(T_n - t))[Y_t(1 - \alpha_{k,T_n}(t) + H_t \alpha_{k,T_n}(t))] \tag{7.61}$$
$$- L \exp(-q(T_0 - t))[Y_t(1 - \alpha_{k,T_0}(t) + H_t \alpha_{k,T_0}(t))]$$

The value of the swap at time t is zero when $H_t = Y_t$ and $q = 0$ or when $k = 1$ and $q = 0$. As with the forward, the delta can be calculated analytically

$$\frac{\partial S(t)}{\partial Y_t} = L \exp(-q(T_n - t))[(1 - \alpha_{k,T_n}(t) + H_t \alpha_{k,T_n}(t))] \tag{7.62}$$
$$- L \exp(-q(T_0 - t))[Y_t(1 - \alpha_{k,T_0}(t) + H_t \alpha_{k,T_0}(t))]$$

Thus, a liquid swap market for real-estate can also be used to replicate the cash-flows of other property derivatives. This is not surprising since swaps are portfolios of forwards.

Pricing forwards and swaps is helped by the linearity of the payoffs of these products. It is not possible to do the same for nonlinear payoffs such as European call and put options. Consider that the options have maturity T and

---

[9] When the returns are total returns the pricing formulae remains valid with $q = 0$.

exercise price K. Formula (7.48) shows that for $k < 1$ the underlying index in the real-estate option is a weighted average of lognormal distributed variables, which we know from the literature on Asian options that is not a lognormal variable. Only when $k = 1$ the formula (7.48) collapses onto $H_t = Y_t = Y_t^*$ which is lognormal distributed and therefore both European call and put options can be priced with a Black-Scholes type formula, with an adjusted implied volatility to account for the effect of stochastic interest rates.

Thus, calculating the price of European call and put on the real-estate index under the BFSP model can be done by pricing the corresponding Asian options on the basket of quantities described by (7.48). Denoting by M_1 the moment of order 1 and by M_2 the moment of order 2, based on (7.48), one can derive

$$M_1 = M_{1,0} + \sum_{i=1}^{T-t} M_{1,i} \tag{7.63}$$

$$M_{1,0} = H_t(1-k)^{T-t} \exp[(\rho_t(T) - q)(T - t)] \tag{7.64}$$

$$M_{1,i} = Y_t k (1-k)^{i-1} \exp[(\rho_t(T) - q)(T - t)] \tag{7.65}$$

$$M_2 = \sum_{i=0}^{T-t} M_{1,i}^2 \exp(\tilde{\sigma}_2{}^2 i) + \sum_{i<j} M_{1,i} M_{1,j} \exp(\tilde{\sigma}_2{}^2 i) \tag{7.66}$$

where $\rho_t(T)$ is the risk-free yield at time t until maturity T.

Knowing these moments one can follow the method developed by Levy (1992) and approximate the forward price of the Asian basket and the associated implied volatility by

$$F_t(T) = M_1, \quad \sigma = \sqrt{\frac{1}{T-t} \ln\left(\frac{M_2}{M_1}\right)} \tag{7.67}$$

Then the approximate European call and put prices for exercise price K and maturity T are given by the Black-type formulae

$$call(t) = \exp[\rho_t(T)(T-t)][F_t(T)N(d_1) - KN(d_2)] \tag{7.68}$$

$$put(t) = \exp[\rho_t(T)(T-t)][KN(-d_2) - F_t(T)N(-d_1)] \tag{7.69}$$

$$d_1 = \frac{\ln(F_t(T)/K) + (\rho_t(T) + \sigma^2/2)(T-t)}{\sigma\sqrt{T-t}}$$

$$d_2 = d_1 - \sigma\sqrt{T-t} \tag{7.70}$$

Other formulae covering multiple lag terms and seasonality are also provided by van Bragt et al. (2009).

Table 7.6. Calibration of the BSFP model to IPD UK Monthly index historical time-series December 1987 to February 2015.

	AR(1)	AR(2)	AR(3)	AR(4)
intercept	0.00070	0.00068	0.00064	0.00077
t-stat	2.70	2.60	2.31	2.61
β_1	0.9028	0.869	0.867	0.88
t-stat	88.33	20.98	21.30	22.24
β_2	NA	0.036	−0.0206	−0.025
t-stat	NA	0.76	−0.35	−0.44
β_3	NA	NA	0.066	0.2529
t-stat		NA	1.385	4.061
β_4	NA	NA	NA	−0.2153
t-stat	NA	NA	NA	−4.07
variance	NA	2.20e-05	2.19e-05	2.09e-05
t-test	NA	25.92	26.17	27.27
AIC	−2658.74	−2657.19	−2656.65	−2670.54
BIC	−2647.27	−2641.90	−2637.53	−2647.60
Jarque-Bera	542.21	560.50	556.93	878.74
p-value	1e-03	1e-03	1e-03	1e-03
Durbin-Watson	2.0651	2.0044	1.9718	1.9840
p-value	0.5863	0.9212	0.6227	0.6389

Numerical example

We consider pricing real-estate derivatives on the IPD index as of 2 March 2015. First we need to calibrate the model using the historical data on the IPD index time-series. Here we are going to use the monthly time series between December 1986 and February 2015. We are going to fit four models with lags up to order four, respectively. The fitting of the AR type models will allow the calibration of the parameters of the model. The results are presented in Table 7.6. The first model with only one lag seems to be as good as the models with more lags and given its simplicity it is preferred here. From this model we infer that $k = 0.0972$, which is a low value of confidence in the observed real-estate values.

The value of the IPD index was $H_t = 1165.113$. First let's use the simplest version of the BSFP model based for the IPD UK index and price the futures prices for the maturities[10] March 2015, March 2016, March 2017, March 2018, and March 2019. We also consider that the risk-free yield is given by a flat curve at 0.5%, the Bank of England base rate in March 2015 while the UK 3-month LIBOR was 0.56963%. It is also assumed that $Y_t \equiv H_t$ so that the observed market index reflects the true value of the real-estate. The results illustrated in

[10] The actual maturities are on a March roll when referring to the publishing of the IPD index and for settling IPD derivatives but the actual calculations for the IPD index are on a December to December roll.

Table 7.7. Pricing IPD futures and options with the BSFP model.

Maturity	EUREX IPD Futures	BSFP futures	Y_t
Mar 2015	117.90	100.50	3304.85
Mar 2016	108.25	106.72	1286.56
Mar 2017	105.25	113.31	1217.65
Mar 2018	104.50	120.32	1199.70
Mar 2019	104.50	127.76	1193.12

the third column of Table 7.7 indicate that the model BSFP, in its simplest form, underestimated the IPD forward curve short term and overestimated the IPD forward curve longer term.

Next, we consider taking advantage of the most advanced side of the BSFP model and reverse engineer the latent hidden level of Y_t that is the true *unobserved* value of the real-estate index such that the BSFP IPD futures price exactly matches the EUREX IPD futures price. The values of Y_t are given in the fourth column of Table 7.7 and it shows that the market believes that the true value of IPD index for March 2015 was a lot higher than the current observed value, but it also implies that this market is likely to catch up with time. The really high value implied for Y_t under the same model for the nearest maturity when compared with its value for more distant maturities should be interpreted with care. It says that the commercial real-estate market in the UK was undervalued in March 2015. The nearest maturity is really one month since the valuation is done at the beginning of March 2015 for a March 2015 expiry. One should expect no property crash coming in March 2015 but the possibility exists for longer maturities, dampening the market expectation of the value of the real-estate index. Hence, the reverse-engineered value of the true value of the real-estate market also incorporates the possibility of an intermediary market crash or market correction.

7.4.3 FABOZZI-SHILLER-TUNARU MODEL

In Fabozzi et al. (2009) and Fabozzi et al. (2012), an advanced framework was developed for pricing real-estate derivatives combining the econometric approach with the no-arbitrage approach. The idea is to use continuous-time mean-reverting models for the real-estate indices that allow us to harness all the properties known for these type of stochastic processes, serial correlation in particular, and also to subordinate the pricing of derivatives to the risk-neutral valuation that is the main pillar of derivatives pricing.

The main ingredients are the real-estate price index $\{I_t\}_{t \geq 0}$, the associated log-price process given for $Y_t = \log I_t$, a long-run trend (LRT) term $\{\Psi_t\}_{t \geq 0}$ such that Ψ_t is deterministic given the information $\mathcal{F}_t$ at time t and smooth enough for $\frac{d\Psi_t}{dt}$ to exist, and an interest rate process $\{r_t\}_{t \geq 0}$ that is generating a risk-neutral money market account described by $B_0 = 1$ and $dB_t = r_t B_t dt$. In addition we permit, if need be, an income/dividends cash-flow process $\{D_t\}_{t \geq 0}$ such that D_t is generated by holding I_t over the infinitesimal interval $[t, t + dt]$.

The Fabozzi-Shiller-Tunaru (FST) model first assumes that

$$dY_t = \left[\frac{d\Psi_t}{dt} - \theta(Y_t - \Psi_t) \right] dt + \sigma \, dW_t^P \tag{7.71}$$

under the physical measure P. Modelling on the log-price scale ensures the positivity of the real-estate index at all moments in time.

Denoting by $\widehat{Y}_t = Y_t - \Psi_t$ the detrended log-price index, the dynamics evolution described in equation (7.71) is given by the solution to the equation

$$d\widehat{Y}_t = -\theta \widehat{Y}_t dt + \sigma \, dW_t^P \tag{7.72}$$

which is just the stochastic differential equation of the well-known OU process. The solution to this equation is given by

$$\widehat{Y}_T = \widehat{Y}_t e^{\theta(t-T)} + \sigma \int_t^T e^{\theta(u-T)} dW_u \tag{7.73}$$

This means that

$$Y_T = \Psi_T + (Y_t - \Psi_t)e^{\theta(t-T)} + \sigma \int_t^T e^{\theta(u-T)} dW_u^P \tag{7.74}$$

which implies that conditionally

$$Y_T | Y_t, \Psi \sim N(m_{y;t,T}; \sigma_{y;t,T}^2) \tag{7.75}$$

with

$$m_{y;t,T} = \Psi_T + (Y_t - \Psi_t)e^{\theta(t-T)} \tag{7.76}$$

$$\sigma_{y;t,T}^2 = \frac{\sigma^2}{2\theta}[1 - e^{2\theta(t-T)}] \tag{7.77}$$

Since $I_t = e^{Y_t}$, applying Itô's lemma to (7.71) gives

$$\frac{dI_t}{I_t} = \left[\frac{d\Psi_t}{dt} - \theta(\log(I_t) - \Psi_t) + \frac{1}{2}\sigma^2 \right] dt + \sigma \, dW_t \tag{7.78}$$

Denoting the drift side by $\alpha(I_t, t) = \left[\frac{d\Psi_t}{dt} - \theta(\log(I_t) - \Psi_t) + \frac{1}{2}\sigma^2\right]$, under the physical measure P,

$$dI_t = \alpha(I_t, t)I_t dt + \sigma I_t dW_t^P \tag{7.79}$$

The income stream, if it is paid, is assumed to follow a diffusion process similar to

$$dD_t = \delta(I_t)I_t + \gamma(I_t)I_t dW_t^P \tag{7.80}$$

Remark that the real-estate price index $\{I_t\}_{t\geq0}$ and the associated income cash-flow process $\{D_t\}_{t\geq0}$ are subject to the same information filtration represented by the one-dimensional Wiener process $\{W_t\}_{t\geq0}$.

A risk-neutral valuation requires changing the dynamics equations from physical measure P to the risk-neutral measure Q. This switch is realized via the market price of risk process $\lambda \equiv \lambda(I_t, D_t, t)$. Then, under the martingale pricing measure Q we would have that

$$dI_t = [\alpha(I_t, t) - \lambda\sigma I_t]dt + \sigma I_t dW_t^Q \tag{7.81}$$

$$dD_t = [\delta(I_t)I_t - \lambda\gamma(I_t)I_t]dt + \gamma(I_t)I_t dW_t^Q \tag{7.82}$$

In our framework λ as a function of the real-estate index, the associated income and time can take a wide variety of functional specifications from constant to linear, affine, quadratic, and so on. For practical purposes we take λ constant, $\delta(I_t) = \delta$ = constant and also $\gamma(I_t) = \gamma$ = constant. This simplification will allow us to derive analytical formulae for vanilla derivatives such as futures and swaps.

Under measure Q it is easier to follow up the modelling on the log-price space. Thus

$$dY_t = \left[\frac{d\Psi_t}{dt} - \theta(Y_t - \Psi_t) - \lambda\sigma\right]dt + \sigma dW_t^Q \tag{7.83}$$

$$dD_t = [\delta - \lambda\gamma]dt + \gamma I_t dW_t^Q \tag{7.84}$$

Therefore, under the risk-neutral pricing measure Q and with constant parameters

$$Y_T|Y_t, \Psi \sim N(\tilde{m}_{y;t,T}; \sigma_{y;t,T}^2) \tag{7.85}$$

where

$$\tilde{m}_{y;t,T} = \Psi_T + (Y_t - \Psi_t)e^{\theta(t-T)} - \frac{\lambda\sigma}{\theta}[1 - e^{\theta(t-T)}]$$

which it can be rearranged as

$$\tilde{m}_{y;t,T} = \Psi_T - \frac{\lambda\sigma}{\theta} + (Y_t - \Psi_t + \frac{\lambda\sigma}{\theta})e^{\theta(t-T)} \qquad (7.86)$$

One can observe that the effect of changing the probability measure from P to Q is equivalent to changing only the mean of the log-price by adjusting the long-run trend from Ψ_t to $\Psi_t - \frac{\lambda\sigma}{\theta}$. The volatility part remains unchanged.

Pricing real-estate futures

Standard asset pricing theory says that the futures prices on the real-estate index I_t with maturity T are given by $F_t(T) = E_t^Q(I_T)$. From (7.85) it is clear that I_t is log-normal distributed with the indicated parameters (see (7.76)) and therefore we get our first important real-estate derivatives pricing results under the FST model

$$F_t(T) = \exp\left(\tilde{m}_{y;t,T} + \frac{1}{2}\sigma_{y;t,T}^2\right) \qquad (7.87)$$

While parameters θ, σ and the quantities Ψ_t and Ψ_T are considered under the physical measure, the parameter λ needs to be calibrated from futures market prices with corresponding maturities.

While the formula (7.87) looks great from an analytical point of view there is a hidden problem. In practice, only looking at the real-estate index I_t will not help us identify the risk-neutral pricing measure Q. This is not caused by the modelling framework offered by the FST model. It has to do with the fact that trading the real-estate index in the spot market is not possible. Hence, our real-estate derivatives, including futures, are written on an observable but not tradable index I_t.

In essence the futures contracts complete the market, allowing traders to fix the pricing measure Q on a tradable instrument. The measure Q is then discovered by reverse-engineering the values of the market price of risk λ from the quoted market futures prices. The parameter λ can be considered to be time dependent with the desired maturity so that λ_1 is recovered from the real-estate futures with maturity T_1, then λ_2 from the real-estate futures with maturity T_2 and so on. More advanced specifications of the market price of risk $\lambda(I_t, D_t, t)$ can be investigated by traders.

Hence, the futures contracts play a fundamental role in real-estate markets. They allow investors, regulators, auditors and so on to recover the implied forward looking market view on futures values of real-estate. Secondly, real-estate futures allow us to fix the pricing measure for other derivatives such as European options, calls and puts, path-dependent options and so on.

The formula (7.87) for the futures price is applicable to a standard difference contract. However, the EUREX futures contract is designed as a total return payoff type of contract. Therefore, in order to be able to compare our futures model prices correctly, we need to calculate the total return model futures price. This is given by the formula

$$F_t^{FST/Eurex}(T) = 100 \times \frac{F_t(T)}{I_t} \qquad (7.88)$$

where $F_t(T)$ is given in (7.87) while I_t is the current level of IPD index.

Example 7.4. *We describe here how to price the IPD UK All Property futures curve, that is for all five annual maturities in the first week of March 2015. For simplicity we assume that there is no income stream.*[11] *First we need to determine the fundamental term Ψ_t to be used for model specification under the real-measure in (7.71). Figure 7.1 shows the fitting of a linear model $\Psi_t = \alpha + \beta t$ on the log-linear scale for the IPD index at monthly frequency. Analysts may use different specifications for Ψ, including those based on lagged real-estate index levels, macroeconomic variables and interest rates as illustrated in Tunaru (2013).*

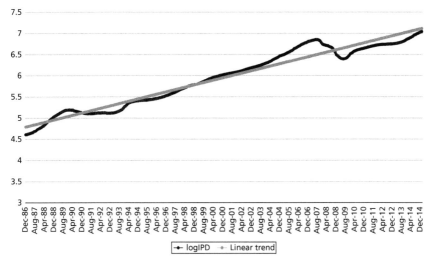

Figure 7.1. The fitting of a log-linear trend for the IPD UK All Property index between December 1986 and February 2015, monthly data series.

Source of Data: Bloomberg.

---

[11] The parameter estimation will become more involved and it may require more advanced estimation methods such as Kalman filtering.

Table 7.8. Regression fitting results for the IPD UK All Property index, monthly between December 1986 and February 2015. The $R^2 = 95.38\%$ indicates an excellent fit.

Coefficient	Estimate	Standard Error	t-stat
α	4.7839	0.0162	295.77
β	0.0827	0.0010	83.35

Table 7.9. Calibration of Fabozzi-Shiller-Tunaru model for EUREX IPD All Property futures prices on 2,3,4,5 March 2015.

Maturity	Dec 15	Dec 16	Dec 17	Dec 18	Dec 19
Futures	117.9	108.25	105.25	104.5	104.5
λ	4.1102	-0.0560	-0.9034	-1.1657	-1.2663

The linear regression fit on the log scale of the IPD index is excellent as illustrated in Table 8. The $R^2 = 95.38\%$ and also the residual analysis indicate an excellent fit.

The next step consists of estimating parameters θ and σ of the OU model (7.73). This can be done by using the exact discretization of the OU process and using again a regression model format, with a monthly frequency. For parameter estimation one can use either OLS or maximum likelihood. In our case the values of parameter estimates are virtually identical $\theta = 0.0554$ and $\sigma = 0.038$.

Now we will show how to price Eurex IPD UK All Property Total Return futures prices for December 2015, December 2016, December 2017, December 2018 and December 2019 on four consecutive days, 2,3,4,5 March 2015. The current values for the IPD index for March 2015 are $I_t = 1165.113$ so that $Y_t = \log(S_t) = 7.0605$ and the fitted fundamental term $\Psi_t = 7.1207$.

The observed Eurex IPD futures prices are calibrated with the help of the market price of risk parameters λ. The calibration is done one-to-one for each maturity and it is repeated each day. The results are described in Table 7.9. The market price of risk indicates a positive outlook for 2015, which is not surprising given that the March 2015 contract was due to expire very soon, followed by a downward negative outlook for the next four years. The futures prices are matched exactly for those values of λ which will fix the pricing measure for other derivatives on the IPD index such as European call and put options.

Pricing real-estate swaps

Now consider pricing a real-estate swap making payments at times $t_1 < t_2 < \ldots < t_n = T$. The pricing is done at time $t \le t_0$ where t_0 is the start date of the swap.

For simplicity we consider first pricing the swaplet over the period $(t_{k-1}, t_k]$. This swaplet will exchange at t_k the total return $I_{t_k} - I_{t_{k-1}}$ *possibly* plus the income over the same period $\int_{t_{k-1}}^{t_k} e^{\int_s^{t_k} r_u du} dD_s$ against a reference interest rate such as LIBOR, operating over the same period, plus a spread ρ, applied to the value of the index at time t_{k-1}. The same set-up was followed in section 7.3.2.

If L_k is the LIBOR rate paid at t_k for the period $(t_{k-1}, t_k]$ and, without reduction of generality, denoting $I_k \equiv I_{t_k}$ for all $k \in \{0, 1, 2, \ldots, n\}$ the swaplet payment is given by

$$S_k = I_k - I_{k-1} + \int_{t_{k-1}}^{t_k} e^{\int_s^{t_k} r_u du} dD_s - \Delta_k(L_k + \rho)I_{k-1} \qquad (7.89)$$

where $\Delta_k = t_k - t_{k-1}$ It is known that $\Delta_k L_k = \frac{1}{p(t_{k-1}, t_k)} - 1$, where $p(s, u)$ is the price of a zero coupon bond at time s and maturity u. This implies that

$$S_k = I_k - \frac{I_{k-1}}{p(t_{k-1}, t_k)} + \int_{t_{k-1}}^{t_k} e^{\int_s^{t_k} r_u du} dD_s - \Delta_k \rho I_{k-1} \qquad (7.90)$$

Denoting by $DF(t, k) = \exp\left(-\int_t^{t_k} r_u du\right)$ the discount factor at time t for maturity t_k the risk-neutral valuation of the swaplet at t is then given by

$$\Pi_k = E_t^Q[p(t, k)I_k] - E_t^Q[p(t, k)\frac{I_{k-1}}{p(t_{k-1}, t_k)}] - \Delta_k \rho E_t^Q[p(t, k)I_{k-1}] \qquad (7.91)$$
$$+ E_t^Q[p(t, k) \int_{t_{k-1}}^{t_k} e^{\int_s^{t_k} r_u du} dD_s]$$

Clearly quite accurate calculations can be obtained for a wide variety of model specifications for short rate r_t and taking into account various day-count conventions for Δ_k. Without a great loss of generality, in order to simplify the exposition, we shall assume that $r_t \equiv r=$ constant and $\Delta_k \equiv \Delta=$ constant. Then, the value of the k swaplet is

$$\Pi_k = e^{-r(t_k-t)} E_t^Q[I_k] - e^{-r(t_{k-1}-t)} E_t^Q[e^{-r(t_k-t_{k-1})} \frac{I_{k-1}}{p(t_{k-1}, t_k)}] \qquad (7.92)$$
$$- \Delta \rho e^{-r(t_k-t)} E_t^Q[I_{k-1}] + E_t^Q[\int_{t_{k-1}}^{t_k} e^{-r(s-t)} dD_s]$$

The second term can be simplified to $E_t^Q[I_{k-1}]$ so that

$$\Pi_k = e^{-r(t_k-t)} E_t^Q[I_k] - \left(e^{-r(t_{k-1}-t)} - \Delta \rho e^{-r(t_k-t)}\right) E_t^Q[I_{k-1}] + E_t^Q\left[\int_{t_{k-1}}^{t_k} e^{-r(s-t)} dD_s\right]$$
$$(7.93)$$

Buttimer et al. (1997) assume that $\gamma \equiv 0$ and $\delta(I_t) = \delta$. Then $dD_t = \delta X_t dt$ and the value of the k swaplet at time t is

$$\Pi_k = e^{rt} \left\{ e^{-rt_k} E_t^Q[I_k] - \left(e^{-rt_{k-1}} - \Delta \rho e^{-rt_k} \right) E_t^Q[I_{k-1}] + E_t^Q \left[\int_{t_{k-1}}^{t_k} e^{-rs} \delta I_s ds \right] \right\}$$

(7.94)

The CREIL swap price is the value of the spread ρ obtained by requiring that

$$\sum_{k=1}^{k=n} \Pi_k = 0.$$

This gives the formula of the CREIL swap rate as

$$\rho = \frac{\sum_{k=1}^{k=n} e^{-rt_{k-1}} E_t^Q[I_{k-1}] - \sum_{k=1}^{k=n} e^{-rt_k} E_t^Q[I_k] - \delta \sum_{k=1}^{k=n} E_t^Q[\int_{t_{k-1}}^{t_k} e^{-rs} I_s ds]}{\Delta \sum_{k=1}^{k=n} e^{-rt_k} E_t^Q[I_{k-1}]}$$

(7.95)

If the real-estate index does not provide any extra income (dividends) and it is only a capital based index, or the swap only covers the capital appreciation/depreciation of the index, all that is required is to take $\delta = 0, \gamma = 0$ in the above and derive the same way that the swap price is

$$\rho = \frac{1}{\Delta} \frac{\sum_{k=1}^{k=n} e^{-rt_{k-1}} E_t^Q[I_{k-1}] - \sum_{k=1}^{k=n} e^{-rt_k} E_t^Q[I_k]}{\sum_{k=1}^{k=n} e^{-rt_k} E_t^Q[I_{k-1}]}$$

(7.96)

One can easily observe that the swap price is a combination of futures prices.[12] This can be rewritten as

$$\rho = \frac{1}{\Delta} \frac{\sum_{k=1}^{k=n} E_t^Q \left[e^{-rt_{k-1}}[I_{k-1}] - e^{-rt_k} I_k \right]}{\sum_{k=1}^{k=n} e^{-rt_k} E_t^Q[I_{k-1}]}$$

(7.97)

As in Bjork and Clapham (2002) then ρ would be equal to zero by applying the martingale condition on the process of a discounted underlying asset so the numerator in (7.97). However, this would only work *if* one could trade costlessly in the underlying "asset" I_t. Shiller and Weiss (1999), Otaka and Kawaguchi (2003), Fabozzi et al. (2009) and Fabozzi et al. (2012) made the point that it is not *currently* possible to trade in the real-estate market as in equity or foreign exchange markets. For a start it is not possible to short sale real-estate directly and furthermore, the real-estate markets are not fungible,

---

[12] Under the assumption of constant risk-free rate r futures prices should also be equal to forward prices.

they present long time transaction costs and trading in the spot real-estate market represented by an index is virtually impossible.

7.4.4 PRICING REAL-ESTATE OPTIONS

Since the conditional distribution of the IPD index under the FST model is lognormal, it is straightforward to derive analytical formulae for pricing European call and put options. Based on formulae (7.85), (7.77) and (7.86) we can derive the following options pricing result.

Proposition 7.5. *Under the Fabozzi-Shiller-Tunaru model, the prices of the European call and put options prices with strike K and maturity T, contingent on the real-estate index I_t are given by*

$$call_t = \exp\left(\widetilde{m}_{y;t,T} + \sigma_{y;t,T}^2/2\right) N\left(\frac{\widetilde{m}_{y;t,T} + \sigma_{y;t,T}^2 - \ln(K)}{\sigma_{y;t,T}}\right) - KN\left(\frac{\widetilde{m}_{y;t,T} - \ln(K)}{\sigma_{y;t,T}}\right)$$

$$put_t = KN\left(\frac{\ln(K) - \widetilde{m}_{y;t,T}}{\sigma_{y;t,T}}\right) - \exp\left(\widetilde{m}_{y;t,T} + \sigma_{y;t,T}^2/2\right) N\left(\frac{\ln(K) - \widetilde{m}_{y;t,T} + \sigma_{y;t,T}^2}{\sigma_{y;t,T}}\right)$$

Proof. Here we shall derive only the formula for the put, the calculations for the call being similar. Since $I_T = e^{\widetilde{m}_y + \sigma_y \times Z}$ where $Z \sim N(0,1)$ is a standard normal variable the event $\{I_T < K\}$ is equivalent to the event $\{Z < \frac{\ln(K) - \widetilde{m}_y}{\sigma_y}\}$. Then

$$put_t = e^{-rT} E_t^Q(\max(K - I_T, 0)))$$

$$= \int_{-\infty}^{\frac{\ln(K) - \widetilde{m}_y}{\sigma_y}} [K - e^{\widetilde{m}_y + \sigma_y z}] \frac{1}{\sqrt{2\pi}} e^{-z^2/2} dz$$

$$= KN\left(\frac{\ln(K) - \widetilde{m}_y}{\sigma_y}\right) - e^{\widetilde{m}_y + \sigma_y^2/2} \int_{-\infty}^{\frac{\ln(K) - \widetilde{m}_y}{\sigma_y}} \frac{1}{\sqrt{2\pi}} e^{-(z - \sigma_y)^2/2} dz$$

$$= KN\left(\frac{\ln(K) - \widetilde{m}_y}{\sigma_y}\right) - e^{\widetilde{m}_y + \sigma_y^2/2} N\left(\frac{\ln(K) + \sigma_y^2 - \widetilde{m}_y}{\sigma_y}\right)$$

□

Example 7.5. *Here we shall continue the above example for pricing futures on the IPD UK All Property at the beginning of March 2015 with pricing at-the-money European put and call options with maturities December 2015, 2016, 2017, 2018 and 2019. The nearest maturity is imminent with less than a month to go. The IPD is published in March but covers, for*

Table 7.10. Calculation of European call and put prices on IPD UK All Property Index.

d_1	d_2	call	put
4.4724	4.4354	208.4624	0.0000
1.5830	1.5321	104.0138	1.9966
0.8732	0.8125	79.4706	10.6801
0.6785	0.6102	79.0786	17.7072
0.6284	0.5540	85.4715	22.1334

Notes: Calculations are for at-the-money strike prices on 2 March 2015, $K = 1165.113$, after estimation of parameters using monthly IPD time-series between December 1986 and February 2015 and calibration on the IPD futures prices traded on EUREX using the Fabozzi-Shiller-Tunaru model. d_1 and d_2 are the values used in the options pricing formula similar to Black-Scholes.

calculation appraisal purposes, the period December to December. Thus, on the 2nd of March 2015 the likelihood that the IPD will show a downturn would have been quite clear. However, for the next December maturities there will be a lot of time and uncertainty that will be reflected in the options prices.

In Table 7.10 we show the calculations for European call and put prices on the IPD UK All Property. All pricing is done under the λ values calibrated on the futures contracts on EUREX. The market suggests an increased likelihood of a market downturn, with call prices decreasing sharply and put prices increasing sharply.

7.5 Summary Points and Further Reading

In this chapter we highlighted the main issues encountered with models proposed for pricing real-estate derivatives. Firstly, the models need to take into account the autoregressive nature of the real-estate markets. Secondly, the real-estate markets are inherently incomplete and one should find a method to find a risk-neutral measure under which forwards/futures and European options should be priced.

Perhaps surprisingly, options on real-estate indices do not always increase with time to maturity when autocorrelated models are used for modelling the underlying index. The Shiller-Weiss model opens a window to a quick pricing platform in this area. Other models published in the literature may carry hidden pitfalls. In particular, equilibrium models may be at odds with no-arbitrage principle. The Fabozzi-Shiller-Tunaru model is more a framework under which many models can be identified for various indices. It allows a flexible methodology for identifying the risk-neutral pricing measure by matching the model futures prices with market futures prices, in the cases where the latter exist.

We showed that real-estate derivatives markets can be also used to extract a possible fundamental value of the index and gauge whether the current market index values are overvalued or undervalued. This could be very useful to policy makers and regulators overseeing stability in financial systems.

The models presented in this chapter can be applied to forwards/futures, swaps, European call and put options. We prefer these models since they lead to analytical formulae. It is straightforward then to calculate other important quantities such as greek parameters but this line of study has been left out of this current text in order to preserve fluency of reading in this area.

Buttimer et al. (1997) employed a two-state model for pricing contingent claims on a real-estate index, mainly total return swaps. Their model combines a real-estate and an interest rate process to generate a bivariate binomial tree designed to capture the volatility in the real-estate market. In a similar fashion Ciurlia and Gheno (2009) propose modelling the risk-free interest rate process and the real-estate asset value process jointly. Since no analytical formula is available for European and American options contingent on the value of the real-estate asset, they suggest using a bidimensional binomial lattice with additive symmetrical upward and downward jumps. They use a Black-Derman-Toy (BDT) model for the interest rates and a geometric Brownian motion for the real asset value. It is not clear how the initial model specified under the historical measure is risk-neutralized. In addition, the volatility of the real-estate asset seems to increase indefinitely with time, in contradiction with the empirical findings in the literature generated by the mean reverting feature of this asset class.

One of the most general models discussed in relation to pricing real-estate securities is Otaka and Kawaguchi (2003). The major advantage of this paper is recognizing the incomplete market character intrinsic to real-estate markets. Their model is spanned by three separate primary markets: the security market—where stocks, bonds, currencies and derivative securities are traded, the space market—this is the market that functions on the back of real properties, deciding the rents of buildings subject to the demand and the supply of commercial or residential space, and the property market—comprising the prices of properties such as buildings and land. In the first market trade occurs without friction. The income and capital returns of properties are determined by the last two markets. The three markets model presented in Otaka and Kawaguchi (2003) may exhibit common factors and in their set-up a real-estate derivative cannot be replicated with a self-financing strategy. This implies that no-arbitrage prices of such derivatives cannot be uniquely derived and the prices are identified through a risk-minimizing strategy.

7.6 Appendix

Here we will prove two of the technical results used in this chapter. Recall that the Shiller-Weiss model is given by the AR(1) model on log-returns.

$$\Delta \ln(H_t) = c + \rho \Delta \ln(H_{t-1}) + \varepsilon_t \tag{7.98}$$

The variable of interest is lognormal with the Gaussian mean and variance given by

$$E_t(\ln H_T - \ln H_t) = (T - t)c + (T - t - 1)\rho c + \rho \frac{1 - \rho^{T-t}}{1 - \rho} \Delta \ln H_t \tag{7.99}$$

where $\Delta \ln H_t = \ln H_t - \ln H_{t-1}$.
and

$$var_t(\ln H_T - \ln H_t) = \frac{\sigma_\varepsilon^2}{1 - \rho^2} \left[(T - t) - \rho^2 \frac{1 - \rho^{2(T-t)}}{1 - \rho^2} + 2 \sum_{1 \le i < j \le T-t} (\rho^{j-i} - \rho^{j+i}) \right] \tag{7.100}$$

In order to prove (7.99) we go through a sequence of calculations.

$$E_t(\Delta \ln(H_{t+1})) = E_t(\rho \Delta \ln(H_t) + c + \varepsilon_{t+1})$$
$$= \rho \Delta \ln(H_t) + c$$
$$E_t(\ln(H_{t+2}) - \ln(H_t)) = E_t(\ln(H_{t+2}) - \ln(H_{t+1}) + \ln(H_{t+1}) - \ln(H_t))$$
$$= E_t(\Delta \ln(H_{t+2}) + \Delta \ln(H_{t+1}))$$
$$= E_t(\rho \Delta \ln(H_{t+1}) + c + \varepsilon_{t+2}) + E_t(\Delta \ln(H_{t+1}))$$
$$= \rho(\rho \Delta \ln(H_t) + c) + c + \rho \Delta \ln(H_t) + c$$
$$E_t(\ln(H_{t+3}) - \ln(H_t)) = E_t(\Delta \ln(H_{t+3}) + \Delta \ln(H_{t+2}) + \Delta \ln(H_{t+1}))$$
$$= c + \rho \Delta \ln(H_t) + \rho(c + \rho \Delta \ln(H_t)) + c$$
$$+ \rho(\rho(c + \rho \Delta \ln(H_t)) + c) + c$$
$$= \dots$$
$$= 3c + 2\rho c + \rho^2 c + (\rho + \rho^2 + \rho^3)\Delta \ln(H_t)$$

By mathematical induction it follows that

$$E_t(\ln H_T - \ln H_t) = (T - t)c + (T - t - 1)\rho c + \rho \frac{1 - \rho^{T-t}}{1 - \rho} \Delta \ln H_t.$$

For the variance calculation observe that

$$var_t(\ln(H_T) - \ln(H_t)) = var_t\left(\Delta \ln(H_T) + \Delta \ln(H_{T-1}) + \ldots + \Delta \ln(H_{t+1})\right)$$

$$= \sum_{j=1}^{T-t} var_t(\Delta \ln(H_{t+j}))$$

$$+ 2 \sum_{1 \leq i < j \leq T} cov_t[\Delta \ln(H_{t+i}), \Delta \ln(H_{t+j})]$$

Clearly $var_t(\Delta \ln(H_{t+1})) = \sigma_\varepsilon^2$. Moreover,

$$var_t(\Delta \ln(H_{t+j})) = var_t\left(\rho \Delta \ln(H_{t+j-1}) + c + \varepsilon_{t+j}\right)$$

$$= \rho^2 var_t(\Delta \ln(H_{t+j-1})) + \sigma_\varepsilon^2$$

$$= \ldots$$

$$= \rho^{2(j-1)}\sigma_\varepsilon^2 + \sigma_\varepsilon^2(1 + \rho^2 + \ldots + \rho^{2(j-2)})$$

$$= \sigma_\varepsilon^2 \frac{1 - \rho^{2j}}{1 - \rho^2}$$

$$cov_t[\Delta \ln(H_{t+i}), \Delta \ln(H_{t+j})] = cov_t[\Delta \ln(H_{t+i}), \rho \Delta \ln(H_{t+j-1}) + c + \varepsilon_{t+j}]$$

$$= \rho cov_t[\Delta \ln(H_{t+i}), \Delta \ln(H_{t+j-1})]$$

$$= \ldots$$

$$= \rho^{(j-i)} cov_t[\Delta \ln(H_{t+i}), \Delta \ln(H_{t+i})]$$

$$= \sigma_\varepsilon^2 \rho^{j-i} \frac{1 - \rho^{2i}}{1 - \rho^2}$$

Summing up the terms gives the formula (7.100).

8 Equity Release Mortgages

8.1 Introduction

The majority of developed economies worldwide experience ageing societies that face significant difficulties posed by insufficient pensions and limited care funding. Reverse mortgages, also called equity release mortgages (ERM) or lifetime mortgages, are financial products, or sale and purchase arrangements, that allow homeowners to make use of any equity they have in their property in order to generate additional cash. Typically a lender provides the homeowner with either a lump sum or instalments (or both) tied up to the value of their home. No repayment is made until a termination or exit event[1] such as voluntary prepayment, the death of the borrower(s) or the borrower(s) move into care. The payments received from the lender accumulate as the outstanding loan balance. There are no underwriting credit-like qualifications but there are some conditions related to age and quality of property that must be satisfied.

In most developed economies the elderly cohorts are expected to increase substantially over the next decade due to increasing longevity and declining fertility. Reverse mortgage loans may provide much needed income security, alleviating two of the most important problems for advanced societies, long-term care and pensions. In general, there is a one-off payment made to the borrower. If the loan is structured such that the lender makes a series of periodic instalments then the product is called a *home income plan*. The borrower must be of at least a certain age, typically over 60. The participation in reverse mortgage programmes increases with age, borrowers over 75 years old being more likely to take up this type of loan. Participation also increases with the house equity and with the ratio of equity to income.

The cash that the borrower can receive on one of these loans can be

- a one-off lump sum
- a periodic (monthly, quarterly, annually) amount of cash, also called a *tenure* payment method, for a given period of time or for as long as the borrower(s) live in the house
- a *line-of-credit* or creditline account allowing the borrower to decide when and how much cash can be withdrawn

---

[1] What can constitute a termination event depends on the jurisdiction; see some other possible events discussed later on in this chapter.

- combinations of the above
- a deferred loan requiring the borrower to use it for payment on house repair and renovation.

The lump-sum option is the most expensive since interest is charged from the first day the contract is issued.

There are few hybrid contracts within the equity release mortgages class.

Line-of-Credit Loans This product pays an initial lump sum and also allows borrowers to take out further draw-downs subject to maintaining a suitable LTV relative to their age. A sudden increase in the house value will allow the borrower to draw more funds.

Shared Appreciation Mortgage It is similar to a reverse mortgage but also charges monthly interest below the standard rate usually charged. The lender takes an equity in the property and agrees to receive a share of any uplift in the value of the property.

Reversion Product The borrower will sell the property to the company who takes legal title and grants the homeowner a life tenancy. Advances are generally higher (the LTV for a 65-year-old may be up to 45%), no interest is charged and the lender will get the entire sum from the property sale upon the death or entry into long-term care of the homeowner. In some cases borrowers may sell only a share of their property and therefore retain a share of the equity.

HECM for Purchase This type of loan allows the borrower to purchase a new home using the loan from the bank and the remaining deposit in cash. Borrowers should switch to the new property as their principal residence. Usually the same LTVs as for the regular reverse mortgages apply.

HECM Saver This is a variant of the standard HECM that carries a lower upfront mortgage insurance premium while allowing larger notional loans. This product is primarily designed for people who only need a small amount of money for a short period of time.

Indexed Reverse Mortgage This product allows future payments to be indexed with inflation.

The reverse mortgage financial instrument can be tracked back to the 1960s in the US, with more activity in the US reintroduced during the early[2] 1980s, before spreading to the UK in the mid- to late 1980s. It has been reinvigorated worldwide in the aftermath of the subprime crisis, this product being popular in the US and the Caribbean, in the UK and some European countries (France), but also in the Far East countries like Japan, Korea, Hong Kong, Singapore, and Australia, see AARP (2005), Addae-Dapaah and Leong (1996),

---

[2] The Federal Home Loan Bank Board approved reverse mortgages in 1979.

Chou et al. (2006), Ma and Deng (2013), Mitchell and Piggott (2004). Under new regulations, reverse mortgages have been endorsed by Robert Merton as a viable source of funding for the elderly, see Rosato (2016). Klein and Sirmans (1994) analysed the Connecticut Housing Finance Authority reverse annuity mortgage program and they found that there was an average annual income increase and that the default rate was very low, this risk being mitigated by the size of the program.

The UK equity release market dried up as a result of the UK property market recession in the late 1980s and early 1990s, but an improved product with embedded no negative equity guarantee and improved economic conditions have led to a revamped interest in this market. Reverse mortgages are called equity release mortgages in the UK. There is often a guarantee embedded in the mortgage contract stipulating that any excess of the accrued loan amount above the sale value of the property after the exit event will be written off by the lender, subject to certain conditions. This is the no negative equity guarantee (NNEG) condition that is the primary concern with reverse mortgages. In the UK, a reverse mortgage must incorporate a NNEG in order to meet the Product Standards within the Statement of Principles of the Equity Release Council.[3]

As of June 2005, the overall UK market – approximately GBP 917 billion, was outstanding in conventional UK mortgages. In the over-65 age group, however, approximately 90% of properties are owned outright with no mortgage. In the UK it is estimated that the over-65s hold approximately GBP 1,100 billion in unmortgaged property equity in 2005. There is no active trading on secondary market of reverse mortgages in the UK but there have been a few securitizations in the past.

Financing a reverse mortgage portfolio poses several challenges, because of the long and uncertain maturity profile of the assets. Securitization used to be a route to get funding and structure the various risks off-balance sheet in a form attractive to medium term note (MTN) investors. Several such securitizations have been launched in the UK.

Reverse mortgages represent a new frontier for real-estate derivatives. We show here how real-estate risk is embedded in this *actuarial* type of mortgage product and how negative equity represents a significant risk associated with this important financial instrument. We describe various frameworks from different parts of the world, the US, the UK, and Korea.

8.1.1 KEY BENEFITS OF REVERSE MORTGAGES

Some reasons frequently invoked for using these type of financial instrument are the hedge against inflation, the investment opportunity in other asset

---

[3] See www.equityreleasecouncil.com/ship-standards/statement-of-principles/.

classes, and taxes. To start with, cashing in early and paying much later on will help the borrower use inflation in her favor, when inflation is positive, that is. The argument will, of course, reverse when the inflation switches to deflation. Using the equity in the house to release cash may help the smart investor put the money in the long term in other asset classes such as equity that traditionally generate more returns than the capital appreciation in the house. For some time it has been thought that the 4% rule: drawing only 4% of the initial portfolio value and immediately investing it at least 50% in equities would allow a person's portfolio not to get depleted over a 30-year period with a confidence of 90%. Recently Wagner (2013) showed that taking tax free monthly sums is a better strategy than taking out credit lines and moreover, drawing even 6% initially would still leave money in the portfolio for a 30-year period with a confidence level between 88% and 92%. Last but not least, depending on the jurisdiction, there could be significant savings on tax.

The principal benefit of a reverse mortgage is immediate access to funds without the necessity of selling the house or having to move out of. These loans are often used to pay off older loans of a different nature. Importantly, in the US the proceeds from the loan are not taxable. Reverse mortgages are also utilized to fund long-term in home care. This situation is typical for a senior couple where one member is ill and needs constant care but the other one does not require it. When neither of them are capable of looking after themselves and they decide or need to move out into care homes then the reverse mortgage is terminated. Reverse mortgages can also be used to buy other property.

There are no income qualifications for a borrower. A very important benefit for the elderly taking reverse mortgages is the possibility increasing their income which otherwise may be below the poverty line.

This financial product can only be used by senior people, who in general cannot access the loan markets due to their reduced income and life expectancy. Allowing elderly people to stay in their homes and receive care in their familiar surroundings will automatically decrease the need for nursing home care, which is usually subsidized by government.

An important benefit of these financial products is their inverse relationship with interest rates and declining property prices. When interest rates fall lower and lower, the borrowers will benefit from a reduced accrual rate. Likewise, when the property prices experience a price correction or market crash that is usually associated with a recession, the borrowers may continue with the mortgage and hope for a property price reversal in the future. Since they do not have to make any payments, even if for the time being they experience negative equity, they can continue to ride the housing markets that are known to be mean-reverting and buy their time to better future periods.

8.2 **Mechanics of Reverse Mortgages**

Reverse mortgages must be the primary debt against the house that is used as collateral. The amount to be borrowed under a reverse mortgage, sometimes called the principal limit, is determined in a direct relationship to the house's value. There are no credit requirements on the borrowers other than they need to keep up with paying their various taxes and maintenance costs. The principal limit is the maximum gross amount lent to the borrower. Overall this is historically about 60% to 70% of the appraised value of the house at issuance.

The termination of the contract and repayment of the loan occurs when the last survivor dies, sells the house, he/she does not live in the house for more than one year or simply repays the loan. The insurer or lender may also trigger repayment in some jurisdictions (in the US in particular) if the borrower is defaulting on paying the property tax or house insurance or fails to repair the property to maintain it to a minimum required standard. Home equity conversion mortgages (HECMs) are non-recourse loans, that is the borrower will not owe to the lender more than the balance or the value of the property, whichever is less. For repayment, the borrower may simply give up the house to the lender and the contract is then closed. If the house is sold the lender will only keep the amount owed and will return any excess to the borrower's estate.

The reverse mortgage can be seen as a portfolio of an income security and a crossover put option that allows the borrower to put the house as collateral in the loan back to the lender even if the accumulated outstanding balance is larger. On the market one can find two categories of reverse mortgage: ones that are publicly guaranteed by government entities and others by private labels. In the US the Department of Housing and Urban Development (HUD) guarantees the reverse mortgages originated in the HECM programme. The HUD provided two ways to cover the lender against crossover default risk. The most popular was the assignment option whereby the HUD buys the loan from the lender whenever the outstanding balance grows to a principal limit. Secondly, the lender may be able to take a shared appreciation position in the house and the HUD will guarantee that position.

The interest rates can be fixed, and many borrowers seem to prefer this route, but it can be very steep, in many cases the rates being in double digit figures such as 12% or 15%. Annually-adjustable rates can be used to link the payments on the reverse mortgages to a reference interest rate. The reference rates that have been used on the market are the 1-year constant maturity treasury, the 1-month and 1-year LIBOR, the 10-year Treasury rate in the US, the certificate of deposit (CD) rate in Korea. In order to avoid liquidity pressures, this rate is usually not allowed to vary by more than few percentage points within a year.

Depending again on jurisdiction there could be a variety of additional costs related to a reverse mortgage. These include upfront costs to pay lawyers and agents for setting up the deal, a monthly charge for securing the funding of the loan, monthly servicing fees if the reverse mortgage is not on a lump sum basis.

In the UK, for reinsurers, the PRA rules on valuation are described in Valuation 2.1 of the PRA Rulebook. For fair valuation the requirement is to value assets at the amount for which they could be exchanged between knowledgeable willing parties in an arm length transaction. The accounting rules depend on the type of reporting. Companies reporting under UK GAAP, FRS 102 employ the fair value as the amount for which an asset could be exchanged, a liability settled, or an equity instrument granted could be exchanged, between knowledgeable, willing parties in an arm length transaction. On the other hand, IFRS 13 defines fair value as the price that would be received to sell an asset or paid to transfer a liability in an orderly transaction between market participants at the measurement date.

Some lenders may include some covenants in the loan contract that allow them to subtract funds from the monthly payment that can be used to pay off all these carrying costs. There could also be an extended list of default conditions covering the borrower's declaration of bankruptcy, abandonment of the house, and misrepresentation of persona. There could also be *acceleration* conditions that may trigger final payment, such as the borrower deciding to rent out parts of the property, changes in the deeds of the property, getting additional loans where the house can be used as a collateral.

For a reverse mortgage the default option can enter into the money domain even when the borrower does not take any action. The negative equity condition may be on and off over the life of the loan, being determined by the house prices and level of accumulated balance.

When premiums were originally set for the HECM loans there was no actual exit data so the assumption made was that loan exits would occur at 1.3 times the rate of mortality, see Rodda et al. (2004). In the UK, equity release mortgages also include as a possible exit event, the possibility of moving into long-term care, also called morbidity. Again, because of lack of availability of morbidity rates, the premia were calculated using a table of adjustment factors of the mortality rates.

Changes in design make it very difficult for borrowers to compare different types of reverse mortgages. The total annual loan cost (TALC) summarizes all costs incurred on a reverse mortgage in one annual average rate. This rate can be used for comparison purposes across lenders and products.

8.2.1 KEY RISKS FOR REVERSE MORTGAGES

Here is an inventory of risks involved in trading a reverse mortgage.

- *Uncertain Maturity.* There is no fixed maturity of this product. The timing is driven by

  1. the death (mortality) or
  2. entry into long-term care (morbidity) of the borrower,
  3. or their decision to repay voluntarily (prepayment).
  4. other possible conditions under the terms of the contract

- *Mortality Risk.* The life of such as mortgage can be lengthy (a 65-year-old will, on average, live for a further 15 to 20 years).
- *Morbidity Risk.* The loan must be repaid following the death or entry into long-term care of the last surviving borrower;
- *Adverse Selection Risk.* This refers to the fact that a borrower who feels that her/his longevity risk is genuinely less than the longevity risk for the average representative of a group category will have an incentive to enter into a reverse mortgage. This also works in reverse for borrowers that feel they have a larger than average longevity risk.
- *House Price Appraisal Risk.* The maximum allowable LTV varies based on the age of the borrower(s) and the appraisal value of the house.
- *House Price Risk.* Another risk factor is the residential property market. For a pool of loans that is diversified geographically, the real-estate price risk is partially diversifiable but there is still exposure to economic recessions at a national level.
- *No Negative Equity: NNE.* This is also called crossover risk and it appears when the value of the house is lower than the value of the loan balance. It is written in the contract that the borrower or his/her heirs are not liable for losses due to property market falls. Crossover risk can either be passed onto an insurer if an assignment option exists in the covenants of the contract or it can be securitized with a portfolio of zero-coupon bonds of various maturities.
- *Transfer Risk.* The loans may be transferable, subject to maintaining a suitable LTV for the age of the borrower at the time of the transfer. The transfer may be in a different geographical location.
- *Interest Rate Risk and Leverage.* The loan interest is added to the capital loan balance so the leverage increases with time. The lender needs to match his assets with liabilities in terms of duration and convexity. There is one rate that is used for loan balance accrual and another rate that is used for discounting.
- *Legal Risk.* The lender gets an equity stake in the property while the borrower retains legal ownership until the loan is paid off.
- *Prepayment Risk.* The borrower may voluntarily prepay the loan, subject to penalty charges.

- *Interest rates and Business Cycles.* Interest rate risk extends over a much longer and more uncertain period than regular RMBS.
- *Cash-flow risk.* The cash flow generated by a portfolio of these assets is very low early on in the transaction and thus there could be liquidity problems.
- *Operational maintenance risk.* The weighted average life (WAL) of these loans gives rise to operational risk in that the condition of the properties that form the security could deteriorate after origination, particularly if the borrower is elderly and/or infirm.
- *Consumer Law Risk.* The market is defined by elderly people, a vulnerable group, and the lender may be subject to various strict consumer protection measures.
- *Default Risk.* This is more related to bankruptcy law and situations when the loan is a crossover of reverse mortgages with bankruptcy.
- *Quick sale discount* In the end, the responsibility for the sale of the property upon exit may be passed, under some conditions, to the lender, who may prefer to reduce the sale price on a vacant property, trying to maximize the price for the owner within a specified timescale. In this situation the value of the NNEG will increase farther and this risk may be correlated to the general direction of the market in house prices.

8.2.2 A FRAMEWORK FOR VALUATION OF REVERSE MORTGAGE IN CONTINUOUS-TIME

Chinloy and Megbolugbe (1994) describe a continuous-time framework for disentangling the various options and risks embedded in a reverse mortgage. This framework is reviewed here.

The loan that is originated when the reverse mortgage is issued has the value

$$L = min(H, \lambda) \tag{8.1}$$

where H is the value of the house and λ is the loan limit. The borrower can draw a maximum of vL where v is the LTV. The rate r is used for discounting. The house price grows at the rate h. The limit of the number of payments (as monthly payments) is η. Hence, in the HECM programme, the maximum limit is considered to be an age 100 and the borrower is at least 62 years old. This implies that $\eta = 456$. Thus, the present value of the borrower's liability is calculated with continuous compounding as

$$vLe^{(h-r)\eta}$$

The borrower will receive a sequence of payments, some of them being possibly zero, at times $t = 0, 1, 2, \ldots, \eta$. The payments may include indexed adjustments for inflation and lump-sum draws on a line of credit. In order for this formula to work, h and r should be transformed into monthly equivalents. Using a slight abuse of notation, in order to keep the exposition simple, we are going to denote by the same notation, h and r, the equivalent monthly rates.

Denoting by $q(t)$ the loan survival at time t, spanned by the various characteristics of the borrowers such as age, sex, correlation (for couples), mortality, morbidity tables and trends, the cash-flow at time t, from a lender perspective, is $q(t)A(t)$. If the inflation index growth rate is i then Chinloy and Megbolugbe (1994) argue that there will be

$$\int_0^\eta q(t)A(t)e^{-(r-i)t}dt$$

Hence, the liabilities and payments will be matched over the life of the product if

$$vLe^{(h-r)\eta} = \int_0^\eta q(t)A(t)e^{-(r-i)t}dt \qquad (8.2)$$

Simplifying the assumptions to have $A(t) \equiv A$ and $q(t) \equiv q$ leads to

$$vLe^{(h-r)\eta} = qA \int_0^\eta e^{-(r-i)t}dt \qquad (8.3)$$

This equation can be solved for the annuity payment A as

$$A = \frac{(r-i)}{[e^{-h\eta}(e^{r\eta} - e^{i\eta}]} \frac{vL}{q} \qquad (8.4)$$

Now we can construct some examples.

Example 8.1. *Assume that for a reverse mortgage loan the following values occur: the property with the initial house price estimation at $L = 500,000$ dollars, an LTV $v = 40\%$, inflation rate $i = 3.25\%$, discount rate $r = 1\%$, house price growth rate $h = 4\%$, constant exit rate (combining mortality, morbidity, prepayment) $q = 6\%$, all rates per annum, and using $\eta = 456$ months as the lifetime of the reverse mortgage that is typically assumed under the HECM programme for a borrower taking the loan at 62 and living until 100 years old. Then, feeding these values into formula (8.4) the value of the annuity A is equal to 173,530 USD.*

In order to gauge the sensitivity of the general annuity formula (8.4) to all input factors involved we have conducted an exercise whereby we varied one input factor at the time. The results are illustrated in Figure 8.1. One can see that, under the simplified framework, the value of the annuity decreases in a convex manner with respect to the discount rate r, as well as with inflation

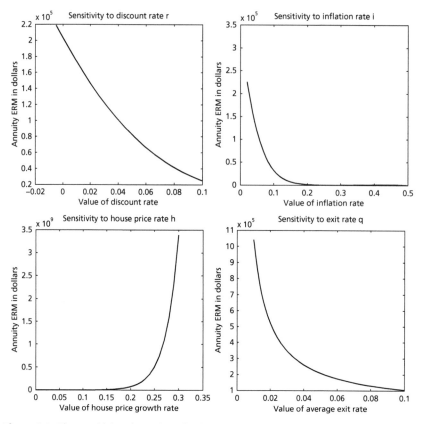

Figure 8.1. The sensitivity of annuity value in an ERM with respect to various important risk drivers, with a constant exit rate over time. The borrower is 62 years old.

rate i. An increase in the flat exit rate q reduces rapidly the value of the annuity but at the same time a small rate of exit that is equivalent to long survivorship of the borrower takes the value of the annuity to a high level, well above the initial house value. The most striking result is the sensitivity with respect to the house price growth rate. If one assumes a house price increase beyond 25% per annum, as observed in some bull periods in some hot real-estate spots like London, New York, Tokyo, Hong Kong, Singapore, the value of the annuity effectively explodes.

Here we recalculate the annuity rate by considering a time evolving exit rate. As in Chinloy and Megbolugbe (1994) we consider that

$$q(t) = b(1 - b)^{t-1} \qquad (8.5)$$

where b is a base exit rate, taken at $b = 0.1$. Thus, the annuity value is calculated from the equation

$$vLe^{(h-r)\eta} = A \sum_{t=1}^{\eta} b(1-b)^{t-1} e^{-(r-i)t}$$

$$= A \frac{b}{1-b} \sum_{t=1}^{\eta} (1-b)^t e^{-(r-i)t}$$

$$= A \frac{b}{1-b} \frac{\omega^{\eta+1} - \omega}{\omega - 1}$$

where $\omega = (1-b)e^{-(r-i)}$. Hence

$$A = \frac{vLe^{(h-r)\eta}}{b/(1-b)} \frac{\omega - 1}{\omega^{\eta+1} - \omega} \tag{8.6}$$

Redoing the sensitivity calculations, under the same initial starting point values, we get the graphs depicted in Figure 8.2. The same conclusions hold as before. One clear difference though is the linearization of the annuity value with respect to variation in inflation and base exit rate, respectively, the decrease and respectively the increase, are almost linear.

One may wonder how the analysis will vary if the borrower is older. Many borrowers of reverse mortgages enter this market when they are 75 years old. This means that instead of 456 months up to a fixed exit maturity of 100 years, one has 300 months up to the same exit time. In Figures 8.3 and 8.4 we illustrate the same calculations as carried out in this section. One can see similar profiles for all input parameters except discount rate where there is a tendency towards more linear profiles suggesting a loss in convexity.

The crossover option at η is determined by the strike price $A \frac{e^{r\eta} - 1}{r}$. The present value of the strike crossover barrier is

$$X(t) = e^{-rt} A \frac{e^{r\eta} - 1}{r} \tag{8.7}$$

Then if $M(H, t; \theta)$ denotes the value of the reverse mortgage, with θ denoting model parameters vector, the payoff of the crossover option at time t is

$$P(t) = \max[X(t) - M(H, t; \theta), 0] \tag{8.8}$$

The assignment option refers to the possibility of transferring the NNEG risk to an insurer. The assignment option is issued relative to a bond $B(r, t; \theta)$ representing the market value of the annuity contract. The fixed dollar annuity has a future value vL. The lender has an option to sell the loan with maturity

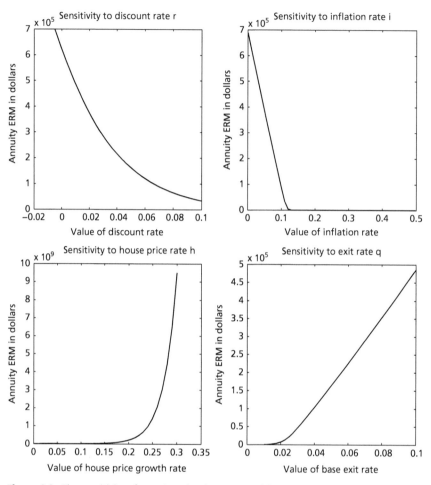

Figure 8.2. The sensitivity of annuity value in an ERM with respect to various important risk drivers, when exit rate evolves geometrically. The borrower is 62 years old.

η to an insurer, for vL. At the term date the value of the assignment option is given by

$$S(r, \eta; \theta) = \max[vL - B(r, \eta; \theta), 0] \tag{8.9}$$

If the accumulating balance reaches vL at some time t prior to the maturity of the loan η then it is optimal that the lender will exercise the assignment option. In this way crossover risk is transferred from the lender to the insurer. What makes the assignment option valuable is the adjustable rates used for growing the outstanding balance. This reinsurance scheme operated in the US with HUD as the insurer for HECM lenders.

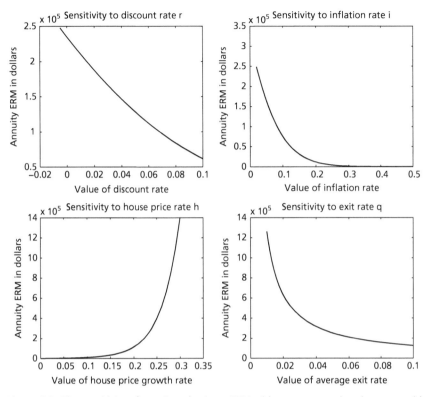

Figure 8.3. The sensitivity of annuity value in an ERM with respect to various important risk drivers, with a constant exit rate over time. The borrower is 75 years old.

8.3 Equity Release Programmes Around the World

8.3.1 THE HECM PROGRAMME IN THE US

The home equity conversion mortgage is a loan that is typical to the US and it is the only reverse mortgage that is covered by the federal government, being issued by the Federal Housing Administration on the primary market and also being supported by the Government National Mortgage Association (GNMA) on the secondary market. Other privately issued reverse mortgages may have smaller arrangement fees but they will have higher interest rates. The HECMs are available to borrowers that satisfy a series of conditions and they are used for a specific declared purpose. The youngest homeowner's age must be 62 in the US for a HECM. The house that is used as collateral in the loan must be the single-family primary residence or an owner occupied two-to-four unit building, and must be also debt-free.

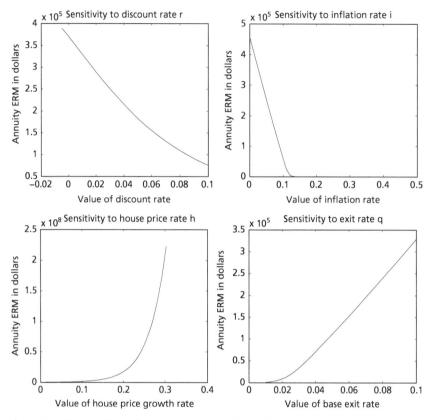

Figure 8.4. The sensitivity of annuity value in an ERM with respect to various important risk drivers, when exit rate evolves geometrically. The borrower is 75 years old.

The home equity conversion mortgage (HECM) programme was introduced in the US in 1989. It has been estimated that the number of Americans over 65 years old will double by 2050 to almost 84 million (Ortman et al., 2014). In the US only 2%-3% of eligible homeowners have a reverse mortgage, over 95% of all reverse mortgages are HECM and the origination is about 70,000 loans a year (Ortiz et al., 2013) although other sources, see Delgadillo et al. (2014), indicate around 119,137 loans between 1990 and 2004, 119,482 loans between 2006 and 2007, and 114,692 loans issued in 2009 alone. This period of boom in the issuance of reverse mortgages in the US was followed by 54,822 loans in 2011 and a similar figure for 2012. The nationwide home value limit for an HECM loan was $625,500 in December 2011. Post 2009 borrowers could only get up to 56% of the home value. In the US alone, between January 2011 and September 2012 around 110,000 loans were funded for a principal of roughly $17.4 billion. As of June 2013 there were 624,318 outstanding HECM loans in the US.

Origination fees and servicing fees are usually ignored when modelling the risks posed by HECMs. They have been in decline in the US but they still represent several thousand dollars in the final pay-back of the loan. Moulton et al. (2015) discovered that in 2014, about 12% of reverse mortgage borrowers in the HECM programme defaulted on their property taxes or homeowners insurance. A possible explanation is that, as opposed to the standard mortgage market, there were no underwriting guidelines for HECMs up to 2014. The high default rate triggered several policy measures including underwriting guidelines.

All HECMs use periodic payments based on either a fixed or variable interest rate, and a fixed or variable notional for the loan (if the borrower is using a creditline then she may draw cash every month). The creditline of a HECM can grow with time, until all credit is used. The rate of growth is usually the same as the rate on a savings account in order to avoid arbitrage.

In 1989 Fannie Mae generated a secondary market by purchasing HECM loans from lenders, loans that satisfied some standards like lump-sum draws against a credit line, fixed interest rates to advance loans from lender to the borrowers, flexible interest rates (one-year Treasury plus a spread) for balance accumulation.

The current regulations for HECM, see Twomey (2015), stipulate that "the owner's obligation to satisfy the loan obligation is deferred until the home-owner's death,[4] the sale of the home, or the occurrence of other events specified in the regulations by the Secretary." When the homeowner dies the house that is the collateral in the reverse mortgage is given to the borrower's heirs by law. The loan become due for payment and the heirs decide whether they will keep the house, sell the house, or give the house up to the lender. In the US the regulations state that the lenders should start proceedings for closing the loan within six months of the mortgagor's death, if the amount due is not fully paid. Twomey (2015) provide an interesting discussion about reverse mortgages used in conjunction with bankruptcy.

8.3.2 THE KOREAN GOVERNMENT SPONSORED REVERSE MORTGAGE MODEL

The minimum age for a borrower should be 60 in Korea for the Korean government-insured reverse mortgage programme. Ma and Deng (2013) describe the model used by the Korean government sponsored reverse

---

[4] If only one spouse is party in the contract as a borrower, upon the death or move into care of that spouse, the reverse mortgage became due. New rules implemented in 2015 allows the spouse who is not listed in the contract to stay in the house as long as it is her/his primary residence.

mortgage. The break-even level of monthly payments can be calculated by equating the present value of the mortgage insurance premium (PVMIP) with the expected loss (PVEL).

To see how this works, we need some notation. Here we denote by $p(x, t)$ the probability that a borrower at age x will survive at $x + t$, by $d^*(x, t)$ the probability that a loan will survive to the age $x + t$ but not to the age $x + t + 1$, P_0 is the upfront mortgage insurance premium. $T(x)$ is the remainder of the payment period until loan termination when the loan starts at the age x of the borrower, μ is the rate of mortgage insurance premium, OLB_t is the outstanding loan balance at time t, pm_t is the monthly payment, H_t is the expected house value at time t, h is the growth rate of housing price, r is the expected value of the actual interest rate of the loan during its period or the discount rate.

Then

$$PVMIP = P_0 + \sum_{t=1}^{t=T(x)} \frac{(OLB_t + pm_t) \times \mu \times p(x, t)}{(1 + r)^{t-1}} \tag{8.10}$$

$$PVEL = \sum_{t=1}^{t=T(x)} \left\{ \frac{\max[(OLB_t - H_t), 0] \times d^*(x, t)}{(1 + r)^t} \right\} \tag{8.11}$$

Requiring that PVMIP = PVEL allows the calculation to be done by a search method of the breakeven level of pm_t.

The evolution of loan balance is given by the equation

$$OLB_t = (OLB_{t-1} + pm_t)(1 + \mu)(1 + r) \tag{8.12}$$

and the house price is supposed to evolve according to

$$H_t = H_0 \times (1 + h)^t \tag{8.13}$$

The Korean government sponsored programme uses a fixed interest rate, the borrowers receiving payments similar to an annuity until the loan is terminated. The expected interest rate μ is used for calculating the outstanding loan balance in each period and the PVMIP and PVEL. As already commented earlier in the chapter there is one rate used to accumulate the balance and another to discount. Commercial lenders in this programme will charge the certificate of deposit (CD) rate plus 1.1%. Hence, the insurer faces interest rate risk.

When payments are like an annuity fixed scheme, using (8.10) and (8.11) and asking that $PVMIP = PVEL$ allows the calculation of the pm_t in closed-form

$$pm_t = \frac{H_0 \times LTV - P_0}{\sum_{t=0}^{T(x)-1} \left[\frac{1}{(1+r)(1+\mu)} \right]^t} \tag{8.14}$$

The Korean programme also allows a *graduate monthly scheme*, with payments indexed to the mean value of the growth rate of consumer prices. What is of interest in this situation is the base amount of graduate monthly payment pm_0 from which payments will be indexed and paid in the future. Once again, by imposing that $PVMIP = PVEL$ one can derive

$$pm_0 = \frac{H_0 \times LTV - P_0}{\sum_{t=0}^{T(x)-1} \left[\frac{1+i}{(1+r)(1+\mu)} \right]^t} \tag{8.15}$$

where i denotes the mean value of the growth rate of consumer prices.

The parameter values used in the Korean programme were reported in Lew and Ma (2012). The housing price growth rate was assumed to be 3.5% per annum, reflecting the average house price growth rate in Korea between 1986 and 2006. The average value of the 10-year government bond rates was 5.12% between 2002 and 2007 so the expected interest rate was calculated as 7.12% after adding 2% lender's margin. Those values were adjusted in Feb 2012 to be 3.3.% for house prices and 6.33% for the expected interest rate. The monthly mortgage insurance premium is 0.5% of the loan's outstanding balance.

Example 8.2. *Suppose that the house price growth rate is $h = 3.5\%$, the lenders margin rate is $\mu = 2\%$ which is added to the discount rate $r = 5.12\%$. The LTV is taken as 40% of a house that costs initially 500,000. In Korea the insurance premium is taken as 2% of the initial value of the house. The inflation rate is estimated as $i = 3\%$. Then for a borrower that is 62 years old and may live up to 100 the fixed monthly coupon that can be paid in the reverse mortgage is equal to $pm_t = 1202.8$ while if a graduate scheme is used $pm_0 = 822.2121$.*

Example 8.3. *Under the same conditions as in Example 8.2. but considering a borrower that is 75 years old and may live up to 100 the fixed monthly coupon that can be paid in the reverse mortgage is equal to $pm_t = 1350.5$ while if a graduate scheme is used $pm_0 = 1011.9$.*

A very important quantity for reverse mortgages is the *total annual loan cost rate* (TALCR). This is an average annual rate at a specific month $t = n$ that absorbs all costs in a reverse mortgage, assuming that the borrowers will reach the age of 100 and ignoring survival probabilities. This rate is used as a yardstick to compare various reverse mortgage products.

For the Korean reverse mortgage programme the TALCR can be calculated for each payment type. For constant monthly payment the equation giving the TALCR is

$$Min(OLB_n, H_n) = pm_t \sum_{t=0}^{t=n} (1 + TALCR)^{n-t} \tag{8.16}$$

or in a more concise form

$$\frac{(1 + TALCR)^{n+1} - 1}{TALCR} = \frac{Min(OLB_n, H_n)}{pm_t}$$

while for graduate monthly payment the equation is

$$Min(OLB_n, H_n) = pm_0 \sum_{t=0}^{t=n} [(1 + i)(1 + TALCR)]^{n-t} \tag{8.17}$$

or in a more concise form

$$\frac{[(1 + i)(1 + TALCR)]^{n+1} - 1}{(1 + i)(1 + TALCR) - 1} = \frac{Min(OLB_n, H_n)}{pm_0}$$

Both equations (8.16) and (8.17) must be solved by searching methods given their high nonlinearity. One can easily prove that both equations have unique solutions.

There is a clear link between the mortality survival probabilities $p(x, t)$ and the termination probabilities $d^*(x, t)$ given by

$$d^*(x, t) = p(x, t) \times d(x, t) = p(x, t) - p(x, t + 1) \tag{8.18}$$

where $d(x, t)$ is a modified mortality rate that takes into consideration the prepayment rate at age $x + t$. For the Korean programme $d(x, t) = 1.2q(x, t)$ where $q(x, t)$ is the 2010 mortality rate for females at age $x + t$.

In Figure 8.5 we illustrate the simulation of the borrower's survival up to a maximum of 100 years and the derived calculation for the probability of loan exit. These calculations are done based on (8.18) and assuming that the base mortality curve $q(x, t)$ evolves geometrically from an initial value of 0.04 and using the recursive calculations

$$q(x, t + 1) = q(x, t)(1 - q(x, t))^{(t-1)}.$$

In Figure 8.6 we present the same calculations but starting from $q(75, 1) = 0.07$ or 7%. Note that all calculations are presented on an annual basis since this is common to actuarial mortality calculations. However, for reverse mortgage valuations a monthly valuation grid is needed.

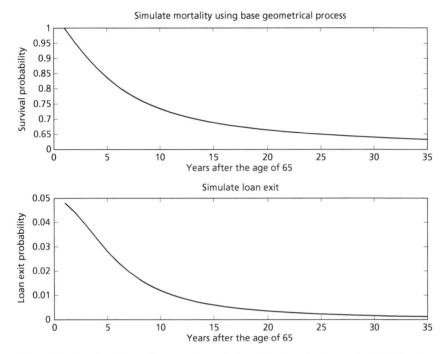

Figure 8.5. The simulation of borrower's survival and loan termination probability. The borrower takes the loan when he is 65 years old.

8.4 **Main Risks with Reverse Mortgages**

8.4.1 INTEREST RATE RISK

The most evident risk affecting reverse mortgages is interest rate risk. Given the long and uncertain maturity of these loans, one may need to rely on models to simulate future paths for interest rates. The recent economic realities where negative interest rates are present worldwide indicate that a very cautious approach must be followed when selecting interest rate models that are calibrated to the market.

A very interesting observation (Pfau, 2016) linked to interest rates is how the line of credit of a reverse mortgage grows. The loan balance typically grows at a rate given by the reference interest rate, say one-month LIBOR, plus a fixed spread reflecting the lender's profit margin and plus a fixed mortgage insurance premium. The sum rate is called the effective rate and is applied to project the growth of the loan balance. The same rate is also applied to increase the overall principal limit, which for line-of-credit reverse mortgage contracts is equal to the balance of the line-of-credit plus the loan balance and plus set-asides.

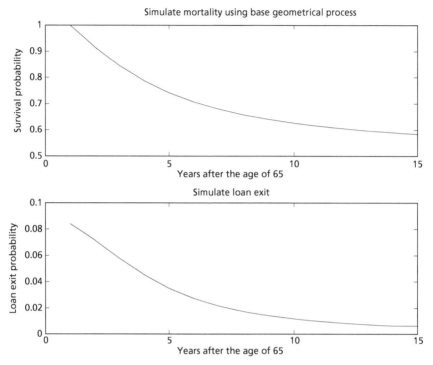

Figure 8.6. The simulation of borrower's survival and loan termination probability. The borrower takes the loan when he is 75 years old.

The design arbitrage is that interest and insurance premiums are charged only to the loan balance. The line-of-credit and set-aside accrue under the effective rate *as if* these rates are also charged to these ledgers.

The line-of-credit decreases only when funds are withdrawn. Voluntary pre-payments will boost the line-of-credit again, and any future evolution is subject to effective rate. Hence, trading a reverse mortgage with a line-of-credit and delaying withdrawing funds from it will have the effect over time to have access later on to a larger balance. The actual level of interest rates, high or low, will of course play a role. Higher rates will imply a higher effective rate and a higher rate of growth.

Tomlison et al. (2016) compared reverse mortgages with a tenure and with a line-of-credit design and concluded that the tenure type is superior in generating sustainable retirement income. However, their interest rate projections were ad hoc and it assumed implicitly that the line-of-credits will be used from the beginning.

On the other hand, from a lender perspective, Cho et al. (2013) advocated using a multi-period cash-flow model incorporating house price risk, interest rate risk and termination delay. They argue that the lump-sum mortgages are

Table 8.1. Longevity expectations based on Immediate Annuities Male and Female Lives.

Expectation	of life at birth		Expectation of life at age 65	
	Male	Female	Male	Female
1841	40	42	11	12
1900	49	52	11	12
2000	76	80	16	19
2020	79	83	18	21

Notes: Derived from Continuous Mortality Investigation Research 00 tables.

more profitable and less risky than the tenure reverse mortgages. One possible explanation is that the analytical valuation of a reverse mortgage with tenure payments is far more complex[5] than a lump-sum mortgage.

Lenders of reverse mortgages use two types of rate. The rate R is the rate charged on the loan. This is the rate at which the loan balance grows. Secondly there is the rate r which is the discount rate used to calculate the present value of the mortgage loan.

8.4.2 LONGEVITY OR MORTALITY RISK

The sellers of reverse mortgages have considered for a long time that longevity risk is diversifiable. Hence, by pooling a large numbers of loans we could use mortality tables to determine the terminations of loans.

The mortality data are derived from the Continuous Mortality Investigation Research (CMIR) 00 mortality tables, to which Norwich Union is a contributor. The tables are referred to as Immediate Annuities Male Lives (IML00) and the Immediate Annuities Female Lives (IFL00), adjusted for cohort effects (i.e. where rates of improvement in mortality have been different for people born in different periods historically). The tables show the probability of death during any year for an individual of a particular age who is alive at the start of that year. Actuarial experience suggests that females live longer than males.

In many instances the loan is given to a living couple. The loan will survive as long as one of the couple survives. Hence, there is correlation built-in as couples can take care of each other and survive longer. There is also a selection bias, people taking up reverse mortgages have more money to look after themselves and therefore live longer than their peers.

---

[5] A valuation framework that takes into consideration the mortality risk, interest rate risk, and housing price risk is detailed in Lee et al. (2012).

If τ is the time of death of the homeowner then this time is a random variable. If $F_\tau(t) = P(\tau \le t)$ is the cdf of τ then we can define the survival probability function that the homeowner lives longer than a time point t as

$$S_\tau(t) = 1 - F_\tau(t) = P(\tau > t) \tag{8.19}$$

Actuaries use a concept called the instantaneous death rate defined by the force of mortality

$$\lambda(t) = -\frac{S'_\tau(t)}{S_\tau(t)} \tag{8.20}$$

If the instantaneous rate of mortality is assumed to be constant then $F_\tau(t) = 1 - e^{-\lambda t}$ and the corresponding probability density function is $f(t) = \lambda e^{-\lambda t}$. The life expectancy is then calculated as

$$E(\tau) = \int_0^\infty t e^{-\lambda t} dt = \frac{1}{\lambda} \tag{8.21}$$

Thus a constant rate of mortality implies a life expectancy that is independent of the current homeowner's age. Clearly this is too simplistic.

Another common assumption made about mortality (Brockett, 1991) is that the death of the homeowner is uniformly distributed in the interval $[0, d]$. Then, if x is the current age of the borrower, conditional that $\tau > x$ the cdf of τ is $F_\tau(t) = \frac{t}{W-x}$ with the density is $f(t) = \frac{1}{W-x}$. The life expectancy in this case is equal to $W/(W - x)$.

8.4.3 MORBIDITY RISK

Morbidity is defined as the movement of people into long-term care. This is defined as the inability to carry out at least two activities of daily living (ADLs). The ADLs test the borrower ability to care for themselves in their own home and include the capacity to feed, clothe and wash themselves, among others. There is very little data available on the movement of people into long-term care as a result of their inability to perform ADLs and making it difficult to accurately predict the rate of morbidity which will affect the timing of the underlying cash flows entering the transaction.

The people who have contracted a reverse mortgage have a greater incentive to remain in their property. Future governmental policies may benefit the owners. The actuarial market practice in the UK calculates morbidity as a percentage of the mortality rate.

Table 8.2. The adjustment factors for deriving the morbidity rates.

Age	Males(%)	Females(%)
≤ 70	2	3
(70, 80]	4	12
(80, 90]	5	13
(90, 100]	4	8

8.4.4 HOUSE PRICE RISK

The house price risk determines the NNE risk which is managed through two channels, by charging a portion of the interest rate risk to cover this potential fall and by insisting on a low LTV. LTVs are in general age-dependent, with lower LTVs for "younger" borrowers and higher LTVs for "older" borrowers, the difference reflecting the expectation of the lender of exit rates. There are lenders who are fine to give larger amounts of cash to borrowers that can prove that they are in poor health.

Although the most common assumption regarding the house price dynamics is the geometric Brownian motion. This is assumed for a real-estate index, for which data is available. Thus, for reverse mortgages, basis house price risk is introduced reflecting the difference in the evolution of the house price index and the price of the particular house that is the collateral in a given loan.

Pu et al. (2014) found a way around basis house price risk by using an N-dimensional vector for all N houses in the loans portfolio. House prices then evolve as a system of GBMs:

$$dH_t^{(i)} = \mu H_t^{(i)} dt + \sigma H_t^{(i)} dW_t^{(i)} \tag{8.22}$$

Miao and Wang (2007) showed that the total level of volatility for real-estate can be decomposed into a systematic volatility component and a idiosyncratic volatility component. Hence Pu et al. (2014) expand the error term into

$$dW_t^{(i)} = \rho_i dZ_t + \sqrt{1 - \rho_i^2} dB_t^{(i)} \tag{8.23}$$

where $\{Z_t\}_{t \geq 0}$ is a GBM that accounts for the systematic component and $\{B_t^{(i)}\}_{t \geq 0}$ is a GBM describing the idiosyncratic shock of the i-th house, the two components being independent between them and across houses.

If $H_t = \sum_{i=1}^{N} H_t^{(i)}$ is the total price of all houses in the portfolio then, exploiting the independence assumption for all processes involved and imposing that $\rho_i \equiv \rho$, we can write

$$\sum_{i=1}^{N} dH_t^{(i)} = \mu \sum_{i=1}^{N} H_t^{(i)} dt + \sigma \sum_{i=1}^{N} H_t^{(i)} dW_t^{(i)} \qquad (8.24)$$

$$dH_t = \mu H_t dt + \sigma H_t \left(\rho dZ_t + \sum_{i=1}^{N} \frac{H_t^{(i)}}{H_t} \sqrt{1 - \rho^2} dB_t^{(i)} \right) \qquad (8.25)$$

Denoting by $\theta = \sqrt{\rho^2 + (1 - \rho^2) \sum_{i=1}^{N} \left(\frac{H_t^{(i)}}{H_t} \right)^2}$ and defining the Brownian process

$$\widetilde{W}_t = \frac{1}{\theta} \left[\rho Z_t + \sum_{i=1}^{N} \frac{P_t^{(i)}}{P_t} \sqrt{1 - \rho^2} B_t^{(i)} \right] \qquad (8.26)$$

it follows that, starting from $H_0 = \sum_{i=1}^{N} H_0^{(i)}$,

$$dH_t = \mu H_t dt + \sigma^* H_t d\widetilde{W}_t \qquad (8.27)$$

where $\sigma^* = \theta \sigma$. Since $\theta < 1$, under this model, the volatility of the entire property portfolio will always be less than the volatility of an individual house, so there is a benefit of portfolio diversification.

If $\frac{H_t^{(i)}}{H_t} = \frac{1}{N}$ for all house prices then $\theta = \sqrt{\rho^2 + (1 - \rho^2)\frac{1}{N}}$ and

$$\widetilde{W}_t = \frac{1}{\theta} \left[\rho Z_t + \frac{1}{N} \sum_{i=1}^{N} \sqrt{1 - \rho^2} B_t^{(i)} \right] \qquad (8.28)$$

Comparing this scenario with the previous heterogeneous scenario it can be observed that the expected house price growth is the same. Thus, under this model, heterogeneity of houses that are collateral in the reverse mortgage loan portfolios only influence the volatility of the future house prices, not their expectation. Moreover, increasing the portfolio size allows us to conclude that $\lim_{N \to \infty} \theta = \rho$. Other extreme cases for this model imply that when $\rho = \pm 1$ then $\theta = 1$ and $\sigma^* = \sigma$. When $\rho = 0$, that is for pairwise independent properties, it follows that $\theta = \sqrt{\frac{1}{N}}$, the minimum value for a given N. In this scenario the idiosyncratic risk of the underlying property portfolio can be diversified the most.

8.4.5 PREPAYMENT RISK

Very little is known about the values of the prepayment rate for reverse mort-gages. In the US in the early days of the HECM programme a flat prepayment rate of 0.3 times the mortality rate of the youngest borrower in the family was used. In Korea a prepayment rate of 0.2 times the 2010 mortality rate for females was chosen based on Korean demographic data.

8.5 **Valuations Considerations for ERMs**

With so many risks bundled together, Monte Carlo (MC) simulation seems the most viable pricing approach. An algorithm for pricing would go through the following steps

1. Calibrate an interest rate model (Hull-White, Vasicek, CIR, Ho-Lee, LIBOR model, market model, etc.).
2. Calibrate a mean-reversion model for a representative house price index HPI.
3. There could be correlation between the two above.
4. Decide on a prepayment model.
5. Calculate the mortality-morbidity migration table for the borrower(s).
6. Simulate the loan termination time for each MC scenario. This is the earliest of the time of death or move into care and the prepayment time.
7. Calculate the payoff to the lender, taking care of the no-negative equity agreement, and discount back to present time.
8. Average the results and obtain the MC price.

8.5.1 MODELLING ISSUES

There are various assumptions that originators of reverse mortgage pro-grammes have made over time.

For the HECM product Szymanowski (1994) discusses the following assumptions that were accepted by lenders.

Assumption 8.1. *The loan termination is independent of interest rate and house prices.*

It should be noticed that lower interest rates are convenient to borrowers since their outstanding balance will grow at a lower rate. There is no sudden ramp-up interest rate charge in monthly payments under the design of HECM. Refinancing is not an incentive due to the transaction costs and crystalliza-tion of payments to be made to the lender. When property prices decline, say through a recession, this motivates borrowers to keep the reverse mortgage alive.

The second assumption refers to the concept of *mutuality* which describes a mechanism for giving back to borrowers excess revenues as dividends when those borrowers as a vintage have been profitable to the insurer. The idea is to incentivize the mortgage seller to be risk averse at the beginning of the programme, and in order to balance it out, pay dividends back to borrowers at the back end. The problem as Szymanowski (1994) remarked is that in the case of reverse mortgages, the borrowers cannot receive the dividends because they will die or move into care.

Hence, another important assumption is:

Assumption 8.2. *The reverse mortgage originating programme is not mutual.*

The third assumption relates to the nature of the reverse mortgage originator. If this is a government-sponsored enterprise then the lenders should only break even. Thus, another important assumption is

Assumption 8.3. *The government backed insurers should be only* risk-neutral.

This last assumption is a bit more tricky since the break-even point is determined based on covering the expected losses on interest rate and house prices.

Earlier models used to price HECM and other reverse mortgages used static mortality tables. Thus, the trends in mortality rates for some vintages as well as more extreme mortality jumps observed in society were largely ignored. Chen et al. (2010) combined a generalized Lee-Carter model with asymmetric jump effects, with an ARIMA-GARCH model for a house price index to evaluate the non-recourse provision of reverse mortgages. They demonstrated that on that basis, the HECM programme in the US is viable. However, somewhat surprisingly they considered the interest rate to be fixed.

Furthermore, the housing prices were modelled with a geometric Brownian motion, see Tsay et al. (2014), in contradiction with serial correlations and possible stochastic volatility effects revealed in the literature. Szymanowski (1994) argued that the dynamics of house prices is well represented by a geometric Brownian motion. This is in contradiction with the findings of Case and Shiller (1989) and a large body of empirical evidence. Using a geometric Brownian motion for house prices is wrong for several reasons. First of all the well-documented serial correlation of returns of property prices is not captured. Secondly, the variance for a GBM increases infinitely with the time horizon. Last but not least, a GBM will not be able to produce a property crash since all paths are continuous. A GBM is used to model house prices in the reverse mortgages literature mainly for convenience.

Ma and Deng (2013) presented an actuarial-based model for pricing the Korean reverse mortgage with constant monthly payments and also with graduate monthly payments indexed to the growth rate of consumer prices. They found that the TALC rates for the graduate payments scheme is more advantageous to the borrower and any shock to house prices may impact the younger borrowers more severely.

Wang et al. (2014) developed an analytical formula for calculating the loan-to-value (LTV) ratio in an adjusted-rate reverse mortgage (RM) with a lump sum payment. In their model, interest rates are modelled jointly with the adjustable-rate RM, and the housing price follows a jump diffusion process with a stochastic interest rate. Assuming that the loan interest rate is adjusted instantaneously with the short rate given by a CIR model, they show that the LTV ratio is independent of the term structure of interest rates, even when the housing prices follow an exponential Lévy process. They raise concerns about the viability of the HECM (Home Equity Conversion Mortgage) at high levels of housing price volatility. Interestingly, when the loan interest rate is based on LIBOR they suggest that the LTV ratio is insensitive to the parameters characterizing the short rate process.

Shao et al. (2015) consider that there are only two main risks that insurers selling ERMs face, real-estate risk, and longevity risk. They investigated the joined effect of real-estate price risk and longevity risk on the pricing and risk profile of reverse mortgage loans. Their stochastic multi-period model was based on a new hybrid hedonic/repeat-sales pricing model and a stochastic mortality model with cohort trends (the Wills-Sherris model). They concluded that using an aggregate house price index and not considering cohort trends in mortality may lead to an underestimation of total risk in reverse mortgage loans.

8.5.2 THE ORTIZ-STONE-ZISSU MODEL

One of the simplest models around for pricing reverse mortgages is the model introduced by Ortiz et al. (2013). Denoting by H_t the house price at time t, by π the rate of inflation, by RM_t the value of the reverse mortgage at time t, by $\delta \in (0, 1)$ the percentage of the property value that is financed under the loan or the LTV, and by r the interest rate charged on the loan, the model assumes that the house price will increase/decrease at the rate of inflation/deflation as described by the equation

$$H_t = H_0(1 + \pi)^t \qquad (8.29)$$

The interest accrues over time and it is added to the outstanding loan balance as follows

$$RM_t = \delta H_0 (1 + r)^t \tag{8.30}$$

Importantly it is assumed that $r \geq \pi$. The two parts of the model represented by the evolution equations (8.29) and (8.30) represent two curves that start from different initial points, at time zero the value of the reverse mortgage is always smaller than the value of the house, but with time the two curves may crossover. The crossover point can be determine by requiring that

$$H_0 (1 + \pi)^t = \delta H_0 (1 + r)^t \tag{8.31}$$

The important curves in the analysis of reverse mortgages are illustrated for this simple model in Figure 8.7. The crossover point determines the negative equity territory. It is important to realize that there is a secondary crossover point between the house price curve and the funding curve, which is very important from the issuer's perspective. Another direct observation is that the excess spread takes at least 15 years to become more substantial. This implies that the mortality trends of various mortgagor vintages are very important, as well as extreme mortality rates that bring the termination point closer to the issuance point.

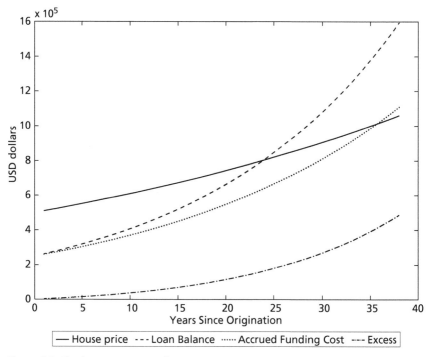

Figure 8.7. The important curves for a reverse mortgage.

This model assumes that the inflation rate and interest rate are exogenous to the system and only δ determines actively the time t^* of the crossover. Solving (8.31) for t^* one gets

$$t^* = \frac{\ln(\delta)}{\ln(1 + \pi) - \ln(1 + r)} \tag{8.32}$$

This function is decreasing and concave as a function of δ.

In Figure 8.8 we plot the crossover time obtained under this very simplified methodology as a function of the LTV for several combinations of the interest rate and rate of house price inflation. It can be observed that the crossover time is a convex function of the LTV for all combinations. Moreover, the smaller the difference between the two rates the steeper the crossover curve. For very large LTVs the crossover point goes to zero.

The model has serious flaws in that there is no possibility of a property price crash, interest rates are assumed constant, and there is no consideration about the determination of the stochastic termination event related to mortality risk.

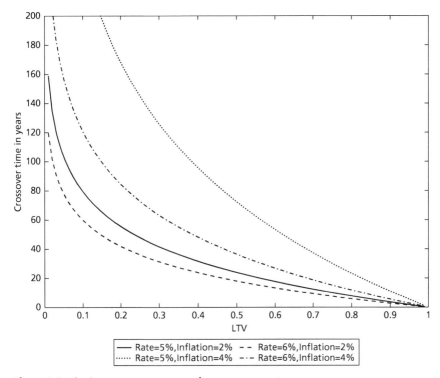

Figure 8.8. The important most curves for a reverse mortgage.

8.5.3 BREAK-EVEN COST CALCULATIONS

Pu et al. (2014) detailed break-even calculations under the assumptions that the exit time from a reverse mortgage loan is fixed at T and that the house prices follow a geometric Brownian motion. In this section we revise these calculations for a lump-sum type of contract for an annuity-like scheme, correcting some typos and discussing some of the issues involved.

Lump-sum scheme

Let L_T be the fixed lump-sum advanced to the homeowner at time t_0. Since the exit time from this loan is fixed at T we can assume, without loss of generality that $t_0 \equiv 0$. The house price that is collateral in this loan evolves according to the process

$$dH_t = \mu H_t dt + \sigma H_t dW_t \qquad (8.33)$$

There are two interest rates to consider: R is the rate charged on the loan and r is the discount rate, taken as a risk-free rate. The balance outstanding at the exit T is calculated using R while any present value calculation is calculated using r, both with continuous compounding. At T the lender will receive

$$H_T - \max[H_T - L_T e^{RT}, 0]$$

The break-even lump-sum of the loan L_T^* is calculated as the solution of the equation

$$L_T = e^{-rT} E(H_T) - e^{-rT} E\left(\max[H_T - L_T e^{RT}, 0]\right) \qquad (8.34)$$

in the unknown L_T.

We know that when the house price follows (8.33) then

$$H_T = H_0 e^{(\mu - \frac{1}{2}\sigma^2)T + \sigma W_T}$$

and

$$E(H_T) = H_0 e^{\mu T}.$$

Calculations similar[6] to Black-Scholes formula give

---

[6] Here we are *not* in a Black-Scholes economy; there is no replication or no-arbitrage argument invoked.

$$E\left(\max[H_T - L_T e^{RT}, 0]\right) = H_0 e^{\mu T} N(d_1(L_T)) - L_T e^{RT} N(d_2(L_T)) \quad (8.35)$$

where

$$d_1(L_T) = \frac{\ln\left(\frac{H_0}{L_T e^{RT}}\right) + \left(\mu + \frac{1}{2}\sigma^2\right) T}{\sigma\sqrt{T}}, \quad d_2(L_T) = d_1(L_T) - \sigma\sqrt{T}$$

The break-even lump-sum equation can be rewritten

$$L_T = H_0 e^{(\mu-r)T} - H_0 e^{(\mu-r)T} N(d_1(L_T)) + e^{(R-r)T} L_T N(d_2(L_T))$$

$$L_T = H_0 e^{(\mu-r)T}\left(1 - N(d_1(L_T))\right) + e^{(R-r)T} L_T N(d_2(L_T)) \quad (8.36)$$

$$L_T \left(1 - e^{(R-r)T} L_T N(d_2(L_T))\right) = H_0 e^{(\mu-r)T}\left(1 - N(d_1(L_T))\right) \quad (8.37)$$

Observe now that there is a value L_T^* such that

$$1 - e^{(R-r)T} L_T N(d_2(L_T)) = 0$$

that is derived as follows

$$N(d_2(L_T)) = e^{(r-R)T}$$

$$d_2(L_T) = N^{-1}(e^{(r-R)T})$$

$$\frac{\ln\left(\frac{H_0}{L_T e^{RT}}\right) + \left(\mu - \frac{1}{2}\sigma^2\right) T}{\sigma\sqrt{T}} = N^{-1}(e^{(r-R)T})$$

$$\frac{H_0}{L_T e^{RT}} = e^{-(\mu - \frac{\sigma^2}{2})T} e^{-\sigma\sqrt{T} N^{-1}(e^{(r-R)T})}$$

and therefore

$$L_T^* = H_0 e^{(\mu - R - \frac{\sigma^2}{2})T)} e^{-\sigma\sqrt{T} N^{-1}(e^{(r-R)T})} \quad (8.38)$$

But, for this solution

$$d_1(L_T^*) = \frac{1}{\sigma\sqrt{T}}\left[\sigma^2 T + \sigma\sqrt{T} N^{-1}(e^{(r-R)T})\right]$$

$$= \sigma\sqrt{T} + N^{-1}(e^{(r-R)T})$$

$$N(d_1(L_T^*)) = N\left(\sigma\sqrt{T} + N^{-1}(e^{(r-R)T})\right)$$

Thus, for L_T^* the left side of (8.37) is zero while the right side is equal to

$$H_0 e^{(\mu-r)T}\left(1-N\left(\sigma\sqrt{T}+N^{-1}(e^{(r-R)T})\right)\right) = H_0 e^{(\mu-r)T}N\left(-\sigma\sqrt{T}-N^{-1}(e^{(r-R)T})\right)$$

which is strictly positive!

Therefore, the assumption of a geometric Brownian motion for the house price and a fixed exit time provides a modelling framework that does not allow specific values for the break-even lump sum.

The ratio $\frac{L_T}{H_0}$ is the loan-to-value (LTV) ratio and it is a fundamental concept in mortgage markets. We have proved that the LTV cannot be equal to the value

$$e^{(\mu-R-\frac{\sigma^2}{2})T)}e^{-\sigma\sqrt{T}N^{-1}(e^{(r-R)T})}$$

Annuity-like scheme

Here we assume that the fixed annuity coupon A is paid every month.[7] As in Pu et al. (2014) we assume a fixed exit time T and that the uncertainty in the house price is driven by a geometric Brownian motion. The months span a payment time grid $\{t_1, t_2, \ldots, t_M\}$ with $t_M = T$. In this case $\Delta \equiv t_{i+1} - t_i = \frac{1}{12}$ year and we assume that $T = M\Delta$.

The balance that will accumulate at exit T will be

$$B(A, R, T) = \sum_{i=1}^{M} Ae^{R(T-t_i)} \tag{8.39}$$

This is equal to

$$\sum_{i=1}^{M} Ae^{R\Delta(M-i)} = Ae^{R\Delta M}\sum_{i=1}^{M} e^{-iR\Delta}.$$

The sum is a geometric progression and we can calculate it in closed form.

$$\sum_{i=1}^{M} e^{-iR\Delta} = \frac{e^{-R\Delta M}-1}{1-e^{R\Delta}}$$

Thus

$$B(A, R, T) = A\frac{1-e^{R\Delta M}}{1-e^{R\Delta}} \tag{8.40}$$

---

[7] It can be any frequency such as quarterly or annually.

At the exit the lender will receive the payoff

$$X_T = \min\left[H_T, B(A, R, T)\right] \tag{8.41}$$

$$= B(A, R, T) - \max(B(A, R, T) - H_T, 0) \tag{8.42}$$

$$= H_T - \max(H_T - B(A, R, T), 0) \tag{8.43}$$

From (8.43) the payoff of a reverse mortgage at maturity is equal to a portfolio of a long position in the house and a short position in a European call option with a time dependent strike $B(A, R, T)$ (dependent on when the borrower(s) exit).

The NPV of the lender's cash flow is

$$NPV = E(e^{-rT}X_T) - E\left(\sum_{i=1}^{M} Ae^{-rt_i}\right) \tag{8.44}$$

$$= E(e^{-rT}X_T) - A\frac{e^{-r\Delta M} - 1}{1 - e^{r\Delta}} \tag{8.45}$$

Therefore, working with $B(A, R, T) - \max(B(A, R, T) - H_T, 0)$, the lender will have a positive NPV if and only if

$$e^{-rT}E\left(B(A, R, T) - \max(B(A, R, T) - H_T, 0)\right)) - A\frac{e^{-r\Delta M} - 1}{1 - e^{r\Delta}} > 0$$

After some algebraic calculations this condition can be written as

$$A\left[\frac{1 - e^{R\Delta M} - 1}{1 - e^{R\Delta}} - \frac{1 - e^{r\Delta M} - 1}{1 - e^{r\Delta}}\right] > E\left(\max(B(A, R, T) - H_T, 0)\right) \tag{8.46}$$

The break-even payment rate A^* is the solution of the equation

$$A\left[\frac{1 - e^{R\Delta M} - 1}{1 - e^{R\Delta}} - \frac{1 - e^{r\Delta M} - 1}{1 - e^{r\Delta}}\right] = E\left(\max(B(A, R, T) - H_T, 0)\right) \tag{8.47}$$

We know from Black-Scholes calculus that

$$E\left(\max(B(A, R, T) - H_T, 0)\right) = B(A, R, T)N(-d_2(A)) - H_0 e^{\mu^T T}N(-d_1(A))$$

where

$$d_1(A) = \frac{\ln\left(\frac{H_0}{B(A,R,T)}\right) + (\mu + \frac{\sigma^2}{2})T}{\sigma\sqrt{T}}, \quad d_2(A) = d_1(A) - \sigma\sqrt{T}$$

8.6 **Summary Points and Further Reading**

Major economies are facing significant problems related to long-term care and pensions cover. Reverse mortgages offer an elegant solution to these difficulties. Banks and governments should work together to develop viable programmes for issuing financial products from the reverse mortgage family.

One of the most important risks for the lenders of these loans is generated by negative equity so implicitly by real-estate risk. Real-estate derivatives would allow lenders to manage this type of risk in a flexible and transparent manner. While there is intensive modelling for mortality rates and of course for interest rates, the financial modelling for real-estate derivatives is only now beginning to emerge.

For reverse mortgages, negative equity is not a trigger for defaults as is the case with standard mortgages. Lenders may be able to overcome negative equity situations if the loans are not terminated during a period of negative equity. Given that mortality risk and the risk of a property market downfall are independent, the design of the reverse mortgage contract is helpful to lenders in the sense that there is no incentive to trigger the termination of the loans. However, if one loan terminates during a period of negative equity, is very likely that other similar loans will terminate at the same time. Hence, it is very important that reverse mortgage portfolios are well diversified across borrowers.

Reverse mortgages open a new frontier for applications of real-estate derivatives. They are an important asset class for the future and they will facilitate a better distribution of risks in society, helping elderly people to overcome cash provision problems and also helping governments to reduce the burden of increasing costs for long-term care.

From an academic perspective the asymmetry of information plays a big role in the risk management of reverse mortgages. An excellent insight is offered by Webb (2009). Cocco and Lopes (2014) analysed how the design of the contract can be improved for the benefit of all parties involved. A very interesting line of research related to reverse mortgages is the insurance of this market. This is very important as the studies US Government Accountability Office (2007) suggest.

9 Conclusions and Where Next

Real-estate markets are here to stay. The stability of financial systems around the world is frequently tested by crises related to property price crashes or price corrections. The quality of livelihood of billions of people is affected by real-estate prices, and governments around the world have not yet found a solution to safeguard the future evolution of property prices. Let's hope that they are actively searching for a solution!

Mortgages provide an important link between the financial markets and the real economy. The design of a robust mortgage contract is very much the subject of intensive research. It is important to recognize the risks embedded in each mortgage and it is also very important to acknowledge that crucial decisions related to real-estate risk such as prepayment, default or curtailments, lie with normal people, individuals who are not actively part of the financial system (capital and derivatives markets) per se. The subprime crisis of 2007 showed that we are not yet fully prepared to contain real-estate risk. At the time of writing of this book it seems that the problems of mortgage defaults and property crashes are in the past. However, this may be only the silence before the storm and finance practitioners, regulators, and academics need to find solutions such that the problems posed by the subprime crisis will remain anchored in the past.

Real-estate risk reappears also in a different context, that of long-term care. The wealth locked in bricks and mortar needs to be released if we are to solve the problem of an ageing population and lack of additional income in challenging economic times. Banks may be able to help funding for long-term care and additional retirement income using the real-estate channel.

The three main directions enumerated above define the trident on which this monograph was built. We have highlighted the sources of problems stemming from real-estate and for all three categories we have only one solution: real-estate derivatives. There are complex issues related to modelling and risk management of these financial products but the benefits would massively outweigh the intellectual cost required to master these techniques. We explored a large set of real-estate indices and we have highlighted that they share a common problem, serial correlation. Any model aiming to price property derivatives should take this feature into consideration. In this monograph we presented many models proposed in this area. I would not make a strong recommendation; I leave the reader the pleasure to adopt any of the models presented in this book and hopefully they will be able to improve them further.

Perhaps what is needed is a joint effort to establish a viable market for vanilla real-estate derivatives, that is futures, total return swaps, and European call and put options. Given the intrinsically slow business clock[1] in real-estate markets, as opposed to foreign exchange markets which have arguably the fastest business clock, liquidity may be considered low. This is wrong in my opinion because liquidity should be measured also relative to the speed of transactions. However, the point I wanted to make here is that real-estate markets need a long vector of maturities, at least ten years into the future, if not longer, in order to facilitate finance agents to trade not only the future levels of the real-estate prices but also the shape of the forward curve. This maturity contract extension may lead to a double benefit, on one side it may help hedge current positions in real-estate derivatives and on the other side it may boost liquidity in those contracts overall.

Real-estate finance seems to be somehow detached from mainstream finance and even more so from quantitative finance. We owe Robert Shiller for bringing real-estate finance into focus and I hope this monograph will help to spark a resurgence of research in this area in the years to come. If not for intellectual endeavor, we should at least remember that the real-estate market is probably the largest market, both in terms of total wealth and also in terms of problems.

What do I think it will happen next? I hope there will be futures contracts introduced in the UK on the two main residential indices, Halifax and Nationwide, and futures contracts introduced in the US on one or two commercial indices. Simultaneously, I hope all these futures curves will go as far as ten years maturity and then hedge-funds will realize the big opportunity they have to trade future evolution of property prices. On the risk-management side, I really wish large banks will be asked to have real-estate hedges in their portfolio linked to their stress results. Top tier banks cannot claim they are fully diversified if they are out of real-estate markets.

On the scientific side, we need more datasets being made available to researchers in academia. I was fortunate to be able to use a great dataset from great companies in the UK. In this respect I was very fortunate to meet Tony Key at Cass Business School in London who knows far more about the main real-estate markets than I will ever learn. Given the problems related to real-estate markets and mortgages in the subprime crisis one would expect to see large databases with information on mortgages, borrowers' characteristics and house prices being collated and made available for research. As far as I know, so far there has not been any initiative in this direction. How can we learn from what has happened from these dramatic events if we do not have any data to look at?

In my opinion, we should not be fully satisfied with the current models for real-estate prices as represented by various indices. It is looking more likely that

---

[1] Here I mean how long it will take two parties to conclude a business transaction in the spot real-estate market.

we need to consider a discrete time model with monthly frequency, the most likely feasible frequency. This would pose additional challenges to the financial engineering part of getting real-estate derivatives prices. There will also be an increased interest in extracting the market sentiment component from the nominal prices but only after identifying a robust method to determine the component generated by fundamentals.

Policy makers should become a lot more interested in real-estate derivatives since they can provide a market orientated forward-looking view of the possible market downturns. Indeed, the Bank of England uses interest rate derivatives markets and equity derivatives markets to determine various percentiles of the risk-neutral density distribution of major market interest rates such as LIBOR and the FTSE100 index. This analysis is done routinely on a daily basis and the results obtained are taken into consideration in the stability analysis of the financial system. I envisage real-estate derivatives being added to the above two asset classes in the not too distant future.

The rapid development of some economies in Asia such as China, Hong Kong, Singapore, and Malaysia will pose interesting problems related to real-estate evolutions in those countries. If anything, all the problems encountered in the US, the UK and Europe will reappear in those parts of the world. There is an opportunity for a joint research effort to introduce real-estate derivatives that will contribute to the stability of these markets and the taming of future property crashes that may have devastating effects on those Asian economies.

Beyond the intellectual challenges posed by real-estate data and the associated real-estate derivatives there is clear contribution that researchers can make by solving *real* problems generated by the real-estate. Stabilizing real-estate markets must be a top priority to all governments and international economic organizations around the world. Taking care of the future of property may require viable property futures.

BIBLIOGRAPHY

AARP (2005). Home made money: A consumers guide to reverse mortgages.

Addae-Dapaah, K. and K. Leong (1996). Housing finance for the ageing Singapore population: the potential of the home equity conversion scheme. *Habitat International 20*, 109–120.

Adelman, I. and Z. Griliches (1961). On an index of quality change. *Journal of the American Statistical Association 56*, 535–548.

Albota, G. and R. Tunaru (2012). *The Handbook of Fixed Income Securities* (8th ed.), Chapter Interest-Rate Caps and Floors, pp. 1525–1538. New York: McGraw Hill.

Asay, M., F. Guillaume, and R. Mattu (1987). *Mortgage Backed Securities*, Chapter Duration and Convexity of Mortgage Backed Securities: Some Hedging Implications from a Prepayment Linked Present Value Model. Probus Publishing.

Bailey, M. A., R. F. Muth, and H. Nourse (1963). A regression method for real estate price index construction. *Journal of the American Statistical Association 58*, 922–942.

Baum, A. E. (2001). *A Global Perspective on Real Estate Cycles*, Chapter Evidence of Cycles in European Commercial Real Estate Markets and Some Hypotheses, pp. 103–115. Massachusetts: Kluwer.

Baum, A. E. and D. Hartzell (2012). *Global Property Investment: Strategies, Structures, Decisions*. Chichester: Wiley-Blackwell.

Bjork, T. (2009). *Arbitrage Theory in Continuous Time* (3rd ed.). Oxford: Oxford University Press.

Bjork, T. and E. Clapham (2002). On the pricing of real estate index linked swaps. *Journal of Housing Economics 11*, 418–432.

Black, D. (1986). Success and failure of futures contracts: Theory and empirical evidence. Monograph Series in Finance and Economics.

Blundell, G. and C. W. R. Ward (1987). Property portfolio allocation: A multi-factor model. *Journal of Property Research 4*(2), 145–156.

Brockett, P. L. (1991). Information theoretic approach to actuarial science: a unification and extension of relevant theory and applications. *Transactions of the Society of Actuaries 43*, 73–135.

Brooks, C. and S. Tsolacos (2010). *Real Estate Modelling and Forecasting* (first ed.). Cambridge: Cambridge University Press.

Buttimer, R., J. Kau, and V. Slawon (1997). A model for pricing securities dependent upon a real estate index. *Journal of Housing Economics 6*, 16–30.

Campolongo, F., K. Jönsson, and W. Schoutens (2013). *Quantitative Assessment of Securitisation Deals*. Springer Briefs in Finance. Heidelberg: Springer.

Cannon, S. and R. Cole (2011). How accurate are commercial-real-estate appraisals? Evidence from 25 years of NCREIF sales data. *Journal of Portfolio Management 37*(5), 68–88.

Cao, M. and J. Wei (2010). Valuation of housing index derivatives. *The Journal of Futures Markets 30*(7), 660–688.

Case, K., E. Glaeser, and J. Parker (2000). Real estate and the macroeconomy. *Brookings Papers on Economic Activity 2000*(2), 119–162.

Case, K. E. and R. J. Shiller (1987). Index-based futures and options markets in real estate. *Journal of Portfolio Management 19*(2), 83–92.

Case, K. E. and R. J. Shiller (1988). The behavior of home buyers in boom and post-boom markets. *New England Economic Review*, 29–47. November–December.

Case, K. E. and R. J. Shiller (1989). The efficiency of the market for single family homes. *American Economic Review 79*(1), 125–137.

Case, K. E. and R. J. Shiller (1990). Forecasting prices and excess returns in the housing market. *Journal of the American Real Estate and Urban Economics Association 18*(3), 253–273.

Case, K. E. and R. J. Shiller (1994). A decade of boom and bust in the prices of single-family homes: Boston and Los Angeles, 1983 to 1993. *New England Economic Review*, 40–52. March-April.

Case, K. E. and R. J. Shiller (1996). Mortgage default risk and real estate prices: The use of index based futures and options in real estate. *Journal of Housing Research 7*, 243–258.

Chen, H., S. H. Cox, and S. S. Wang (2010). Is the home equity conversion mortgage in the United States sustainable? Evidence from pricing mortgage insurance premiums and non-recourse provisions using the conditional Esscher transform. *Insurance: Mathematics and Economics 46*, 371–384.

Chinloy, P. (1989). The probability of prepayment. *Journal of Real Estate Finance and Economics 2*(3), 267–283.

Chinloy, P. (1991). The option structure of a mortgage contract. *Journal of Housing Research 2*(1), 21–38.

Chinloy, P. and I. F. Megbolugbe (1994). Reverse mortgages: Contracting and crossover risk. *Journal of the American Real Estate and Urban Economics Association 22*(2), 367–386.

Cho, D., K. Hanewald, and M. Sherris (2013). Risk management and payout design of reverse mortgages. working paper, Australian Research Council Center of Excellence in Population Ageing Research (CEPAR), Sydney.

Chou, K.-L., N. W. Chowa, and I. Chib (2006). Willingness to consider applying for reverse mortgage in Hong Kong Chinese middle-aged homeowners. *Habitat International 30*, 716–727.

Chow, Y.-F., C. Huang, and M. Liu (2000). Valuation of adjustable rate mortgages with automatic stretching maturity. *Journal of Banking & Finance 24*, 1809–1829.

Ciurlia, P. and A. Gheno (2009). A model for pricing real estate derivatives with stochastic interest rates. *Mathematical and Computer Modelling 50*, 233–247.

Clayton, J. (1997). Are house price cycles driven by irrational expectations? *Journal of Real Estate Finance and Economics 14*(3), 341–363.

Clayton, J., D. Ling, and A. Naranjo (2009). Commercial real estate valuation: Fundamentals versus investor sentiment. *Journal Real Estate Financial Economy 38*, 5–37.

Cocco, J. and P. Lopes (2014). Reverse mortgage design. working paper, London Business School.

Cocco, J. F. (2013). Evidence on the benefits of alternative mortgage products. *Journal of Finance 68*(4), 1663–1690.

Coval, J., J. Jurek, and E. Stafford (2009). The economics of structured finance. *Journal of Economic Perspectives 23*(1), 3–25.

Cox, J., J. Ingersoll, and S. Ross (1985). A theory of the term structure of interest rates. *Econometrica 53*, 385–407.

De Wit, I. and R. Van Dijk (2003). The global detereminants of direct office real estate returns. *Journal of Real Estate Finance and Economics 26*(1), 27–45.

Delgadillo, L., C. Stokes, and J. Lown (2014). Descriptive analysis of reverse mortgage counseling clients. *Journal of Financial Counseling and Planning 25*(2), 115–128.

Dobson, S. and J. Goddard (1992). The determinants of commercial property prices and rents. *Bulletin of Economic Research 44*(4), 301–321.

Epstein, D. and P. Wilmott (2002). A note on the pricing of index amortising rate swaps in a worst-case scenario. *International Journal of Theoretical and Applied Finance 5*(5), 447–454.

Fabozzi, F. J., R. J. Shiller, and R. S. Tunaru (2009). Hedging real estate risk. *Journal of Portfolio Management 35*, 92–103.

Fabozzi, F. J., R. J. Shiller, and R. S. Tunaru (2010). Property derivatives for managing European real-estate risk. *European Financial Management 16*(1), 8–26.

Fabozzi, F. J., R. J. Shiller, and R. S. Tunaru (2012). A pricing framework for real-estate derivatives. *European Financial Management 18*, 762–789.

Fisher, J. D., D. Gatzlaff, D. Geltner, and D. Haurin (2004). An analysis of the determinants of transaction frequency of institutional commercial real estate investment property. *Real Estate Economics 32*(2), 239–264.

Fisher, J. D., D. Geltner, and B. R. Webb (1994). Value indexes of commercial real estate: A comparison of index construction methods. *Journal of Real Estate Finance and Economics 9*, 137–164.

Fisher, J. D., M. E. Miles, and B. R. Webb (1999). How reliable are commercial appraisals? Another look. *Real Estate Finance Fall*, 9–15.

Fleming, M. C. and J. G. Nellis (1981). The interpretation of house price statistics for the United Kingdom. Environment and Planning A, 13, 1109–24.

Forum, I. P. (2008). Getting into property derivatives. report, Investment Property Forum.

Foster, C. and R. V. Order (1984). An option-based model of mortgage default. *Housing Finance Review 3*(4), 351–372.

Frame, W. S., K. Gerardi, and P. S. Willen (2013, April). Supervisory stress tests, model risk, and model disclosure: Lessons from OFHEO. working paper.

Galaif, L. (1993). Index amortising rate swaps. *FRBNY Quarterly Review Winter*, 63–70.

Geltner, D. (2007). Transaction price indexes and derivatives. *Research Review 14*(1), 16–22.

Geltner, D. and J. Fisher (2007). Pricing and index considerations in commercial real estate derivatives. *Journal of Portfolio Management 33*(5), 99–118.

Geman, H. and R. S. Tunaru (2012). Commercial real-estate inventory and theory of storage. *The Journal of Futures Markets 33*(7), 675–694.

Ghysels, E., A. Plazzi, and R. Valkanov (2007). Valuation in US commercial real estate. *European Financial Management 13*(3), 472–497.

Goodman, L. S. and F. J. Fabozzi (2005). CMBS total return swaps. *Journal of Portfolio Management*, 162–167.

Gorton, G. (2009). The subprime panic. *European Financial Management 15*, 10–46.

Green, R. K. and S. M. Wachter (2005). The American mortgage in historical and international context. *Journal of Economic Perspectives 19*(4), 93–114.

Gu, A. (2002). The predictability of house prices. *Journal of Real Estate Research 24*(3), 213–233.

Gyourko, J. (2009). Understanding commercial real estate: How different from housing is it? *Journal of Portfolio Management Special Real Estate Issue*, 23–37.

Hill, R., C. Sirmans, and J. Knight (1999). A random walk down main street? *Regional Science and Urban Economics 29*(1), 89–103.

Hoag, J. (1980). Towards indices of real estate value return. *The Journal of Finance 35*(2), 569–580.

Iacoviello, M. and F. Ortalo-Magné (2003). Hedging housing risk in London. *Journal of Real Estate Finance and Economics 27*(2), 191–209.

Im, K. S., M. H. Pesaran, and Y. Shin (2003). Testing for unit roots in heterogeneous panels. *Journal of Econometrics 115*, 53–74.

Kamra, A., L. Hayre, and S. Chiluveru (2012). Modeling prepayments and defaults for UK Non-conforming RMBS. *Journal of Fixed Income*, 61–77.

Kau, J. B., D. C. Keenan, and T. Kim (1994). Default probabilities for mortgages. *Journal of Urban Economics 35*(3), 278–296.

Kinlaw, W., M. Kritzman, and D. Turkington (2014). The divergence of high- and low-frequency estimation: Causes and consequences. *The Journal of Portfolio Management 40*(5), 156–168.

Klein, L. S. and C. F. Sirmans (1994). Reverse mortgages and prepayment risk. *Journal of the American Real Estate and Urban Economics Association 22*(2), 409–431.

Kuo, C. (1996). Serial correlation and seasonality in the real estate market. *The Journal of Real Estate Finance and Economics 12*(2), 139–162.

Kupiec, P. and A. Kah (1999). On the origin and interpretation of OAS. *The Journal of Fixed Income 9*(3), 82–92.

Lecomte, P. and W. McIntosh (2005). Is this a revolution? What property derivatives need to succeed. *Institutional Real Estate Letter 17*, 10.

Lecomte, P. and W. McIntosh (2006). Designing property futures contracts and options based on NCREIF property indices. *Journal of Real Estate Portfolio Management*, 119–153.

Lee, Y.-T., C.-W. Wang, and H.-C. Huang (2012). On the valuation of reverse mortgages with regular tenure payments. *Insurance: Mathematics and Economics 51*, 430–441.

Levin, A. (2009). *Home Price Derivatives and Modeling. Quantitative Perspectives.* Andrew Davidson & Co.

Levin, A. and C. F. Lin (1993). Unit Root Test in Panel Data: New Results, University of California at San Diego, Discussion Paper 93–56.

Levin, A., C.-F. Lin, and C.-S. J. Chu (2002). Unit root tests in panel data: Asymptotic and finite-sample properties. *Journal of Econometrics 108*, 1–24.

Levy, E. (1992). Pricing European average rate currency options. *Journal of International Money and Finance 14*, 474–491.

Lew, K. and S. R. Ma (2012). A study on evaluating total loan cost rate of the reverse mortgage products. *Housing Studies Review 20*(3), 77–102.

Ling, D. C. and A. Naranjo (1996). Economic risk factors and commercial real estate returns. *Journal of Real Estate Finance and Economics 14*, 283–307.

Lizieri, C., G. Marcato, P. Ogden, and A. Baum (2010). Pricing inefficiencies in private real estate markets using total return swaps. *Journal of Real Estate Finance and Economics 45*, 774–803.

Lybeck, J. A. (2011). *A Global History of the Financial Crash of 2007-10.* Cambridge: Cambridge University Press.

Ma, S. and Y. Deng (2013). Evaluation of reverse mortgage programs in Korea. *Seoul Journal of Business 19*(1), 137–160.

Maddala, G. S. and S. Wu (1999). A Comparative Study of Unit Root Tests with Panel Data and a New Simple Test. Oxford Bulletin of Economics and Statistics *61*, 631–652.

McDonald, R. and D. Siegel (1984). Option pricing when the underiying asset earns a below-equilibrium rate of return: A note. *Journal of Finance 39*, 261–265.

Miao, J. J. and N. Wang (2007). Investment, consumption and hedging under incomplete markets. *Journal of Financial Economics 86*, 608–642.

Miles, M., R. Cole, and D. Guilkey (1990). A different look at commercial real estate returns. *AREUEA Journal 18*, 403–430.

Mitchell, O. S. and J. Piggott (2004). Unlocking housing equity in Japan. *Journal of the Japanese and International Economies 18*, 466–505.

Mitchell, P. and S. Bond (2009, August). The IPF UK consensus forecast and the returns implied by property derivative pricing: Evolution, record and influences. IPF Research Programme Short Papers Series 2, Investment Property Forum.

Moulton, S., D. Haurin, and W. Shi (2015). An analysis of default risk in the home equity conversion mortgage (HECM) program. *Journal of Urban Economics 90*, 17–34.

Ortiz, C. E., C. A. Stone, and A. Zissu (2013). When do securitized reverse mortgages become liabilities. *Journal of Structured Finance* (Spring), 57–64.

Ortman, J. M., V. A. Velkoff, and H. Hogan (2014). An aging nation: The older population in the United States. Population estimates and projections. Current Population Reports. P25–1140.

Otaka, M. and Y. Kawaguchi (2003). Hedging and pricing of real estate securities under market incompleteness. mimeo Meikai University Working Papers Series.

PDIG (2015, October). Property future contracts: An introduction. discussion paper.

Pfau, W. D. (2016). Understanding the line of credit growth for a reverse mortgage. *Journal of Financial Planning* (March), 37–39.

Pu, M., G.-Z. Fan, and Y. Deng (2014). Breakeven determination of loan limits for reverse mortgages under information asymmetry. *Journal of Real Estate Finance and Economics 48*, 492–521.

PWC (2016). Emerging trends in real estate: Asia pacific 2016. report, Urban Land Institute.

Quantum Alpha Limited (2013). Safer mortgage financing for sustainable growth: A 2013 budget submission to HM treasury. www.quantumalpha.com.

Quercia, R. G. and M. Stegman (1992). Residential mortgage default: A review of the literature. *Journal of Housing Research 3*(2), 341–379.

Raynes, S. and A. Rutledge (2003). *The Analysis of Structured Securities*. Oxford: Oxford University Press.

Richard, S. F. and R. Roll (1989). Prepayments on fixed-rate mortgage backed securities. *Journal of Portfolio Management 15*(Spring), 73–82.

Rodda, D. T., K. Lam, and A. Youn (2004). Stochastic modeling of federal housing administration home equity conversion mortgages with low cost refinancing. *Real Estate Economics 32*(4), 589–617.

Rosato, D. (2016). A safer way to tap home equity. *Money.Com*, 45.

Rosen, S. (1974). Hedonic prices and implicit markets. *Journal of Political Economy 82*(1), 33–55.

Schindler, F. (2013). Predictability and persistence of the price movements of the S&P/Case-Shiller house price indices. *The Journal of Real Estate Finance and Economic 46*(1), 44–90.

Schwartz, E. and W. Torous (1989). Prepayment and the valuation of mortgage backed securities. *Journal of Finance 44*(2), 375–392.

Shao, A., K. Hanewald, and M. Sherris (2015). Reverse mortgage pricing and risk analysis allowing for idiosyncratic house price risk and longevity risk. *Insurance: Mathematics & Economics 63*, 76–90.

Shiller, R. J. (1993). Measuring asset value for cash settlement in derivative markets: Hedonic repeated measures indices and perpetual futures. *Journal of Finance 68*, 911–931.

Shiller, R. J. (2008a). Derivatives markets for home prices. Working Paper/Disscussion Paper 46/1648, Cowles Foundation, Yale.

Shiller, R. J. (2008b). Macroshares: Functions and pricing.

Shiller, R. J. (2008c). *Subprime Solution: How Today's Global Financial Crisis Happened and What to Do about It*. Princeton: Princeton University Press.

Shiller, R. J. (2014, January). Why is housing finance still stuck in such a primitive stage. Discussion paper 1934, Cowles Foundation For Research In Economics Yale University, New Haven, Connecticut.

Shiller, R. J. and A. Weiss (1999). Home equity insurance. *Journal of Real Estate Finance and Economics 19*(1), 21–47.

Shiller, R. J., R. Wojakowski, M. S. Ebrahim, and M. Shackleton (2013). Mitigating financial fragility with continuous workout mortgages. *Journal of Economic Behaviour and Organization 85*, 269–285.

Staiger, R. (2015). *Foundations of Real Estate Financial Modelling*. New York: Routledge.

Stanescu, S., M. R. Candradewi, and R. S. Tunaru (2014). Forward-futures price differences in the UK commercial property market: Arbitrage and marking-to-model explanations. *International Review of Financial Analysis 34*, 177–188.

Stiglitz, J., J. Orszag, and P. Orszag (2002). Implications of the new Fannie Mae and Freddie Mac risk-based capital standard. *Fannie Mae Papers 1*(2).

Stulz, R. (2004). Should we fear derivatives? *Journal of Economic Perspectives 18*, 173–192.

Syz, J. M. (2008). *Property Derivatives*. Chichester: Wiley.

Syz, J. M., P. Vanini, and M. Salvi (2008). Property derivatives and index-linked mortgages. *Journal of Real Estate Finance and Economics 36*, 23–35.

Szymanowski, E. (1994). Risk and the home equity conversion mortgage. *Journal of the American Real Estate and Urban Economics Association 22*(2), 347–366.

Thomas, G. R. (1996). Indemnities for long-term price risk in the UK housing market. *Journal of Property Finance 7*(3), 38–52.

Tomlison, J., S. Pfeiffer, and J. Salter (2016). Reverse mortgages, annuities, and investments: Sorting out the options to generate sustainable retirement income. *Journal of Personal Finance 15*(1), 27–36.

Tsay, J.-T., C.-C. Lin, L. J. Prather, and R. J. Buttimer Jr. (2014). An approximation approach for valuing reverse mortgages. *Journal of Housing Economics 25*, 39–52.

Tunaru, R. S. (2013). The fundamental economic term of commercial real-estate in UK. In M. B. J. Berg (Ed.), *Property Prices and Real Estate Financing in a Turbulent World*, Volume 4, pp. 27–40. SUERF STUDIES.

Twomey, T. (2015). Crossing paths: The intersection of reverse mortgages and bankruptcy. *American Bankruptcy Law Journal 89*, 363–395.

US Government Accountability Office (2007). Long-term care insurance partnership programs include benefits that protect policyholders and are unlikely to result in Medicaid savings. Report to Congressional Requesters 02-231, US Government.

van Bragt, D., M. Francke, B. Kramer, and A. Pelsser (2009, October). Risk-neutral valuation of real estate derivatives. Technical paper 2009-02, ORTEC Finance Research Center, Rotterdam.

van Bragt, D., M. Francke, S. Singor, and A. Pelsser (2015). Risk-neutral valuation of real estate derivatives. *Journal of Derivatives 23*(1), 89–110.

Wagner, G. (2013). The 6.0 percent rule. *Journal of Financial Planning* (December), 46–54.

Wang, C.-W., H.-C. Huang, and Y.-T. Lee (2014). On the valuation of reverse mortgage insurance. *Scandinavian Actuarial Journal*, 1–25.

Webb, B. R. (1994). On the reliability of commercial appraisals: An analysis of properties sold from the Russell-NCREIF index (1978–1992). *Real Estate Finance 11*(1), 62–65.

Webb, B. R., M. E. Miles, and D. K. Guilkey (1992). Transactions-driven commercial real estate returns: The panacea to asset allocation models? *AREUEA Journal 20*(2), 325–357.

Webb, D. (2009). Long-term care insurance, annuities and asymmetric information: The case for bundling contracts. *Journal of Risk and Insurance 76*(1), 53–85.

Wenzlick, R. (1952). As I see the fluctuations in the selling prices of single-family residences. *The Real Estate Analyst 21*, 541–548.

Wyngarden, H. (1927). An index of local real estate prices. *Michigan Business Studies 1*.

■ AUTHOR INDEX

■ SUBJECT INDEX

Introductory Note
References such as '178–9' indicate (not necessarily continuous) discussion of a topic across a range of pages. Because the whole of this work is about 'real-estate derivatives', use of this term (and certain others which occur throughout) as an entry point has been restricted. Please look under the appropriate detailed entries. Wherever possible in the case of topics with many references, these have either been divided into sub-topics or only the most significant discussions of the topic are listed.